GOD
INTERVENES
IN THE MIDDLE EAST

Second Edition

"God's Precision Timing in History"

by Marion F. Kremers

D1414276

Discover
God's Precision Timing during the last six millennia

See
How God rescues Israel from the Coming Invation

Learn
How a False King (Anti-Christ)
deceives the world and rises to power

Know
The Real Messiah is coming

"When the Lord shall build up Zion,
He shall appear in His glory."
— *Psalm 102:16 KJV* —

First printing: September 1992
Second printing: April 1995
Third printing: March 1996
© Copyright 1992—Marion Fleming Kremers

Unless otherwise identified, Scripture quotations are from the New International Version of the Bible.

Requests for information should be directed to:
God Intervenes, Inc.
P.O. Box 10695
Burke, Virginia 22009-0695

Library of Congress Catalogue Card Number: 95-090106

ISBN 1-56043-483-X

The watchman must blow the horn to warn the people.
(cf. Ezekiel 33:1-6)

The watchman cried blow the horn to warn the people.
(cf. Ezekiel 33: 1-9)

DEDICATION

To Bring Glory to the God of Heaven and Earth.

To You Who Want to Know God!

To honor my godly grandparents and my beloved parents, Selwyn and Agnes, who taught me to worship the God of the Bible; my encouraging and supportive husband, Marc, children, and son-in-law; and kind friends for their help.

and

To offer a profound debt of gratitude to my pastor, Ellen K. Blackwell, and my fine publication staff.

Contents

DEAR READER

What is man that you are mindful of him, the son of man
that you care for him?   (Psalm 8:4)

Many people have sought to cope with emptiness and a vague, unexplainable longing at times. Existence has to be more than work, leisure and survival. After a lifetime search in diverse areas, I found the seemingly unattainable, which brings harmony with God, others, and self—in the midst of a very "real world" with all its challenges.

This inner peace creates a clearer horizon...the liberty to pursue another impossibility, another quest: **Since *precision timing* is basic to the functioning of the universe, is there an ordering of events in man's history as well? Is there any structure behind the endless roll of the years?**

To my amazement, the Old Testament does present a master framework. In fact, it is God's signature, written across the spectrum of life. The evidence is visible from the monumental to the miniscule. The Lord's schedule is embedded in the gestation of a baby; Israel's harvests; and pre-Mosaic, Jewish and Christian history. His hand can be seen, even in the smallest details of timing. This sweeping perspective can change your understanding of God and of yourself. It is truly awesome.

This book demonstrates that God has followed a predetermined schedule over a long period. The Lord's plans do not deprive us of free will. Knowing our choices in advance, He fits our lives into His larger design, while still permitting us freedom to choose. His execution of events demonstrates His overarching control of time.

In the *"fullness of time"* events will start to converge. This is not only due to divine initiative, but also to the culmination of man's cumulative actions on earth. A seven-year transition period will usher in the Jewish Messiah-Deliverer with His reign of righteousness and justice on earth. We will lose the privilege of coming to a loving God if we continually ignore, resist, and grieve His Holy Spirit. He will not always strive with us (Genesis 6:3). He will stop restraining evil for a brief period and will ultimately destroy it.

The mystery of God will be accomplished, just as He announced to his servants the prophets. (Revelation 10:7)

A discussion of divine intervention is not intended to project dogmatic views or "place God in a box," but rather to provoke thought and challenge you to compare the Bible with history, especially from the 1880s to the present.

Two hundred years of archaeology have uncovered artifacts, ancient writing and structural foundations that have provided Scripture with a new dimension. As we draw close to the climax of this age, God is showing us that His Word is factual and must be taken seriously.

You may argue that certain historical facts have been selected to illustrate Bible timing; but can the repeated parallels all be mere coincidence? They illustrate an undeniable order and direction behind events.

God's Word is logical. This research focuses upon what He has already done. Through repetition, the Lord teaches us what to expect in the future. I challenge the most ardent skeptic to examine God's blueprint of history which at times He fine-tunes to "the self-same day"!

We are also the generation that has seen the formation of Israel (the fig tree):

> *Now learn this lesson from the fig tree...this generation will certainly not pass away until all these things have happened. Heaven and earth will pass away, but my words will never pass away.* (Matthew 24:32ff; cf. Mark 13:28ff; Luke 21:29ff; Psalm 102:16, KJV)

The Jewish nation will occupy center stage. It is God's timepiece by which we can understand world events today. The prophesied events build in intensity, bringing us to the culmination of many centuries. **While many are unaware of Scripture, God's intervention will overtake us.**

The prophet Daniel and King Nebuchadnezzar, the most powerful man of the Gentile world, agreed that Daniel's God was *"a revealer of mysteries"* (Daniel 2:28, 29, 47). Daniel set himself to gain understanding and humble himself before his God and his words were heard (Daniel 10:12).

In 539 B.C., three years before the Jews were to be released from Babylonian captivity, the prophet understood from the Scriptures (Jeremiah 25:11f) the exact length of his people's exile (Daniel 9:2f).

Cannot God's people learn from the Scriptures the approximate time before Israel's full restoration? I believe the Lord will do so through His Holy Spirit, as we humbly study His Word. We see the Jews from many nations returning to Israel. Just because this restoration is happening in our daily lives does not reduce its eternal significance.

God's intervention for Israel when they are invaded will be His warning. Then, we will understand we are in the countdown of a terminal contest. My intention is to:

1. Warn Jews about the false king-messiah who follows God's great deliverance of Israel from a few nations. This man will precede their real Messiah by seven years.

2. Inform Christians and others who want perspective on the world today from the Biblical standpoint.

For what they were not told, they will see; and what they have not heard, they will understand. (Isaiah 52:15b)

These things happened to them [the Israelites] *as examples and were written down as warnings for us on whom the fulfillment of the ages has come.* (1 Corinthians 10:11)

But you, brothers, are not in darkness; so that this day [of the Lord] *should surprise you like a thief.*
(1 Thessalonians 5:4)

This book does not claim infallibility on a subject as vast as prophecy. As noted, the emphasis is on presenting precedents from history so that you may gain perspective on the future.

The one thing that is extremely clear is that the unfulfilled prophecies of the Bible have been coming to pass for over a century. They have followed the sequence that begins in the last 12 chapters of Ezekiel.

The Lord tells us all that **when He builds up Zion, He will appear in His glory (Psalm 102:16, KJV).** This thought is repeated in three of the four gospels of the New Testament.

You and I are God's highest order of creation and are greatly loved by Him. He wants to communicate with us through His Word. We gain a new dimension as we understand the Lord's program for mankind.

Marion Fleming Kremers

NOTE

The *NIV Study Bible* is used throughout, except where stated "KJV" (*King James Version*). The "f" or "ff" following the number of a verse or page indicates the inclusion of the following verse or verses. An italicized quote is from the Bible. Bold words in the quotes are used for emphasis.

The *Mishnah* of the *Talmud* is divided into tractates (treatises) which are referred to here by name only. Some of these are: *Abodah Zarah* (Idolatry), *Arachin* (Estimations), *Berachoth* (Benedictions), *Middoth* (Dimensions), *Pesachim* (Passovers), *Sanhedrin* (Courts), *Shabbath* (Sabbath), *Sukkah* (Booth), *Taanith* (Fast), and *Yoma* (The Day).

Italicized foreign words in parentheses indicate the Hebrew equivalent. *"Erez Israel"* (Land of Israel) was the name used before it became an established nation in 1948-1949.

Please note the charts at the end for an explanation of the Jewish months and an outline of the Feasts of Israel. Of special interest is Chart Three—Multiple Historic Fulfillments of the Feasts of Israel.

Chapter One

THE OVERVIEW

The thrust of this book is to provide perspective. This will enable us to judge the significance of events swirling around us that will impact on everyone alive today.

The seven transitional years that herald the arrival of the Jewish Messiah are analyzed. The Jews are given two key events, after which their Messiah will come to Jerusalem seven years later. God has always given Israel, as a nation, specific prophecies to give them hope in times of exile and to prepare them to recognize the real Messiah before He comes.

We who have seen Israel come alive before our eyes are profoundly comatose if we do not wake up and scrutinize these prophecies, as well as prior prophetic fulfillments. **Discovery of God's exquisite precision throughout history illuminates the issues of today.**

We are fast approaching the end of the sixth millennium. Historians generally agree that recorded history (not creation) began in the Tigris-Euphrates river valley in the Middle East about 4000 B.C. and continues with the 2,000 years of this era. The Bible promises 1,000 years of worldwide peace and harmony under the rule of Messiah, who is called the *"Prince of Peace"* (Isaiah 9:6). This would encompass a 7,000-year period.

2 God Intervenes in the Middle East

God's sacred cycle of seven is foundational throughout Scripture. The governing principle of six units of work and one of restoration is also a part of the Ten Commandments (the Creator's will, or "Manufacturer's Handbook," on how man must live to be at peace with God, himself, and each other). God calls observance of the Sabbath *"a sign"* between Him and the Jews for generations to come (Exodus 31:13).

Here are some key prophecies that God announced through His prophets long in advance:

1. To Abraham: 400 years—The length of Hebrew captivity in Egypt (They were not enslaved for the first 30 of the total 430 years.) (Genesis 15:13).

2. To Jeremiah: 70 years—The length of Israelite exile in Babylon (Jeremiah 25:11f).

3. To Isaiah: Cyrus—The name of the king who would release them from Babylon (Isaiah 44:28; 45:13).

4. To Daniel: Seven "sevens" (49 years)—The time it would take to rebuild Jerusalem, once the decree to do so was issued (Daniel 9:25). A "seven" (*shemittah*) comprises seven years of 360 days each (30 days per month).

5. To Daniel: 2,300 sacrifices (1,150 days)—The number of Temple sacrifices (two per day) that would be stopped by a tyrant (Antiochus Epiphanes) before the Jews regained the Temple (164 B.C.) (Daniel 8:14).

6. To Daniel: 69 "sevens" (483 years)—The total number of years (after the issuance of the decree to rebuild Jerusalem) until Messiah would be killed in the 69th seven-year period (Daniel 9:26).

7. To Ezekiel: One final "seven" will follow the invasion of Israel by specified countries. Israel will burn the enemy's war materiel for the one remaining seven-year period (Ezekiel 39:9). The invaders will be buried between the Mediterranean Sea and the Dead Sea (Joel 2:20; Ezekiel 39:11). Logically, this attack should happen

immediately prior to Israel's final seven years before Messiah's arrival.

8.   To Daniel: One "seven" will follow Israel's confirmation of a covenant with a leader. In this interval, a wicked king will rule and cause worldwide destruction in the second half of his reign. Then the Most Holy will be anointed; the Jewish people and Jerusalem restored; and everlasting righteousness established on earth at the coming of Messiah (Daniel 9:24, 27).

Note: **There is only one seven-year period remaining for Israel's spiritual restoration.**

Since God gave the Jews such specific information about their prior restorations, it is not surprising that He would give them two events to mark the start of this awesome seven-year interval, which will precede their permanent reinstatement. It is so simple that a child will be able to pinpoint the year Messiah will deliver the Jews and restore the world after these two actions take place.

Once the seven years begin, the timing of other major events within this period has been clearly defined. Such knowledge will be a veritable life preserver for each of us as humanity's problems escalate.

At the ascension of Jesus, the apostles were told that:

This same Jesus who has been taken from you into heaven, will come back in the same way you have seen him go into heaven.   (Acts 1:11)

The Old Testament teaches that Messiah will come bodily, touching down upon the Mount of Olives with *his feet* (Zechariah 14:4), *the soles of his feet* (Ezekiel 43:7).

It is clear that He will have to come at the start, not at the end, of the 1,000 years, if He is to reign for that period on earth. It is so important for people to understand that there is a millennium that it is repeated six times in succession (Revelation 20:2-7).

The New Testament holds out a future "day of rest" that has not come yet:

For if Joshua [Yeshua, Jesus] *had given them rest, God would not have spoken later about another day. There remains, then, a Sabbath-rest for the people of God.*

(Hebrews 4:7)

The length of God's *"day"* is defined as 1,000 years, whether it refers to the past, present, or future (Psalm 90:4; 2 Peter 3:8). It seems that God is allowing equal time, for the Jews and the Church, or approximately 2,000 years each.

It is highly possible that the transition to God's new order could happen around the start of the coming seventh millennium. This would, of necessity, place the seven years in the near future. All but a small percentage of unfulfilled prophecy focuses upon these particular seven years, which are called the *"birth pains"* of the Kingdom of God coming on earth.

You may ask, **"But what about the Jewish calendar?"** The year 2000 A.D., added to 4,000 years B.C., totals 6,000 years in the civil calendar. However, 2000 A.D. is the Jewish year, 5760/5761, causing a discrepancy of 240 years between the two calendars.

After the time of the Second Temple, the rabbis defined the date of Creation as *Tishri* 1, October 6, 3761 B.C.E. (Before the Common Era). The Talmud (*Abodah Zarah,* 9b, p. 46f) refers to this date in citing that 470 A.D. (400 years after the destruction of the Second Temple) was the year 4231 (3761 B.C. + 70 A.D. + 400 years = 4,231 years) after the Creation. The rabbis made their date of Creation official in the 10th century, according to Fred Reiss, author of *The Standard Guide to the Jewish and Civil Calendars.*

In addition to the difference of 240 years, the civil calendar does not specify that the creation of the universe is the calendar's point of origin. If God intervenes in this decade, that would prove that the year, 2000 A.D., is the start of the next millennium as the civil calendar indicates. The civil calendar will be followed here.

Even if the 6,000th year after the creation of Adam should not come precisely in this decade, we are given another bench mark or point of reference. God promised the Jewish nation that He would revive them at the end of two "days" and restore them on the third (Hosea 6:2). Two millennia after their nation was destroyed, God is rebuilding Israel. So, we can expect their spiritual restoration at the dawn of the "third day."

Jesus (Acts 10:40) and Jonah (Jonah 1:17) both provide precedents for this restoration on the third "day" (see p. 213f). Assuredly, the Lord will restore Israel, at the dawning of the third "day" as He promised.

For if their rejection is the reconciliation of the world, what will their acceptance be, but life from the dead?
(Romans 11:15)

The pivotal factor is: when will the invasion of Israel happen? The prophecies, history, and current events point to the blitzkrieg of Israel by Russia and specified countries on *Rosh Hashanah*. If this is quickly followed by Israel "confirming the covenant" with a brilliant leader, we know for certain that the seven-year countdown to Messiah, King of Kings, has begun.

Then, the prophecies, those ancient markers of time, will no longer be glanced at as irrelevant images, projected against an obscure horizon. They will become tangible and three-dimensional. In an instant, God will put to rest all of men's conflicting interpretations. No longer will truth be wrenched around, due to our lack of knowledge or our unbelief.

Observe coming events and compare them with God's precedents and the seven Feasts of Israel, His "appointed times." The schedule of the Feasts governs time. To man's oft-repeated question:

How long will it be before these astonishing things are fulfilled?   (Daniel 12:6)

God responds:

See, the former things have taken place, and new things I declare. Before they spring into being, I announce them to you.   (Isaiah 42:9)

I have not spoken in secret from somewhere in a land of darkness. I have not said to Jacob's descendants, "Seek me in vain." I, the Lord, speak the truth; I declare what is right.   (Isaiah 45:19)

He [Gabriel] *said: "I am going to tell you what will happen later in the time of wrath, because the vision concerns the appointed time of the end."*   (Daniel 8:19)

You may say to yourselves, "How can we know when a message has not been spoken by the Lord?" If what a prophet proclaims in the name of the Lord does not take place or come true, that is a message the Lord has not spoken.   (Deuteronomy 18:21f)

Do not seal up the words of the prophecy of this book.
                                      (Revelation 22:10)

The 17th-century scientist, Sir Isaac Newton said, "About the time of the end, a body of men will be raised up who will turn their attention to the prophecies, and insist upon their literal interpretation." This gifted man spent much time studying Bible chronology in the prophecies.

Chapter Two

PERSPECTIVE FROM THE PAST

Call to me and I will answer you, and tell you great and unsearchable things which you do not know.

(Jeremiah 33:3)

The Lord confides in those who fear Him. (Psalm 25:14)

The Big Picture

Only as we comprehend what is happening to the ancient nation of Israel today, will we grasp the significance of world events that are unfolding with astounding rapidity. Such an overview can help people avoid the deception that will take hold in Israel, then Europe, and finally, the world. Examining occurrences from their Biblical perspective will provide us with an anchor of the utmost importance in the days ahead and enable us to do our part.

A synthesis of the prophecies of God is presented. No one prophecy can be taken out of context to illustrate a point of view. They all interrelate and provide one consistent picture.

The start of the seven-year period prior to Messiah's arrival will not be certain until it begins. Therefore, the real purpose of the book is not to set dates, but rather to make people aware of the precise correlation between Bible prophecy and world events, past and present. It will be demonstrated that God has been following **a predetermined schedule over the last 6,000-year segment of time.** It seems logical to assume that the remaining prophecies will be fulfilled according to the same undeniable pattern.

Ours is not merely an intellectual search. We will ask God's Holy Spirit to lead and enable us to receive His wisdom and discernment. Without Him, even God's words will not come alive for us. Whether we believe the Bible or not will not delay its fulfillment. The prophecies will be revealed before our eyes. As Matthew Henry said, **"Truth is the daughter of time."**

We will mainly focus on God's Holy Land. Strategically, it is at the intersection of the continents of Africa, Asia and Europe. "God's land," for so He calls it, was on the highway connecting the two centers of the Fertile Crescent, the Nile and the Euphrates river valleys. It was at this crossroads of people and power that God chose to situate Israel among the nations.

Even today, countries west of Israel are referred to as western, and those east of her, as eastern. Geologically, she is the navel of the globe, containing the deepest rift valley in the world.

God says He has set Jerusalem *"in the center of the nations"* (Ezekiel 5:5), which ancient maps depict. There, His presence with His outshining glory will once again fill the Temple in Jerusalem (Ezekiel 43:4, 5).

The Bible is not the history of the universe or even of earth. Its purpose is to describe the restoration of man to his original state of perfection. This renewal can only be accomplished in those who will believe, repent, and obey God.

The Lord's plan was to place man on earth to populate, subdue and rule over it under divine guidance (Genesis 1:28). God loves His creation and wants to be loved in return. In order for man's response to have meaning, man was given free will. Only those who desire to worship the Lord, do so. To indicate the closeness of the relationship between God and His people, they were called His *"wife"* in the Old Testament (Jeremiah 3:14; Ezekiel 16:32) and His *"bride"* in the New (Matthew 25:6; Revelation 19:7).

Our Inheritance from Adam and Eve

Adam and Eve, made in God's image, were the only creatures possessing God's Spirit and they were created last. Skeletons of man-like creatures from the past may be found. However, without the Spirit of God resident in them, there would be a profound difference.

Adam and Eve were created perfect and with God's power to discern and live above all the deceptions and wiles of the original rebel, Satan. However, when their free will was put to the test, the couple betrayed the Lord's trust in them.

They were then cast out of God's presence, and lost their direct communication with Him. Sin always causes guilt, hardness, and blindness, which separate us from God and others. The light that had shone forth from their perfect bodies disappeared, and they felt naked. They at once tried to cover themselves and hid from God (Genesis 3:7, 8).

Disconnected from God, their spirits stopped functioning. An inoperative spirit could no longer act as governor and guide for the soul (mind, emotions, and will) and body. The spiritual leadership was gone. The untamed passions of the body could now dictate to the soul.

God knew that our first parents would disobey and had already prepared a way by which He would restore men. Through this plan, an individual's spirit could be revitalized. Man would then be able to live in peace with God, himself, and others. Since we can never make ourselves good enough to meet God's standards of holiness (Isaiah 64:6), we must receive the righteousness He offers us. It is free to us, but it cost Him the life of His Son.

The Bible starts with a perfect, but unproven, man and woman who failed the test. It ends with the restoration of flawed people into *"new creations"* (2 Corinthians 5:17) with whom God is pleased to dwell. He does this by offering to fill our nonfunctioning spirits with His Spirit or breath, as one might charge a dead battery.

Notice that Adam's son, Seth, was not created in God's likeness as was Adam. Instead, *"Adam had a son in his own likeness, in his own image"* (Genesis 5:3; cf. 1:27).

God did not destroy His opponent, the devil, and his evil influence at once. Had the Lord done so, men would have been like robots, stripped of free will. The crowning gift that the Creator bestowed upon man was "choice." Although freedom involves risk and temptation, without free will, our choices are meaningless.

The Lord is demonstrating to all creation that within a predetermined period of time, and despite the efforts of His arch enemy to entice, deceive, and ensnare men, the Lord will still find a remnant of people among Jews and Gentiles who love Him. Some people will choose to live to please God rather than self or Satan. The Lord cannot be accused of force or partiality, as people decide for themselves.

A 6,000-Year Segment of Time

The assumption is that time did not necessarily come into existence with the creation of the universe or of man. Time can be seen as a series of "slices" of God's infinite consciousness. **We will limit ourselves to the last 6,000 years, upon which the Bible focuses.**

Archaeology and ancient history bring civilized man upon us somewhat of suddenness, and well-established in homelands of recent formation. Whence came these peoples, whose great works and thoughts are found near the beginning of an era...?[1]

You may question how long it would take for a sizeable population to come forth if there are only two people at the start. For example, if we use a hypothetical period of 14 generations of 40 years each (560 years) with every couple bearing an average of six children; and few deaths due to the great longevity in the pure pre-Flood environment: there would be over 4.78 million people. If all the couples had an average of eight children under similar conditions, the number would climb to over 1.38 billion people over the same interval.[2]

Complex societies in different cradles of civilization arose in approximately 3500 B.C. in Mesopotamia (Tigris-Euphrates river valley), 3200 B.C. in Egypt, and 2500 B.C. in the Indus Valley.[3]

In his book *The Tigris Expedition,* Thor Heyerdahl, explorer and author of *Kon Tiki,* reminded us of the extraordinary coincidence that civilizations emerged in Mesopotamia, Egypt, and the Indus Valley at roughly the same time. "Why this impressive, seemingly overnight blossoming in three places simultaneously?" he asked.[4]

The period from 4000–3300 B.C., the Chalcolithic Age, yielded little written materials. There is indication of organized society due to existence of stratified cities in those times.[5]

Archaeological evidence seems to indicate that the earliest actual writing originated in Mesopotamia after the middle of the fourth millennium B.C. (c. 3500 B.C.). The oldest deciphered inscriptions in existence are probably in the Sumerian language. Writing, if not created by the Sumerians, was utilized by them for

1.   Orr, p. 644.
2.   Morris, pp. 416–419.
3.   *U.S. News and World Report,* April 2, 1990, p. 49.
4.   *Ibid.,* p. 57.
5.   Schultz, p. 19.

administrative purposes very early in the third millennium B.C. Writing evidently developed from pictographs. Probably the oldest example of pictographic script occurs on a small limestone tablet from Uruk dated about 3000 B.C. The popularity of writing spread throughout the Near East by the second millennium B.C.[6]

The non-Semitic Sumerians controlled the lower Euphrates in Mesopotamia and enjoyed an advanced culture by 3000 B.C. Archaeologists have discovered cities and large buildings, at Ur, Eridu, Uruk (Erech), Nippur, Kish, and Lagash. Society centered around temples run by priests. Records were kept on clay tablets with cuneiform writing. Irrigation and plows were used in addition to potter's wheels and kilns. They trained goldsmiths and gem-cutters. Chariots and the phalanx were employed in battle; and extensive trade was carried on.[7] Next, came the Semitic Akkadians c. 2400 B.C. on the plain of Shinar (Babylon or modern Iraq).

Most scholars place the Jewish patriarchal period in "the first half of the second millennium" (2000–1550 B.C.).[8] The discovery and publication of the Nuzi (Nuzu) tablets and other archaeological information since 1925 has replaced the belief that the patriarchs of Genesis were fabricated legends. The data demonstrates numerous parallels between life in northern Mesopotamia in the 15th century B.C. and specific social and legal customs practiced by Abraham, Isaac and Jacob.

Abraham is thought to have lived about 2000 B.C.[9] For most of his career, archaeologist Albright struggled with the dating of Abraham. He finally concluded that the patriarch "could not have lived before the 20th or after the 19th century B.C."[10] The Jewish and Arab nations began with Abraham's sons, Isaac and Ishmael.

6.   Blaiklock and Harrison, ed., p. 476.
7.   Schultz, p. 22.
8.   *Encyclopaedia Judaica,* Vol. 8, p. 572, 766a; Schultz, p. 29.
9.   *The World Book Encyclopedia,* Vol. 10, p. 388b.
10. Johnson, p. 11.

Bible history can be divided into three distinct eras of 2,000 years each. The first was from Adam to Abraham, the second from Abraham to Jesus Christ, and the third from Christ until the present (see Chapter 13).

Though difficult to absorb in the midst of our commonplace but urgent lives, we are going to encounter the direct intervention of God on a worldwide scale. Its magnitude will astound the world. He has declared:

I will once more shake the heavens and the earth, the sea and the dry land. I will shake all nations, and the desired of all nations will come, and I will fill this house [the Jewish Temple] *with glory.*   (Haggai 2:6f; cf. Hebrews 12:26)

Who is the *"desired of all nations?"*

God's unfulfilled prophecies telescope through several millennia to focus upon the generation alive when the Jewish people are regathered as a nation to their homeland. It is the prerogative of God, and God alone, to reveal the future. He scoffs:

Bring in [your idols] *to tell us what is going to happen...Or declare to us the things to come. Tell us what the future holds, so we may know that you are gods.*   (Isaiah 41:22f)

Scripture repeatedly uses the yardstick of 40 years to express one generation. In addition, most women do not bear children after age 40. Since the Biblical "lifespan" is about 70–80 years (Psalm 90:10, Isaiah 23:15f), *"this generation"* is still present that saw the rebirth of Israel in 1947–1949.

Look at the fig tree and all the trees. *When they sprout leaves, you can see for yourselves and know that summer is near. Even so, when you see these things happening, you know that the kingdom of God is near* [right at the door]. *I tell you the truth, this generation will certainly not pass*

*away until all these things have happened. Heaven and
earth will pass away, but my words will never pass away.*
(Luke 21:29f; Matthew 24:32f; Mark 13:28f)

The prior verses are so important that they are repeated three
times, almost verbatim.

*When I saw your fathers, it was like seeing the early fruit
on the fig tree.*
(Hosea 9:10; cf. Jeremiah 24:1–10; Amos 8:2f)

Nations are compared to trees (Ezekiel 31). In the Old Testament, the fig tree represents Israel as a national entity.[11] The olive tree, known for its persistent life, refers to Israel's religious aspect. (For example, there are several 2,000-year-old olive trees growing in the Garden of Gethsemane in Jerusalem today.) The budding of the tree speaks of the restoration of the nation.[12]

The sprouting of *"all the trees"* (Luke 21:29) represents the other nations that have come to life (independence). There are about 170 nations, of which 98 have been formed since 1945. This is due to the breakup of the Turkish, British, and French empires in this century. And now we see the crumbling of the Soviet empire. This gaining of national sovereignty by many nations is another sign that Messiah's arrival is soon.

The responsibility for every country's policy toward Messiah's brothers must rest upon each country itself. When Messiah comes in all His glory, He will sit on His throne and all the nations will be gathered before Him. Then, He will judge the people according to their treatment of *"the least of these brothers of mine"* (Matthew 25:31–46). He defines His "brothers" as being those who do the will of His Father in heaven (Matthew 12:48f).

11.   *Berachoth* 57a; Midrash on Canticles i.1.
12.   Edersheim, *The Life and Times of Jesus The Messiah*, Book II, p. 247; Wilson, p. 179.

Prophecy—The Warning Call to Safety

The more carefully one searches the Bible prophecies, the more integrated they become. Though the Old Testament is for us all, it is written to the Jewish people. "Israel" must not be spiritualized to mean the "Church," as some do.

Twenty-seven percent of the Bible is predictive.[13] God's standard by which we judge prophecy is that it must come to pass, and a false prophet must be put to death. Since the Lord has equal access to the future and the past, His prophets speak the truth. Prophecy is to be approached with the greatest sincerity (Deuteronomy 18:20f; Jeremiah 28:9; Zechariah 13:3).

When men tell you to consult mediums and spiritists, who whisper and mutter, should not a people inquire of their God?   (Isaiah 8:19)

God intends that those who obey Him should know His plans ahead of time. One of David's chief desires was to seek the Lord (Psalm 27:4). What God has revealed in His Word is for the benefit of all. Prophecy is not given to tickle itching ears, but to teach us the steps by which God's redemption will be accomplished. It is imperative that we be forewarned. A watchman who sees destruction coming, but does nothing to alert others will be held accountable (Ezekiel 33:6).

Surely the Sovereign Lord does nothing without revealing his plan to his servants the prophets.   (Amos 3:9)

I make known the end from the beginning, from ancient times, what is still to come. I say: My purpose will stand

---

13.   Payne, p. 681.

*and I will do all that I please.... What I have said, that will
I bring about; what I have planned, that will I do.*

(Isaiah 46:10f)

See, I have told you ahead of time.   (Matthew 24:25)

*I have told you now before it happens, so that when it does
happen you will believe.*   (John 14:29)

The Spirit of truth...will tell you what is yet to come.

(John 16:13b)

Compare the difference between the instructions given to the
Old Testament prophet, Daniel, and to the New Testament apostle,
John. God revealed one final seven-year period for the Jewish nation to both men. Since this last interval did not happen during the
2,000-year Jewish era, Daniel was told:

...the words [of this prophecy] *are closed up and sealed
until the time of the end...You will rest, and then at the end
of the days you will rise to receive your allotted
inheritance.*   (Daniel 12:9, 13, cf. 4)

God described the same seven-year interval in great detail to
John in Revelation, the last book of the Bible, written c. 90 A.D.
John was told:

Do not seal up the words of the prophecy of this book.

(Revelation 22:10)

The very first words of Revelation indicate that it was given for
John to show to God's servants. It is the only book of the Bible that
extends an additional blessing to those who read, hear, and take its
words to heart, so important is the information (Revelation 1:1f).
God has provided a plan of escape, so that we can avoid His
coming punishment of evil on earth.

In Noah's generation, God's period of warning before His judgment was the 120 years it took to build the ark. All who believed the Lord's warning through Noah could have entered.

My Spirit will not contend with man forever, for he is mortal; his days will be a hundred and twenty years.

(Genesis 6:3)

...who disobeyed long ago when God waited patiently in the days of Noah while the ark was being built.

(1 Peter 3:20)

As it was in the days of Noah, so it will be at the coming of the Son of Man.   (Matthew 24:37)

At the end of the construction, the Lord gave them one final, brief chance to repent and come to Him before He instigated the Flood. He will again give one last warning call before removing His people prior to His wrath.

How can we be aware of His warning if we ignore His words? However, we must employ great discernment as false conclusions dishonor God, confuse people, and carry grave consequences for their author. As stated in "The Overview," no person can know with certainty the date of the invasion of Israel by some nations (Ezekiel 38 and 39); nor of God's evacuation (*natzal*) of His people from earth (1 Thessalonians 4:15f; 1 Corinthians 15:51) until it happens. However, we can be aware of the parallel restoration of both Israel and the Church since the 1880s.

Jesus Christ expected the people to recognize the signs of spiritual crisis in their day because of the eternal consequences for each person. Surely, He says no less to us today!

How foolish you are, and how slow of heart to believe all that the prophets have spoken!   (Luke 24:25)

Hypocrites! You know how to interpret the appearance of the earth and the sky. How is it that you don't know how to interpret this present time?   (Luke 12:56f)

Rejection of the Jewish Nation from Israel

As God's intended agents on earth, the Jews have always been given definite lengths of time of exile before God's intervention comes. Everyone else, including the Church, must look to His ancient nation, to understand His timing.

Abraham was told that his descendants would be enslaved for 400 years in Egypt before deliverance (Genesis 15:13; Exodus 12:40; Acts 7:6). They were in Egypt for 30 years with Joseph before the bondage began. Jeremiah was instructed that his people would be exiled in Babylon for 70 years (Jeremiah 25:11; 29:10; 2 Chronicles 36:21).

It was predicted that the Jews would be dispersed and Jerusalem destroyed (Deuteronomy 28:64; Daniel 9:26; Hosea 3:4f; Zechariah 11:12f; 13:7). Jesus confirmed this (Luke 19:42f; 21:20f; Matthew 23:37–39).

However, Moses (Deuteronomy 4:30f) and many of the prophets promised that Israel would be restored in the latter days (Isaiah 2:40; Hosea 3:5 etc.). This would come seven years after their nation "confirms the covenant" with a leader. The end of sin and transgression would then have arrived and everlasting righteousness would be brought in (Daniel 9:24, 27). The prophets were not told how long the interval would last between the killing of *"the Anointed One"* and this final seven years.

The journey from Egypt to the Promised Land should have taken 11 days (Deuteronomy 1:2). Instead, they did not arrive in the land until the next generation. In the same sense, the acceptance of the Messiah should have happened when He was first proclaimed. Instead, it will probably be the second generation (**as a nation**) after Jesus' ministry on earth that will accept Him. (As mentioned, the Biblical lifespan is 70–80 years.)

The God of Israel graphically warned their first national leader, Moses, of the terrible price they would pay if they departed from Him. Israel is the only nation ever called out by the Lord as a group. (Otherwise, people are chosen one by one as they turn to Him.) Israel was to be His *"treasured possession...a kingdom of priests and a holy nation"* (Exodus 19:5f).

However, if they disobeyed Him, they would not continue under His blessing. He could not endorse rebellion. The Israelites were given constant demonstrations of God's love through His miraculous protection and provision. If they persisted in rebellion after repeated warnings and reinstatements, God would turn His face from them as a nation and scatter them until the time came for Him to restore **all** things. The Jewish people went into worldwide dispersion in 70 A.D.

If...you do not accept my correction but continue to be hostile toward me, I myself will be hostile toward you and will afflict you for your sins **seven times over.**
(Leviticus 26:23)

But if you turn away and forsake the decrees and commands I have given you...then I will uproot Israel from my land, which I have given them, and will reject this temple I have consecrated for my Name.   (2 Chronicles 7:19f)

Therefore will the Lord wait, that he may be gracious unto you...and have mercy upon you.   (Isaiah 30:18, KJV)

I am like a moth to Ephraim, like rot to the people of Judah...I will tear them to pieces and go away; I will carry them off, with no one to rescue them. Then, I will go back to my place until they admit their guilt. And they will seek my face; in their misery they will earnestly seek me.
(Hosea 5:12ff)

He must remain in heaven until the time comes for God to restore everything, as he promised long ago through his holy prophets.   (Acts 3:21)

People today have no concept of how extensively the miraculous attended Jewish life. "Signs" were an integral part of their relationships with God and were a method by which He guided them (Exodus 34:10; Numbers 14:11). This is the reason the four gospels of the New Testament all report that the Jews sought *"a sign"* from Jesus. The Apostle Paul summarized it:

Jews demand miraculous signs and Greeks [Gentiles] *look for wisdom* [intellectual conviction].   (1 Corinthians 1:22)

The *Talmud* mentions ten miracles which were considered the norm in the Temple. However, the Divine Presence (*Shekinah* glory) was not restored to the Holy of Holies in the Second Sanctuary with the return of the exiles from Babylon. The ark of the covenant and the cherubim were also gone.[14] After the later prophets, Haggai, Zechariah, and Malachi, the Spirit of prophecy departed from Israel; but the *Bath Kol,* the divine voice of guidance, remained.[15]

Independent sources confirm the signs which preceded the ruination of the Jewish nation and their Sanctuary: the Jerusalem *Yoma* 43c and Babylonian *Yoma* 39b, Tacitus, Josephus and earliest Christian writings.[16]

The *Talmud* reports that the Jews had warnings of moral disintegration and impending catastrophe for 40 years before the dispersion of the Jewish nation. In the 40 years from 30 A.D. (the year many scholars believe Jesus was rejected and *"cut off"* or killed) until 70 A.D.:

---

14.   *Yoma* 21a, b, p. 91ff.
15.   *Yoma* 9b, p. 41.
16.   Edersheim, *The Life and Times of Jesus the Messiah,* Book 2, p. 610; Josephus, p. 582.

(1) The Supreme Court (*Beth Din or Sanhedrin*) was banished from meeting in the "Chamber of Hewn Stones" erected in the Temple enclosure.[17] Then, the court sat in a trading station (bazaar). They "wandered to ten places of banishment" and ended up in Tiberias.[18]

(2) The lot for "the Lord's goat" never came up in the right hand of the High Priest on *Yom Kippur* (see p. 241), as it had during the 40 years of Simeon the Righteous (c. 300 B.C.).[19] Between Simeon and the final 40 years, the lot came up in either hand, intermittently.

(3) The crimson-colored strap tied on the door of the Temple did not turn white to indicate God's forgiveness on *Yom Kippur* (Isaiah 1:18).[20]

(4) The westernmost light, from which the other lights of the golden candlestick (*menorah*) were lighted, did not shine all the time.[21]

(5) The great doors of the Temple (*hekal*) would open by themselves. (It normally required 20 men to open these heavy portals.) The Talmudic rabbis[22] considered that this predicted the Temple's destruction in fulfillment of:

Open thy doors, O Lebanon, so that the fire may devour your cedars.   (Zechariah 11:1)

Lebanon means "white" and refers to the white Temple. The cedar paneling of the Temple also came from Lebanon and was, indeed, demolished by fire.

(6) The pile of wood for the altar did not burn strongly all day, as before, but had to be replenished often.[23]

---

17. *Shabbath* 15a, Vol. 1, p. 63.
18. *Rosh Hashanah* 31a, b, p. 149.
19. *Yoma* 39a, p. 184; 39b, p. 186.
20. *Yoma* 39b, p. 186; 67a, p. 314; 68b, p. 321.
21. *Yoma* 39a, p. 185.
22. *Yoma* 39b, p. 186.
23. *Yoma* 39a, p. 185.

Note: God says He will again *"show wonders in the heaven above and signs on the earth below"* in the last days (Acts 2:19; cf. Joel 2:30). However, Satan will also display counterfeit miracles in his attempt to imitate God and so deceive people (2 Thessalonians 2:9; Revelation 13:13ff).

The reason the *Talmud* gave for the destruction of the First Temple was Jewish "idolatry, immorality, and bloodshed." The rabbis believed that since Jews were studying and practicing the Torah (the first five books of the Bible) during the time of the Second Sanctuary, the reason for its destruction was Jewish "hatred without a cause."[24] Jesus said that those who had seen His miracles and yet despised Him, hated Him *"without reason,"* which fulfilled Scripture (John 15:25; cf. Psalm 35:19; 69:4).

The Jewish people were told four times (Leviticus 26) that they would be punished *"seven times over"* (a complete cycle) if they did not obey God. Following their original refusal to enter the Promised Land (*Av* 9, c. 1280 B.C.) seven major disasters have all happened on the same day to the Jewish people (see p. 307).

> *The people of Israel went into exile for their sin, because they were unfaithful to me. So I hid my face from them and handed them over to their enemies.*   (Ezekiel 39:23)

> *Then, the Lord will scatter you among all nations, from one end of the earth to the other...Among those nations you will find no repose, no resting place for the sole of your foot.*   (Deuteronomy 28:65)

> *Day after day you will be oppressed and robbed, with no one to rescue you...an object of scorn and ridicule.*   (Deuteronomy 28:15, 37)

> *I will forsake my house* [Temple], *abandon my inheritance.*   (Jeremiah 12:7)

---

24.   *Yoma* 9b, p. 39.

For the Israelites will live **many days** *without king or prince, without sacrifice or sacred stones, without ephod or idol. Afterward the Israelites will return and seek the Lord their God and David their king. They will come trembling to the Lord and to his blessings in the last days.*

(Hosea 3:4f)

The Israelites angered God gravely on two separate occasions in the first 17 months after leaving Egypt: worship of the golden calf and refusal to enter the Promised Land. The Lord told Moses both times that He would *"destroy the people and make Moses into a great nation...greater and stronger than they* [the Israelites]" (Exodus 32:10; and Numbers 14:12). It was also said about Messiah:

It is too small a thing for you to be my servant, to restore the tribes of Jacob, and bring back those of Israel I have kept. I will also make you a light for the Gentiles, that you may bring my salvation to the ends of the earth.

(Isaiah 49:6)

Scripture foretold that God would justify the Gentiles by their faith, and announced in advance to Abraham:

All nations will be blessed through you. So those who have faith are blessed along with Abraham, the man of faith.
(Galatians 3:8f; see also Genesis 12:3; 18:18; 22:18)

The Jews Outside of Their Homeland

Evil forces have done everything possible to annihilate the Jews and prevent their return to the area God swore to give them.

Whoever found them devoured them. Their enemies said, "we are not guilty," for they sinned against the Lord...the hope of their fathers.   (Jeremiah 50:7)

They are targeted by Satan to receive full-force his hatred for God, and their land has suffered equally. Whether a Jewish person serves God or not, he is still identified as a Jew. Nahmanides, a famous Jewish sage from Spain, wrote this mournful description in a letter to his son in 1268 A.D. about the land of Israel:

> And what can I say about the country? Much of it is deserted; the desolation is overwhelming. As a rule, whatever is sanctified by the sword is destroyed by the sword, but Jerusalem is more devastated than all else.[25]

In the 17th and 18th centuries, influential Christians believed in the restoration of the Jews to their homeland while many leading Jews did not.[26] Understandably, many Jews have not been eager to leave their countries of birth for the Spartan, pioneering existence required to rebuild Israel, until their survival depended upon it.

> *In the time of my favor I will answer you, and in the day of salvation I will help you...to restore the land and to reassign its desolate inheritances.*   (Isaiah 49:8)

"The time of my favor" refers to the restoration that will happen in *"the year of the Lord's favor,"* the *Year of Jubilee,* the fiftieth year spoken about in Leviticus 25:8–55; Isaiah 61:1, 2.

> *See, I will send you the prophet Elijah* [to prepare the way] *before that great and dreadful day of the Lord comes. He will turn the hearts of the fathers to their children, and the hearts of the children to their fathers.*
> (Malachi 4:5f; see also Matthew 17:11 and Luke 1:17)

The Lord says that only if the sun, moon, stars and sea should cease to exist or the universe could be measured will He reject all

---

25.   Ben-Dov, p. 355.
26.   Prince, p. 33.

the descendants of Israel because of all they have done (Jeremiah 31:35f).

I will not accuse forever, nor will I always be angry...but I will heal him and restore comfort to him.   (Isaiah 57:16f)

I take no pleasure in the death of anyone...Repent and live!
(Ezekiel 18:32)

For God's gifts and his call are irrevocable.
(Romans 11:29)

In that day, the Root of Jesse will stand as a banner for the peoples; the nations will rally to him, and his place of rest will be glorious. In that day the Lord will reach out his hand **a second time to reclaim the remnant** *that is left of his people from...*[many nations].   (Isaiah 11:10f)

When God led the Israelites out of Egypt, He brought out the entire nation, not the remnant. The only time He has gathered a portion of them was from one nation, Babylon. There has not been **a second regathering of the remnant from many nations** until our day!

I will take the Israelites out of the nations where they have gone. I will gather them from all areas and bring them back into their own land. I will make them **one nation** *in the land, on the mountains of Israel.*   (Ezekiel 37:21f)

From the end of Solomon's reign, c. 930 B.C., the Holy Land was divided into two regions, ten tribes in the north (Israel) and two tribes in the south (Judah). Today it is one nation again.

That there should be Jews to regather is indeed miraculous in the light of: their massacre and exile by Spanish Moors (11th century); the mass murders in European Jewish communities by the Crusaders (1096–1202); the banishment of all Jews from England in 1290 by Edward I; the massacres, confiscation of property, and expulsion of Jews from Spain in 1492 and Portugal in 1498; catastrophes in Poland and the Ukraine in 1648; and excessive taxation, boycotts, exile of their children, and *pogroms* (devastations) of entire Jewish ghettos in Russia (1881–1921). And this list is certainly not complete.

There have been wicked people who masquerade behind the name of Jesus Christ, like the Nazis and the Russian *Pamyat* of today. Tragically, the Church has had a sad history of anti-Semitism itself. God says:

> *I will bless those who bless you, and whoever curses you, I will curse.*   (Genesis 12:3)

> *Israel was holy to the Lord, the firstfruits of his harvest. All who devoured her were held guilty, and disaster overtook them.*   (Isaiah 2:3)

> *Though I completely destroy all the nations among which I scatter you, I will not completely destroy you.*
> (Jeremiah 30:10)

Within one century of casting the Jews out, the Spanish Empire reached its height and declined under Philip II. He lost the Spanish Armada in his attempt to conquer England. His invincible navy was wrecked through a combination of providential events, such as two gales, low tides and no wind.

Queen Elizabeth I of England had a monument set up and silver medals struck saying "Jehovah," in Hebrew and the words, "He blew and they were scattered."[27] Another Armada was gathered in 1597, but was entirely defeated by the weather. England did not start to prosper as a world power until the reign of Oliver Cromwell, when the Jews were allowed to return in 1655.

The Jewish people had no recourse, no hope for justice. The cruelty to them reached demonic, sub-human depths in our own "civilized" day with the systematic elimination of one third of all

---

27.   Gardner, Vol. 2, p. 39.

Jewish people by Hitler's Germany. There was little intervention from the world at large. President Franklin D. Roosevelt organized a conference in July 1938 at which 32 countries met in Evian-les-Bains, France, to decide how to rescue the Jews from Germany and Austria. Since these desperate people could still get out of Europe, where would they go?

Golda Meir described listening to each delegate stand one by one and explain why his country could not accept the refugees. Only Holland and Denmark opened their doors to them.[28] Hitler interpreted this refusal of the nations as justification of his policy to eradicate Jewry. His program started in earnest on November 9, 1938, "Crystal Night." Nazis went on a rampage, killing Jews and setting fire to hundreds of their homes and synagogues and smashing thousands of their store windows all over Germany. Because there were no objections of any consequence to this widespread violence, Hitler's evil continued unrestricted.

The Nazi movement arose in the midst of a so-called "Christian" nation with little active opposition (see page 168). In Berlin at Wannsee on January 20, 1942, fifteen top German officials mapped out the Final Solution, i.e., "the identification, transportation, and murder of every Jew in Europe."[29]

Can we ever forget this genocide of six million members of the human family? The Holocaust did not end until Germany was defeated in 1945. No other group of people has been singled out for such sustained hatred throughout the last 2,000 years.

The Jewish claim to their homeland rests on the will and power of God to finalize it.

But now, I will send for many fishermen...and they will catch them. After that, I will send for many hunters, and

---

28.   Dixon, p. 117f.
29.   *The Washington Post,* May 9, 1990, p. A-1.

*they will hunt them down on every mountain, and hill...My
eyes are on all their ways. They are not hidden from me...*
                                        (Jeremiah 16:16f)

*Return faithless people, for I am your husband. I will
choose you—one from a town and two from a clan—and
bring you to Zion.*   (Jeremiah 3:14)

The last words of a great leader to his people would be considered most significant. Among Moses' final words to the Israelites,
before he went up to die on Mount Nebo, were:

*The Lord will judge his people and have compassion on his
servants, when he sees their strength is gone and no one is
left, slave or free.*   (Deuteronomy 32:36)

*When the power of the holy people has been finally broken,
all these things will be completed.*   (Daniel 12:7)

*For my own name's sake, I delay my wrath...I hold it back
from you, so as not to cut you off...I have tested you in the
furnace of affliction.*   (Isaiah 48:9f)

Return to me and I will return to you.   (Malachi 3:7)

*When you are in distress and all these things have hap-
pened to you, then in later days you will return to the Lord
your God and obey him. For the Lord your God is a merci-
ful God; he will not abandon or destroy you or forget the
covenant with your forefathers, which he confirmed to
them by oath.*   (Deuteronomy 4:30f)

A result of World War I was to force Turkey out of Palestine,
followed by formal recognition of a homeland for the Jews in Palestine under the British Balfour Declaration. After World War II,
there was a mass migration of Jews to their homeland.

God's Covenants with the Jewish Nation

Now that the Jewish people are established in their ancient land, no power under the sun will be able to dislodge them. To attempt to prevent the restoration of Israel spells destruction.

When all these blessings and curses I have set before you come upon you and you take them to heart wherever the Lord your God disperses you among the nations; and when you and your children return to the Lord your God and obey him with all your heart...then the Lord your God will restore your fortunes, and have compassion on you, and gather you again from all the nations where He scattered you...He will bring you to the land that belonged to your fathers, and you will take possession of it. He will make you more prosperous and numerous than your fathers.

(Deuteronomy 30:1–5)

I will bring back my exiled people Israel; they will rebuilt the ruined cities and live in them...They will make gardens and eat their fruit. I will plant them upon their land and they shall never again be plucked up out of the land which I have given them, says the Lord, your God.   (Amos 9:14f)

The Lord has bound Himself under oath to fulfill this **unconditional promise,** which even sin would not cancel:

On that day, the Lord made a covenant with Abram and said, To your descendants I give this land, from the Wadi of Egypt to the great river, the Euphrates.   (Genesis 15:18)

The United Kingdom of David and Solomon did extend from the River of Egypt (Wadi el Arish in the Egyptian Sinai) to the Euphrates River, the kingdom's northeasterly border. The future boundaries of Israel are found in Ezekiel 47.

The Lord remembers his everlasting covenant with Abraham; the oath He swore to Isaac; and the decree He confirmed to Jacob and their descendants to give them the land of Canaan as the portion they will inherit.

(Psalm 105:8f)

The word of our God stands forever.   (Isaiah 40:8)

The Lord's land grant to Abraham was not based on the other party's performance to remain in effect. By contrast, the covenant made at Mt. Sinai with Israel and her descendants depended on total commitment to God and to His purposes. Israel would receive His blessings only if they walked in obedience to Him (Exodus 19:5–8; 24:7; Leviticus 25:18). If not, the land itself would *"vomit"* them out (Leviticus 18:28).

The Law received at Sinai was to train the Jews in righteousness and prepare them for their Messiah. The Law serves: to reveal sin, which alienates man from God, and to demonstrate the need for a Savior from sin (Galatians 3:19–22).

The New Covenant (Jeremiah 31:31–34) is unconditional to men, because someone else has already met its terms. God offers to forgive a person his sins and to establish a new relationship with him on a new basis. The Lord will write His requirements directly on the "tablets" of our hearts instead of the original tablets of stone. The fulfillment of this covenant did not depend upon the performance of sinful men, but upon that of God's own Son, in Whom there was no failure. To benefit from this New Covenant, foretold in the Old Testament, one has to receive what the Son did on our behalf.

God's unconditional covenants with Israel were made with:

Abraham   —the land grant (Genesis 15:9–21) and the survival of descendants who would not become extinct or assimilated in exile, but would "take possession of the cities of their enemies" (Genesis 22:17f).

Phinehas	—a lasting, faithful priesthood (Numbers 25:10–13).
David	—a Davidic king who will bring rest in their Promised Land forever (2 Samuel 7:11–16; 1 Kings 4:20f; 5:3f).
New	—a new relationship with God (executed by God's Son, but not accepted by Israel yet) (Jeremiah 31:31–34; Ezekiel 11:19f; 36:26).

These are immutable, legal terms, and the Lord does not break His word. So far, we have witnessed the first steps in the enforcement of God's land covenant by the return of Jews to their land.

Even if you have been banished to the most distant land under the heavens, from there the Lord your God will gather you and bring you back.   (Deuteronomy 30:4)

Moreover, He is the only One who has the power to establish Israel's boundaries and bring peace to the land forever. The sovereignty of God demands that His land grant to Abraham and to his descendants be established fully and without question. To accomplish this, He will use force.

In those days, at that time...search will be made for Israel's guilt, but there will be none...I will forgive the remnant I spare...the Lord has opened his arsenal and brought out the weapons of his wrath...He will vigorously defend their cause, so that he may bring rest to their land.
                    (Jeremiah 50:20, 25, 34)

The Holy Land in the Last 2,000 Years

Israel was reborn legally by the majority vote of the United Nations on November 29, 1947; formally, with the Jewish Proclamation of Independence on May 14, 1948; and effectually by the cease-fire on January 7, 1949. Thus, the nation resurrected into a functioning body politic. To understand better the formation of Israel, we need a brief sketch of the last 2,000 years.

Jerusalem was first controlled by the Romans from 63 B.C.–324 A.D., followed by the Byzantine Christians until 638 A.D. Then, the Arabs took over until the Crusaders overwhelmed them in 1099. The European knights were displaced in 1244. Tartars, Mongols, and Turkish tribes from Asia and China swarmed in, spreading devastation until 1291.

Next, Mameluke sultans from Egypt ruled Palestine and built Jerusalem into a Muslim holy city. They were ousted by the Ottoman Turks who were ensconced from 1517–1917. The city fell into a state of pitiful neglect after the reign of Suleiman the Magnificent (1520–1566). The British had control from 1917–1947 when they relinquished Palestine to the United Nations. Of course, Israel became a state between 1947–1949.

Escalating over the last five centuries, a series of events have led up to the restoration of Israel. A new haven was granted to the Jews and a fresh start to all the peoples of earth with Christopher Columbus's discovery of the New World.

Note: Evidence suggests that Columbus was a *Converso,* a Jewish convert to Christianity.[30] His personal survival and that of his mission depended on the total suppression of all evidence of his Jewish background. His first name means "Christ bearer."

Columbus' sailors, some of whom were Jewish, boarded ship before midnight on August 2 (*Av* 9). It was illegal for a Jew to remain in Spain past that hour. Luis de Torres, a Hebrew translator, also set sail at dawn with Columbus.[31]

---

30.   Wiesenthal, p. 108ff.
31.   *Ibid.,* p. 3, 171.

The voyage was sponsored by two *Conversos,* Luis de Santangel and Gabriel Sanchez, to whom the explorer sent word of his successful voyage, even ahead of Ferdinand and Isabella.[32] The impetus behind the expedition may have been a desperate search for a haven for the Spanish Jews, the largest body of Jews in Europe. The maps were drawn by Jewish cartographers. Columbus' marginal notes in his books demonstrate extensive familiarity with Jewish terms.[33]

Palestine's importance as a bridge to international trade routes declined after the discovery of America. However, after Napoleon's Middle East campaign in 1799, Palestine started to gain importance, especially after the opening of the Suez Canal in 1869. There was much rivalry among the European powers over the declining Turkish Empire, which included Palestine.

The Turkish Empire reached its height under Sultan Suleiman. It was later called the "sick man of Europe." Four European nations kept it from collapsing throughout the 1800s. They did not want Russia to control the Balkans of Turkey and extend Russian influence to the Mediterranean Sea.

In 1877, Russia declared war on Turkey and defeated her within a year. The European powers met at the Congress of Berlin in 1878 and forced Russia to give up most of her gains, especially the Balkans. The breakup of the entire Turkish Empire did not come until the end of World War I, at which time Palestine came under British administration.

The Vision of Zionism—1880

Within Jewish thought, Rabbi Judah Alkalai (1798–1878) was a precursor of modern Zionism. He was denounced for his pamphlets in the 1840s, and 1850s, which suggested that international recognition and Jewish settlement of *Erez* Israel was

---

32.   *Ibid.,* p. 177.
33.   *Ibid.,* p. 107.

the best solution to the Jewish situation in Europe. He saw the need for the revival of the Hebrew language and Jewish agriculture.

Some found it necessary to abandon the traditional Jewish hope for Messiah in order to convince themselves that God would use human effort to rebuild Israel. On the other hand, assimilated Jews had to recognize Judaism's real political necessity to establish a separate Jewish state.

Zevi Hirsch Kalischer (1795–1874), a rabbinic scholar, maintained that redemption would be manifest in two stages: the "natural one" with the return to Israel and agriculture, followed by "the supernatural" phase.[34]

In the year of the Turkish defeat, 1878, the first Jewish agricultural communities, Rosh Pinnah ("cornerstone") and Petah Tikvah ("door of hope") were founded in Palestine. They became part of the "new *yishuv*" or Jewish community, which started evolving in 1880. It was the *pogrom*-impelled masses of Russia and Eastern Europe who immigrated to Zion (*Hovevei Zion*—lovers of Zion) and provided the manpower that rebuilt *Erez* Israel.

They found the visual fulfillment of Moses' prophecy:

> ...*a burning waste...nothing planted, nothing sprouting, no vegetation growing on it.*   (Deuteronomy 29:23)

Drought was one of the covenant curses (Deuteronomy 28:22ff). God withheld rain from Israel in the past. (He promises to do so in the future to any nation that does not come up to worship the King, the Lord Almighty—Zechariah 14:17ff). Mark Twain, who visited the Promised Land in 1867, described it as a veritable "dust bowl."

> ...a country...given over wholly to weeds—a silent mournful expanse...a desolation is here that not even imagination can grace with the pomp of life and action...We never saw a human being on the whole

---

34.   Rubinstein, ed., p. 8.

route...Hardly a tree or a shrub anywhere...Even the olive and the cactus...had almost deserted the country.[35]

For many centuries, Palestine was sparsely populated, largely nomadic, poorly cultivated and generally neglected. The trees had been cut down under Turkish administration and the topsoil had long since disappeared. The physical restoration began as the Jews bought and drained the malarial swamps and cultivated the barren, stony land. Agriculture had to be well established to support the nation.

The newcomers clashed with the "old *yishuv*" settlers, who were mainly Orthodox and opposed modern trends. In 1897, the secular, nationalist groups and the strictly religious ones reached a mutual agreement which enabled them to coexist.

Note: As a matter of conscience, some pious Jews in Israel today will not pay taxes. They do not recognize the existence of Israel, as they believe that only Messiah can establish the state upon His arrival.

In addition to reclaiming the land, millions of trees have been planted since 1900, which play an important role in the area's atmospheric water (hydrologic) cycle. The trees help retain moisture and stop erosion. The land has become highly productive under Jewish labor, irrigation, and fertilizer. This is the more amazing, since they were denied land ownership for so many centuries in Europe.

Israel now ranks high in the export of citrus fruits, vegetables, and flowers. It seems as if the earth itself is "rejoicing" and coming back to life with the return of its people. Rashi (1040–1105), one of the most revered teachers in Jewish history, said that "when Israel becomes so very fertile, there can be no clearer sign that Messiah's advent is near." This is based on:

---

35. Mark Twain, *The Innocents Abroad;* Davis, p. 12.

But you, O mountains of Israel, will produce branches and fruit for my people, Israel, for they will soon come home. I am concerned for you and will look on you with favor. You will be plowed and sown. I will multiply the number of people upon you, even the whole house of Israel. The towns will be inhabited and the ruins rebuilt. I will increase the number of men and animals upon you as before and they will be fruitful...Then you will know that I am the Lord. I will cause people, my people Israel, to walk upon you. They will possess you, and you will be their inheritance. You will never again deprive them of their children.

(Ezekiel 36:8ff)

Never in the memory of mankind has a people, scattered to every corner of the earth, returned about 1,900 years later to their ancient homeland to speak their long defunct language! Since the Jewish people immigrated to Israel from many diverse countries, national unity would have been impossible without Hebrew. European Jews spoke the Yiddish dialect. This was not a pure language, and not all Jews knew it.

Revival of Hebrew as the spoken language by 1948 in Israel was due to the heroic, fanatic fight of one Eliezer Ben-Yehuda. The Russo-Turkish War (1877–1878) and the Balkan nations' contending for their freedom inspired Ben-Yehuda to think that the Jews could return to their ancient homeland as well. He went to Paris in 1878 where he contracted tuberculosis.

With little money and in frail health, he moved to Jerusalem in 1881. In 1909, he published the first of 16 volumes of his Hebrew dictionary. He devoted his entire life to reconstructing this language out of a limited number of words. He fulfilled the prophecy:

For then will I turn ["haphak" - return] *to the people a pure language, that they may all call upon the name of the Lord, to serve him with one consent.*

(Zephaniah 3:9, KJV)

At his death in 1922, there was material for eleven of the volumes and Hebrew was spoken fluently in Palestine. He also published a newspaper, which was a voice for Zionism, the Jewish independence movement. Zionism had become well-established in world politics by this time.

The Zionists conceived of an independent Jewish state because of their despair among the nations. The father of political Zionism was Theodor Herzl, a doctor of law, a journalist, and a playwright. He was shocked out of the complacent belief in Jewish assimilation while covering the trial of the French officer, Alfred Dreyfus, and the reaction of the violent Parisian mob in 1895.

There were also anti-Semitic riots in Herzl's home of Vienna in 1895 when the city elected a mayor on an anti-Jewish platform. This, combined with multiple Russian *pogroms* and German agitation, convinced Dr. Herzl that Jews would not be assimilated in Europe.

At the same time, William Hechler, the Anglican chaplain of the British Embassy in Vienna, concluded from his study of Bible prophecy that the restoration of the Jewish state was imminent. He read Herzl's *Der Judenstaat* ("The Jewish State") right after publication in 1896, and immediately offered Dr. Herzl his help.

Hechler, the son of a Hebrew scholar, had excellent connections with the German royal family, to whom he introduced the journalist. Reverend Hechler and British Christian Restorationists remained Herzl's strongest non-Jewish allies. The Orthodox rabbis, the Reform movement, and many wealthy Jews were outright hostile or ignored Herzl altogether.

He convened the First Zionist Congress in Basel, Switzerland, on August 29, 1897. The flag that flew on that day was later to become the national flag of Israel. After the Congress, Dr. Herzl stated:

> At Basel I founded the Jewish state! If I said this out loud today, I would be greeted by universal laughter. In five years, perhaps, and certainly in fifty years; everyone will perceive it...[36]

Hechler influenced Herzl against accepting the British Foreign Office's offer of Uganda in 1903 to alleviate the urgent need of Russian Jewry, due to the *pogroms*. Such an acceptance by the Congress might have made it impossible for Jews to settle in their Biblical homeland.[37] It was Dr. Chaim Weizmann who led the opposition against Uganda.

The evangelical clergyman was one of the instruments God used to help bring Israel back into being. Hechler followed Herzl everywhere and encouraged him in this work of destiny. Dr. Herzl mentioned the minister more than any other person in his diaries, according to Rev. Claude Duvernoy in *The Prince and the Prophet*. No doubt due to the strenuous battle, Dr. Herzl died at an early age on July 4, 1904.

The vision of the Jewish state began to take more shape by 1917. Dr. Chaim Weizmann's valuable discoveries in chemistry helped Britain win World War I. Thus, he gained prestige and influence among British statesmen, such as Prime Minister David Lloyd George and Foreign Secretary Arthur Balfour.

Weizmann's crucial contribution, the diplomatic talents of journalist Nahum Sokolow, and the influence of other Jews caused the British government to respond with the Balfour Declaration. Lord Balfour spoke out against persecution of the Jews, saying it had been "a disgrace to Christendom." The British also wanted control of Palestine and knew that Jewish backing would

---

36. Prince, p. 35.
37. *Ibid.,* p. 37.

strengthen their case. The Balfour Declaration was issued on November 2, 1917.

His Majesty's Government view with favor the establishment in Palestine of a National Home for the Jewish people...

Five weeks later, the English general, Lord Edmund Allenby, liberated Jerusalem from Turkey on December 10, the first day of *Hanukkah.* This was accomplished without firing a shot.

On April 24, 1920, the Balfour Declaration was approved by the Allies' Conference at San Remo and incorporated into the British Mandate on Palestine by the League of Nations on July 24, 1922. However, the struggle to implement the Declaration lasted until the British left Palestine in 1948.

The League of Nations conferred upon Britain the British Mandate of Palestine in 1920. It included the land west of the Jordan River as well as a much larger area, east of the river. Turkey surrendered all rights in Palestine to Britain under the Lausanne agreement of 1923.

With only his signature, British Colonial Secretary Winston Churchill transferred 77.6% of the total British Mandate of Palestine to the Arabs. The new entity of Transjordan came into being in 1921. The British appointed Abdullah the emir of this state, east of the Jordan River, and made Faisal, king of Iraq. These were two sons of the prominent Arabian leader, Sherif Hussein. ("The King [Hussein] can trace unbroken descent from the prophet Mohammed.")[38]

Britain recognized Transjordan as an independent state in 1928 and granted it complete independence in 1946. The agonizing formation of Israel stands in utter contrast to that of Jordan.

After 1922, the Arabs began to come into the Jewish area of Palestine from Syria, Iraq, Lebanon, Transjordan and Egypt due to better wages and living standards. Prior to this, Palestine's Arab

---

38.   *The Europa World Year Book* 1991, Vol. 1, p. 1,547.

population had been declining. Arab immigration was never restricted and "the non-Jewish population in the country soared by 75.2%" between 1922 to 1939.[39]

In the calm 1920s, the Jews did not go to Palestine in large numbers. Nevertheless, by the end of the decade, there were 110 agricultural colonies, farming 175,000 acres.[40]

As the Jews' economic and political status began to deteriorate in Europe, beginning in 1929, so did their personal security. Jewish immigration into Palestine increased, causing a violent Arab reaction. The British government severely limited Jewish immigration into the Mandate in 1921, 1929, and 1939. Jews were "severely restricted from purchasing land on a large scale, even at exorbitant prices."[41]

The Arab population increased in areas of intense Jewish development, such as Haifa, Jaffa, and Jerusalem. There was a much lower Arab increase in non-Jewish areas such as Nablus, Jenin, and Bethlehem.[42]

After a major Arab uprising in April 1936, the British Peel Commission suggested on July 7, 1937 a reduction in Jewish immigration to no more than 12,000 people per year, restrictions on Jewish land purchases, and a three-way partition of Palestine. The Arabs vehemently rejected the Peel plan and staged another revolt.

In August 1937, Heinrich Himmler, head of the SS, reported to Hitler that the concentration camps had been reorganized with four in Germany alone. The Nazi regime had been sending Jews and others to these camps since March 1933. The number of camps had increased to eighteen by the end of the war.

By October 20, 1937, the British government in Palestine had issued an ordinance limiting Jewish immigration according to

---

39.   Davis and Decter, p. 13.
40.   Johnson, p. 444.
41.   Davis and Decter, p. 6.
42.   *Ibid.*, p. 7 quoting: Fred Gottheil, *Arab Immigration into Pre-State Israel,* 1922–1931; *Palestine Royal Commission Report,* 1937, p. 279.

local political conditions.[43] Therefore, hundreds of thousands of Jews who might have found refuge in Palestine were denied entry and murdered in Germany instead.[44]

The position of the Central Conference of the American (Reform) Rabbis (CCAR) underwent a radical change at their Columbus, Ohio, convention in 1937.

> The Pittsburgh Platform (1885)...which rejected all Torah (the first five books of the Bible) laws "such as are not adapted to the views and habits of modern civilization," became the standard creed of Reform Judaism until 1937. It...denied the resurrection, heaven, and hell; dismissed a return to Zion; and presented messianism as the struggle for truth, justice, and righteousness in modern society.[45]

The CCAR had originally declared its "total disapproval of an attempt to establish a Jewish state" a month prior to the First Zionist Congress in 1897. These leaders were concerned that such a state would add to anti-Semitism by causing people to view Jews as aliens in their country of birth. This remained their position until the rise of Hitler. His actions convinced them in 1937 that it was the obligation of all Jews to build a Jewish homeland as a haven for refugees and as a Jewish spiritual and cultural center.[46]

A pan-Arab conference in Cairo in 1938 pledged all Arab states and communities to take international action to prevent the development of the Jewish state. Because of the failure of the Tripartite Conference (Jews, Arabs, and British) in London in 1939, the Balfour Declaration was shelved and replaced in May

---

43. *Chronicle of the 20th Century,* p. 475.
44. Davis and Decter, p. 13.
45. Johnson, p. 369f.
46. Rubinstein, ed., p. 61.

1939 by the British MacDonald White Paper limiting Jewish immigration during the following five years to 75,000 with none thereafter, except by Arab consent.[47]

Why was the life-blood of European Jews utterly poured out before the formation of Israel? What was God's adversary trying to prevent?

It was the "second generation" of Israelites (those under 20 years of age—Numbers 14:29-31; 1:45) who entered the Promised Land under Joshua. We are still in the lifetime (70-80 years—Psalm 90:10) of those under 20 years old when Israel won its independence in 1949. They are the "second" Jewish generation **as an entire nation** since Judea was destroyed in 70 A.D.

Of course, the 19-year-olds in 1949 would have been born in 1930. The most demonic annihilation in history was perpetrated against the Jewish people by the Nazi regime between 1933 and 1945. The Holocaust reveals the hideous depths to which the forces of evil will go to prevent the fulfillment of God's plan for humanity. Despite all opposition, the Word of the Lord will prevail in His preordained time.

---

47.   Johnson, p. 445.

Chapter Three

PERSPECTIVE FROM THE PRESENT

I will bless those who bless you, and whoever curses you I will curse. And all the peoples on earth will be blessed through you.   (Genesis 12:3)

Israel—1948

After World War II, the world confronted the horror of the Holocaust. There arose international demands to resettle the survivors in a Jewish state. The Palestine Partition Plan, creating Israel, passed by a 33 to 13 vote in the United Nations on November 29, 1947. This was 50 years after the First World Zionist Congress as Dr. Theodor Herzl had prognosticated. Though extremely hostile to Zionism, the Soviet bloc saw this as an opportunity to oust Britain from this most strategic area. Therefore, this bloc cast a total of four votes in favor of partition.

The Partition Plan offered the Jews only **16.1%** of the 1920 British Mandate of Palestine. Over three-quarters of the mandated territory had already been given to the Arabs in 1921 with the creation of Transjordan at **the first division of Palestine.** Land was not given to the Jewish people in spite of the Balfour Declaration (1917) which, as we have seen, was approved by both the Allies' Conference (1920) and by the League of Nations (1922). Britain located its military bases in the Arab states and not in the Jewish area.[1]

There had been no Arab or Jewish nations in Palestine, as it had belonged to Turkey for 400 years until 1917. Palestinian Arab nationalism started to develop after World War I. The U.N. Partition Plan (1947) offered self-determination to both Arabs and Jews in Palestine. The former could have created their own state in the area allotted to them. Instead, the Arab nations unanimously rejected the second division of Palestine and mobilized for war.

The Jewish people decided to accept the Partition Plan and formulated a government. Six months later, the Jews declared statehood on May 14 (*Iyyar* 5), 1948.

Can a country be born in a day or a nation be brought forth in a moment?   (Isaiah 66:8)

After the last British troops departed at midnight, Egypt, Transjordan, Syria, Lebanon, Saudi Arabia, and Iraq attacked on May 15. The Jewish state held West Jerusalem but had to surrender the Jewish Quarter in East Jerusalem.

The Israelis suffered casualties of 6,000, almost one percent of a population of 650,000. (This would equal the death of 2.25 million Americans in the United States today.)

The U.N. partition boundaries were obscured by the Arab invasion, in which the Arab neighbors were unsuccessful in aborting the birth of the legally authorized Jewish state. After the cease-fire of January 7, 1949, Transjordan took the West Bank, the Old City (East Jerusalem) with the Temple Mount and the Jewish Quarter. Egypt obtained the Gaza Strip, and Israel proclaimed West Jerusalem as the capital and the seat of the Knesset. Jerusalem remained

---

1.   Davis, p. 7.

divided by a north-south cease-fire line until June 7 (*Iyyar* 28) 1967. This is:

> *...a land that has recovered from war, whose people were gathered from many nations to the mountains of Israel, which had long been desolate.*   (Ezekiel 38:8)

Israel has arisen from the ashes of Jewish suffering. Historian Paul Johnson uses the image of a jigsaw puzzle to show how each event relates to the following one. The massacres in eastern Europe of 1648 led to the return of the Jews to England and thence to America, where they were free to develop in all areas. Without the American Jewish community, Israel would have lacked tremendous political and financial support.

Israel—1967

War broke out again between the Jews and Arabs in 1956 and in the Six-Day War in 1967. The Israelis did not instigate the battle for Jerusalem in 1967, but retaliated against Jordan's attack. Israel captured Jerusalem in **the first 30 days of the 20th year** after becoming a nation in May 1948. The remarkable timing of the unification of Jerusalem is of great significance in God's plans and follows this amazing precedent:

The Persian King Artaxerxes granted Nehemiah's request to rebuild Jerusalem in order to provide safety for the Jewish exiles who had returned from Babylon. This decree was issued in **the first month of the 20th year** in 445 B.C.

> *In the month of Nisan* [the first month] *in the twentieth year of King Artaxerxes'* [Jewish Queen Esther's stepson] *reign...I* [Nehemiah] *answered the king...send me to the city in Judah so that I can rebuild it...the king granted my requests.*   (Nehemiah 2:1ff)

Can this precise parallel be due to mere chance? In keeping with this parallel, Israel herself is being rebuilt in the 20th, in this case, century (cf. Hosea 6:2).

There are other similarities between the Jewish capture of Jerusalem in 1967 and history. Exactly 1900 years earlier, the Roman Empire began to subdue the Jewish Revolt (66–70 A.D.) in the northern district of Galilee in October 67 A.D. The climax came in 70 A.D. when the Roman General Titus attacked Jerusalem on her vulnerable northern side. The Temple was set afire on *Av* 9 (the end of July), the very day on which the First Temple had been burned in 586 B.C.

One of the two Jewish leaders, Simeon ben (son of) Giora, protected the Upper City (the northern side). After being defeated, the two men were marched in chains along with 700 other prisoners in Titus' triumphal procession through Rome in 71 A.D.[2]

When Israel fought the Jordanians in Jerusalem in 1967, the battle began on the northern side. Of great interest is the name of the company commander who led two of the Jewish breakthroughs. It was "Giora!"[3]

On the eve of the ninth of *Av* in 1970, the Temple Mount archaeological team uncovered a column with "a Tenth Legion dedicatory inscription to Titus himself." Nineteen hundred years ago to the day, Titus was briefing his troops on storming the Temple Mount.[4]

As a result of the Six-Day War against Jordan, Egypt, Syria, and Iraq in 1967, Israel gained the Old City, the Sinai Peninsula, the Gaza Strip, the West Bank, and the Golan Heights. Jerusalem was immediately unified under Jewish control for the first time since the days of Bar Kokhba (132–135 A.D.), who had control of the city for a brief time.

---

2.   *Encyclopaedia Judaica,* Vol. 9, p. 1,399; Keller, p. 416.
3.   Gur, pp. 19, 41, 342.
4.   Ben-Dov, p. 189.

Israel allowed the Temple Mount area of the city to remain under Islamic control. The Israelis annexed the Golan Heights for security reasons, but occupied the Gaza Strip and the West Bank.

In the *Yom Kippur* War in 1973, Israel penetrated deeper into Egypt and Syria than in 1967. The Israeli forces stopped about 40 miles from Cairo and 22 miles from Damascus. Sinai was returned to Egypt in the Peace Treaty of 1979. This is the allocation of all the land of the 1920 British Mandate of Palestine:

Mandated Area	Square Miles 1920 Mandate	Percentage of Original	Year Gained
Jordan	37,737	77.6%	1921
Israel	7,847	16.1%	1947
East Jerusalem	626	1.3%	Annexed by Israel, 1967
West Bank	2,270	4.7%	Occupied by Israel, 1967
Gaza Strip	146	0.3%	Occupied by Israel, 1967
British Mandate of Palestine	48,626 Total	100.0%	
Golan Heights	454		Occupied by Israel in 1967; annexed in 1981 from Syria

(Source: Central Bureau of Statistics, Hakirya, Givat Ram, December 1987).

Indeed, Jewish prayers were answered, but what is lacking? Rather than immigrate (*aliyah*—ascend) to build Israel, many Jews prefer to move to the United States. The settling of Israel has been a fierce fight, calling for determination and sacrifice every step of the way.

> By the year 2020, Jews will constitute a minority of 48 percent inside Israel…According to the estimate, every hundred thousand extra Jews will delay that demographic balance by one year.[5]

The best product of Zionism, the offspring of the *kibbutzim* (collective farms) is leaving. To exist under the constant pressure,

---

5.   Newsletter of the International Christian Embassy, January–February 1991, p. 6.

an Israeli needs full comprehension of why his country has been summoned back into existence. "Going home to Israel" transcends statehood, as essential as that is. The Jewish nation will not be complete until it fulfills its spiritual purpose as well.

In the words of their national anthem *"Hatikvah"* (The Hope): "So long our hopes are not yet lost." In whom does their real hope lie?

For on my holy mountain, the high mountain of Israel...the entire house of Israel will serve me, and there I will accept them.   (Ezekiel 20:40)

All 21 Arab nations surround Israel. Six were granted independence between 1918 and 1948, and the remaining 15, since 1948. They include a total of 216.55 million people and 5.29 million square miles (41 people per square mile).

Israel's population (1992 estimate) is 5.20 million with 7,847 square miles (665 people per square mile) or about the size of New Jersey. Israel is the equivalent of 0.1% (0.00148) of the total Arab land mass or about 21% the size of Jordan (37,737 square miles).

After Transjordan took the western bank of the Jordan River in 1948, the name was changed to "Jordan." Today, "60% of Jordan's population of 2.4 million are Palestinian and there are 1.3 million Palestinians living in the West Bank."[6]

Israel—Today

Though many nations have recognized the existence of Israel, only Costa Rica and El Salvador accept Jerusalem as the capital of Israel. Remember that without Israel, there would be no state in which to regather the exiles, and no Jewish nation to which Messiah would come. Jesus Christ said to the Jewish people:

6.   *The Europa World Year Book 1991*, Vol. 1, p. 1,537.

For I tell you, you will not see me again until you say, "Blessed is he who comes in the name of the Lord."
(Matthew 23:39; cf. Psalm 118:26)

This is the well-known Jewish messianic proclamation.

Israel's reappearance is of such pivotal significance that it captures constant attention in the United Nations and the media. The possibility of a Jewish state was fought decades before it ever came into being.

Over more than forty years, Arab neighbors have waged four unsuccessful wars against Israel. Arab extremists have been unrelenting in their bitter opposition. Two Arab heads of state, Anwar Sadat and Bashir Gemayel, were assassinated for making peace with the Jewish state.

Moderate Palestinians have been accused of collaborating with Israel and murdered. The extremists exert much pressure.

They [Israel's enemies] *do not speak peaceably, but devise false accusations against those who live quietly in the land.*
(Psalm 35:20)

The land resonates with tension. The unresolved conflict formally erupted again on December 9, 1987, as the Palestinian *intifada* (uprising). The United States is bringing Jews and Arabs to the peace table.

They dress the wound of my people [the Jews] *as though it were not serious. Peace, peace, they say, when there is no peace.*   (Jeremiah 6:14)

The settlement of Russian immigrants in the West Bank alarms the Arab world. Jewish preparations over the last few years for the future Temple also infuriate Moslems. "Jerusalem's Temple Mount is potentially the most volatile 35 acres on earth."[7]

---

7.   Ostling, p. 64.

Although Israel maintained overwhelming military superiority over its Arab adversaries, this is shifting due to new Arab weapons and missiles. Israel will not return to the security from land and air attack she once had. Iraq scourged Israel 39 times with Scud missiles over a 40-day period (January 17 to February 25, 1991).

Note: Under the limit imposed by the Jewish law (Deuteronomy 25:3), the Jews gave 39 lashes (*malkot*) as a punishment.

With the exception of Egypt and Turkey, Arab nations have been in a state of war and boycott of the Jewish state since its founding. A nation that attempts to broker peace in the Middle East dare not disregard God's Word that He Himself is restoring the Jews to their entire ancient homeland.

Some Moslems believe they are fighting a "holy" war for Allah, a war in which Israel will be wiped off the map. They tolerate no compromise or coexistence. Instead of men initiating war on God's behalf, it will be the reverse. God will defend Israel, as she will not be able to stand against the overwhelming forces that will attack her.

> *"Come," they say, "let us destroy them as a nation that the name of Israel be remembered no more." With one mind they plot together. They form an alliance against you.*
> (Psalm 83:4f)

> *Melt away, all you Philistines!...The Lord has established Zion, and in her his afflicted people will find refuge.*
> (Isaiah 14:31f)

Is this primarily a problem of land ownership, or of spiritual dominance? Until men accept that it is God who is gathering the Jews back to Israel, they will fight. Only God can convince anyone of this. When did the contention between these half brothers originate? We need to return briefly to their mutual father, Abraham.

The Half Brothers—Isaac and Ishmael

Because of the advanced age of Abraham's wife, Sarah, the couple was concerned over the lack of the heir that God had promised. The long waiting period was due to Abraham's incomplete obedience to God's explicit instructions to leave his country, Ur in the Chaldees, **and** his father's polytheistic household (Joshua 24:2). Abraham was to go to a land God would show him (Genesis 12:1f). Instead of this, his father, Terah, *"took Abram"* and influenced his son to settle in Haran, a flourishing caravan city, far short of God's destination of Canaan (Genesis 11:31).

It was not until Terah's death, that Abraham started to follow God's orders again at age 75 (Genesis 12:4; Acts 7:4). God waited until Abraham and his wife were in the Promised Land before allowing Abraham to father the first Hebrew, Isaac.

God was initiating the Hebrew nation, the first step in His program to free mankind from enslavement to sin. He would have a holy people with a land in which to live. Through them, He would reveal His nature and laws and bring salvation at the appointed time for all people. To the Jews belong: the adoption as sons, the divine glory, the covenants, the receiving of the law, the Temple worship, the promises, the patriarchs, and the human ancestry of the Messiah (Romans 9:4).

After arriving in Canaan, Sarah, who remained barren, contrived the plan to give Abraham her Egyptian bondswoman, Hagar, according to the custom of those days described in the Nuzi Tablets. Hagar became with child, and the angel of the Lord told her that her son, Ishmael ("God hears"), would be:

> *...a wild man. His hand will be against everyman, and everyman's hand against him. And he shall* [future tense] *dwell* ["shakan," live permanently] *in the presence of all his brethren.*   (Genesis 16:12, KJV)

Here, we have God's marvelous declaration that the Jews and Arabs, will eventually abide together in peace. The Jews and Arabs will become partners and bless all nations.

In that day Israel will be the third, along with Egypt and Assyria, a blessing on the earth. The Lord Almighty will bless them saying, "Blessed be Egypt my people, Assyria my handiwork, and Israel my inheritance." (Isaiah 19:24f)

Abraham loved Ishmael and said to God, *"If only Ishmael might live under your blessing!"* God agreed, but said that it would be Sarah's son and his descendants with whom He would establish His everlasting covenant.

As for Ishmael, I have heard you: I will surely bless him; I will make him fruitful and will greatly increase his numbers. He will be the father of twelve rulers, and I will make him into a great nation. (Genesis 17:20)

Ishmael was circumcised at thirteen and was fourteen years old at the birth of Isaac. Ishmael's twelve sons are mentioned by name and became the rulers of the Arab people (Genesis 25:12f).

His [Ishmael's] *descendants settled in the area from Havilah to Shur,* [Sinai and north-west Arabia] *near the border of Egypt, as you go toward Asshur. And they lived in hostility toward all their brothers.* (Genesis 25:18)

Finally, God sent Isaac ("he laughs"), the son for whom Abraham and Sarah waited 25 years after God's promise of an heir. His birth was certainly supernatural, as he came from a barren woman, who was ninety years of age.

(The birth of Isaac, the first Hebrew child, symbolizes that God's children, people who believe in Him and obey His Word, have a miraculous birth. This is not the result of natural descent, but is due to the will and intervention of God (John 1:13). When a person is born of God, the individual's spirit comes to life.)

Abraham himself never owned any of the Promised Land, except the small area in which he was buried (Genesis 49:30).

Abraham left everything he owned to Isaac. But while he was still living, he gave gifts to the sons of his concubines and sent them away from his son, Isaac, to the land of the east.   (Genesis 25:5f)

Sarah provides a cameo of the Jewish nation, which also will bring forth strong male progeny in her later years (see p. 154).

Society Today

A new order of society is overshadowing the old. The times of turbulence that bring forth this new era are referred to as *"birth pangs"* (Matthew 24:8) or *"hevlei Mashi'ah"* by the rabbis. The nations *(goyim),* not the Church, will have control of Jerusalem until the times of the Gentiles are over:

But now our enemies have trampled down your sanctuary.
(Isaiah 63:18)

Jerusalem will be trampled on by the Gentiles until the time of the Gentiles are fulfilled.   (Luke 21:24)

They [the Gentiles] *will trample on the holy city for 42 months* [the last three-and-one-half years of this era].
(Revelation 11:2)

The days are coming...when this city [Jerusalem] *will be rebuilt for me...the city will never again be uprooted or de-molished.*   (Jeremiah 31:38ff)

In the United States, cracks in the foundation of Gentile society started to appear in the 1960s. On the other hand, in that decade:

(1) The Jews gained control of Jerusalem.

(2) The Catholics and Protestants were revived and united by the Holy Spirit in the Charismatic Renewal (see p. 305f).

First, a minority of people began to throw off the restraints of morality and law in the 1960s. The longer this spirit permeates society, the more people it affects. They become more bold; demand their point of view; and will not tolerate a God who requires righteousness of them. Once moral fiber has been destroyed, it is no longer there to protect young people and guide their maturation. A decadent nation will eventually be destroyed by forces from within.

Regardless of the arena, today's events point to a climax. We live under the external threat of nuclear war and wrestle with the internal breakdown of the family. This most basic unit of society is being bombarded by divorce, child abuse, and immorality.

Females in the U.S. labor force, as a percent of the female population, have risen steadily from 29.8% in 1947 to 55.9% in 1988.[8] The 1990 Census shows that the number of married-couple households dropped as a proportion of the population in the Washington, D.C. area.

U.S. public schools now have the dual job of educating and parenting the students, as both parents of many households work. In the 1960s, U.S. universities and colleges dropped many of their residential regulations. Alcoholism, drug abuse, and homosexuality abound. Cocaine and crack, which have ravaged American society, are now inundating Western Europe.

AIDS is pandemic. The first published case report by the Centers for Disease Control was in Los Angeles on June 5, 1981. A million people in the United States are thought to be infected

---

8. Bureau of the Census: *Historical Statistics of the U.S.*, Part 1, Chart D 49–62, p. 133; and *Statistical Abstract of the U.S.—1990*, Chart 635, p. 384.

with this virus now.[9] The World Health Organization of the United Nations estimates that up to 10 million are infected globally.[10]

Now, some churches are beginning to ordain homosexuals and to marry them. All of this is in direct disregard for the Bible, which calls this behavior *"wicked," "detestable," and "vile"* (Genesis 19:7; Leviticus 18:22; Judges 19:23; Romans 1:24ff).

> *If a man lies with a man as one lies with a woman, both of them have done what is detestable. They must be put to death; their blood will be on their own heads.*
>
> (Leviticus 20:13)

> *In a similar way, Sodom and Gomorrah and the surrounding towns gave themselves up to sexual immorality and perversion. They serve as an example of those who suffer the punishment of eternal fire.*
>
> (Jude 7)

> *In the same way the men also abandoned natural relations with women and were inflamed with lust for one another. Men committed indecent acts with other men, and received in themselves the due penalty for their perversion.*
>
> (Romans 1:27)

> *Although they know God's righteous decree that those who do such things deserve death, they not only continue to do these very things, but also approve of those who practice them.*
>
> (Romans 1:32)

In another arena, "the homicide rate in the United States first soared in the 1960s and 1970s." A sharp increase began in 1986 with the availability of crack cocaine and guns. Between 1982 and 1988, the amount of cocaine confiscated went up a hundredfold.

9.   *The Washington Post*, April 2, 1991, p. A-1.
10.   *Ibid.*, August 1, 1990, p. A-1.

More than 100,000 rapes were reported in the U.S. in 1990. The rate of these assaults is increasing four times faster than the overall crime rate. All these elements demonstrate a mentally and physically ill society. And how do we deal with the manipulation of society that is inherent in genetic engineering and euthanasia? The latter has been legal in Holland since 1972.

Financially, the U.S. has gone from being a creditor to a debtor nation. Disobedience causes a people to be removed from blessings (Deuteronomy 28:12f, 44).

Due to instant communications, rapid transportation and dependence on foreign oil, nations have been propelled into the closeness of a global village. However, man's explosion of knowledge and brilliant inventions do not guarantee our peaceful co-existence.

Seal the words of the scroll until the time of the end. Many will go here and there to increase knowledge.

(Daniel 12:4)

It is well-known that the Bible and prayer have been removed from the U.S. public schools. The Church of England has declined to 3% of England's population.[11] In contrast, the number of Islamic mosques has exploded from one in 1945 to over 1,000 in 1989 in England and one in 1934 to over 500 in the United States in 1989. "It is the fastest-growing religion in the U.S., especially among black Americans."[12] This is also true worldwide.

Islam is predicted to double in size around the year 2020. If estimates hold up, Muslims will at that time number approximately 1.9 billion or 25 percent of humanity.[13]

Ishmar Schorsch, the chancellor of the Jewish Theological Seminary of America, lamented the "disintegration of the greatest

11.   *Ibid.,* November 3, 1990, p. G-11.
12.   *Ibid.,* June 22, 1991, p. C-6.
13.   Otis, p. 61.

Jewish community in our history." Judaism, which could never be destroyed in Jewish hearts by the fire of persecution in the ghettos, is now losing ground to the lure of Western materialism. "Recent surveys showed a 52 percent intermarriage rate among American Jews and a higher rate of conversion out of Judaism than into the faith." One congregation in Cincinnati has applied for membership in the Union of American Hebrew Congregations "whose liturgy eliminates all references to God."[14]

And there is abortion. God says:

From each man, too, I will demand an accounting for the life of his fellow man.   (Genesis 9:5)

Midway through the 50-year period since the establishment of Israel, the U.S. Supreme Court legalized abortion in 1973. Under pressure, the high court allowed the state legislatures greater freedom to limit abortion in July 1989. In effect, the nine justices were allowing the issue to rest with the voters themselves. This issue has convulsed American politics. Subsequent anti-abortion laws passed since 1989 have been enjoined until they go through the court system.

We are better informed than the ancient pagans, who feared the forces of nature, and thought they could placate their gods through child sacrifice. Today, we destroy millions of infants at the altar of personal convenience. Is there a Biblical precedent that informs us about God's justice on this subject?

God told Abraham that his descendents would return to Canaan when the sin of the Amorites (of Canaan) had *reached its full measure* (Genesis 15:16). This was given to them as a turning point.

What was this most detestable of practices found in the archaeological artifacts and the epic literature of Ras Shamra (Ancient Ugarit) on the Syrian Coast? It was the abhorrent sacrificing of their children to their god, Molech (*"melek"*, king).

---

14.   *The Washington Post.*, November 9, 1991, p. G-13.

Palestinian excavations have uncovered evidences of infant skeletons in burial places around heathen shrines. [15]

This, of course, was strictly forbidden to the Hebrews, who were to be stoned to death for such action (Leviticus 18:21; 20:2–5). Because of such practices, the Lord caused several nations to be driven from Canaan when the Israelites entered the land (Deuteronomy 18:9–12). Centuries later, Jewish children were burned as sacrifices to Molech in the Hinnom Valley in Jerusalem as well. Then, God declared that this valley would become a place of slaughter of the people themselves by invaders (Jeremiah 7:30–33; 32:35).

> *Was your prostitution* [spiritual and physical] *not enough? You slaughtered my children and sacrificed them to idols...Woe! Woe to you!*
> (Ezekiel 16:20ff; also Ezekiel 23:37)

Many nations sanction abortion. Have we filled God's heart with pain, because of our terrible wickedness? At the time of *"restitution of all things"* (Acts 3:21, KJV), He will remember the unborn babies, the most innocent and helpless members of humanity. Does their blood not cry out to Him from the ground (Genesis 4:10)?

Our Environment

An area once thought to be the province of environmentalists is now recognized as the greatest global challenge of our times, the survival of our planet. We are destroying our surroundings by: depleting our protective ozone layer; polluting oceans, rivers, lakes, and air; destroying forests and the underground water supply; and causing acid rain, toxic wastes, oil spills, and the warming "greenhouse effect." Many feel that humanity is "sitting on an environmental time bomb."

---

15.   Unger, p. 416.

In 1986, British scientists discovered a hole in the Antarctic ozone layer. Alarming new observations of ozone depletion have been released by the National Aeronautics and Space Administration and others. Depletion allows the entrance of ultraviolet radiation which causes skin cancer, human immune-system damage, and destruction of microscopic marine organisms.

Apollo 9 Astronaut Rusty Schweickart gave us this rare view.

At the edge of the Earth, at the horizon, you see this thin, brilliant, blue band and above it pure black. The whole environment is in that thin, iridescent, blue band that goes all the way around the horizon. That's our whole environment and above it is this pure black, absolute infinite deep black.[16]

Our planet seems so vulnerable, viewed from space. The astronaut also described seeing the forest fires all over the Amazon basin.

Massive fuel consumption of industrialized nations and destruction of forests increase carbon dioxide and other gases which trap heat and warm the planet, causing the "greenhouse effect." Weather patterns may be altered, generating ferocious storms.[17] Little is known about the long-term effects of this chemical pollution.

In February 1990, President George Bush was presented with an "Appeal by American Scientists to Prevent Global Warming" signed by 52 Nobel laureates and over 700 members of the National Academy of Sciences. It is the consensus of the scientific

---

16.   *Eastern Airlines Review,* June 1990, p. 48.
17.   *Time,* April 20, 1987, p. 69.

community that this is the most serious environmental threat of the 21st century.[18]

On the other hand, sulfur dioxide pollution, which causes acid rain, may be cooling the planet. Acid rain kills trees and aquatic life.[19]

"We believe that the '90s may be our last chance to reverse the trends that are undermining the human prospect... The world has deteriorated markedly in the two decades since the first Earth Day."[20]

In the Shadow of the New World Order

A New World Order has been crafted in the utmost secrecy over many years. Americans are not affected by massive waves of change yet, but consider the English. Being separate from the continent, England fought the hardest against the European Union (E.U.). Of course, European unity is requisite for global control.

Since Margaret Thatcher lost the battle and resigned (1990), many Englishmen feel robbed of nationhood, culture and some individual rights. The British now have access to the World Court in Luxembourg, which overrules even the highest English court. Internet, the computer information highway, is being implemented as fast as possible in Brussels, the headquarters of the Council and Commission of the E.U.

Gradually advancing according to plan, the New World Order will take control over the world (possibly three-and-a- half years after God annihilates the Russo-Islamic-German confederation. We should not be surprised about the march toward global government! Scripture declares that it will appear in the generation that sees the fig tree (Israel) come back to life. This system will engulf every aspect of life: trade and finance, government and religion.

---

18.   *Union of Concerned Scientists' Newsletter,* June 1990.
19.   *The Washington Post,* September 17, 1990, p. A-10.
20.   *The Worldwatch Institute Newsletter,* April 1990.

The "New World Order" is an expression that has been used in secret, top echelon Freemasonry since the days of Adam Weishaupt. He founded the Illuminati (Enlightened Ones) a secret Luciferic order in Ingolstadt, Bavaria on May 1, 1776. The Illuminati was created as a special Order within high Freemasonry. The Masonic historian, H.L. Haywood, included Weishaupt in his book, *Famous Masons and Masonic Presidents.*[21]

The book, *Morals and Dogma of the Ancient and Accepted Scottish Rite of Freemasonry* by Albert Pike is perhaps the most complete history of organized occultism. A major leader of Freemasonry, "Pike traced the growth and spread of the Mysteries over the earth *from ancient Babylon down to the present-day Masonic Order.*"[22]

As the Sovereign Pontiff of Universal Freemasonry, Pike set up the Holy See of the Dogma for the whole Masonic world at Charleston. He said, "The Masonic religion should be, by all of us initiates of the high degrees, maintained in the purity of the *Luciferic* doctrine."[23]

[**NOTE:** Lucifer (Morning Star) was the original name for Satan (Hebrew for "adversary") before he rebelled against God and fell from his high estate (Isaiah 14:12-15; Ezekiel 28:12-17)

Satan said he would make himself like the Most High God. He desires to sit on the Temple Mount in Jerusalem, receive worship as God, and control the earth (Isaiah 14:13,14). He will achieve his ends through a tyrant and prideful people who reject a personal God to whom they must give account.

How unusual that the Freemasons have laid a claim to Solomon's Quarries in Jerusalem on a plaque at the entrance! What right do they have to this immense cavern that extends under a large part of God's Holy City?]...

---

21.   *En Route to Global Occupation*, Gary Kah, p.107
22.   Ibid., p. 95
23.   Ibid., p.113f

Today, only those promoted to the highest level of Freemasonry know that Lucifer is worshipped as god with a capital "G". In *Occult Theocracy* historian Edith S. Miller states that in the New and Reformed Palladian Rite, Lucifer is considered divine. They deify man. In the Royal Arch degree of the York Rite the candidate is asked, "Brother, Inspector, what are you?" He replies, "I AM THAT I AM." This is the name for God! (Exodus 3:14).[24]

In *The Lost Keys of Freemasonry*, Manley P. Hall says that the seething energies of Lucifer are in a Mason's hands, but he must prove his ability to apply this energy ... "Man is a god in the making...he receives the triple crown of godhood.[25]

Economist Larry Bates describes a large stained glass window at the entrance to the Meditation Room of the United Nations. It depicts the religions of the world uniting as one with a *serpent* conspicuously placed at the center. In history a snake is often depicted on the back of a ruler's throne, seal, or symbol of authority. The serpent or dragon represents Satan from the first to the last book of the Bible.

Satan showed Jesus Christ all the kingdoms of the world. The devil said that all their authority and splendor has been given to him (Satan) and that he could give it to anyone he chose. Jesus did not disagree with this statement (Luke 4:5ff).

An illuminized Freemason's secret symbol was placed on the back of the Great Seal of the U.S. in 1782. Under Franklin D. Roosevelt, a 33rd degree Mason, this same symbol appeared on our one-dollar Federal Reserve Note. It includes a divided pyramid, an all-seeing eye and the words, "*Novus Ordo Seclorum*" (New World Order). The capstone will be joined to the rest of the pyramid once the system is made public and the dictator takes his seat of power.

---

24.   Ibid., pp.113, 127
25.   Ibid., pp.123, 126

In the late 1700s, European banking interests allied themselves with Freemasonry and the latter's extensive business and political contacts. Freemasonry, on the other hand, needed money to finance its efforts to build the *New World Order*. The history, connections, and center of direction spanning: Freemasonry, One-World interests, the Media and the New Age movement is a vast subject. For a comprehensive grasp of the matter, please refer to *En Route to Global Occupation* which offers extensive documentation. [The book has been quoted here with the publisher's permission.]

Some of the tangible building blocks implementing global government have appeared in this century:

> Federal Reserve System (1913)
> League of Nations (1920)
> Royal Institute of International
>   Affairs (1920-1921)
> Council on Foreign Relations (1921)
> Institute for Pacific Relations
> Institut fur Auswartige Politik
> Centre d'Etudes de Politicque Etrangere
> United Nations (1945)
> The Bilderberger Group (1954)
> Club of Rome (1968)
> Trilateral Commission (1973)[26]

Each of these organizations has had its own role to play in laying the groundwork for global government. For example, the Club of Rome (COR) was founded the year after the watershed event, the *unification of Jerusalem under Jewish control for the first time in two millennia.*

The Club is charged with establishing the regionalization and unification of the entire world. Aurelio Peccei, the Club's founder states: "Their world model... *divides the world into TEN interdependent regions.*"[27] A COR report (9-17-73) refers to

---

26.   Ibid., p. 50
27.   Ibid., p. 41

these regions as ten kingdoms, the same term used in Revelation 17:12ff. Each of these trading areas will have a king who will support the world dictator (cf. Daniel 7:7,8,24).

The divisions suggested were: 1-North America, 2- Europe, 3-Japan, 4-Australia and South Africa, 5-Old Soviet Union and Siberia, 6-Latin America, 7-North Africa, Saudia Arabia and other Muslim countries, 8-Africa, 9-India and Southeast Asia, 10-China. Does this relate to the eleven seats placed in the Meditation Room of the United Nations, the body set-up for world government? Do these seats point to the tyrant and the ten kings under him spoken of by the Old and New Testaments and now by the Club of Rome?

Global control must be accompanied by world trade and centralized banking. The expanded world trade pact, General Agreement on Tariffs and Trade (GATT), passed Congress in a rare post-election session (1994). Signed by 124 nations, it will reduce trade barriers and create a World Trade Organization (WTO) to *enforce compliance.*

The WTO will have unprecedented power to arbitrate disputes among GATT's members. WTO has the power to create and regulate the rules of global trade and authorize sanctions and fines. No matter what the trade benefits, *this is an unspeakable assault upon our national sovereignty!* Under the WTO, all countries, regardless of size, will have the same vote. The mechanism is now firmly in place. Ex-House Speaker Thomas S. Foley said that along with the North American Free Trade Agreement (NAFTA), GATT/WTO provide the most important trade liberalization of this century.

In the area of finance, centralized banking began in the late 1970s. New interstate banking laws have allowed big banks to acquire smaller ones. Finally, regional banks merge with the super-banks.

The American banking industry is already indirectly controlled by the Federal Reserve System. This has been true ever since the Owen-Glass Act was rammed through Congress on December 23,

1913. The Federal Reserve is not a government institution, but *a privately held corporation owned by stockholders.*

Until recently, the names of the owners of the Federal Reserve were unknown due to a proviso of the Act stating that the Fed's Class A stockholders may not be revealed. Eight major banks worldwide own the Federal Reserve through approximately 300 stockholders. Only four of the eight banks are located in the U.S., all in New York City[28].

Many conservative congressional leaders have tried unsuccessfully to put a stop to the forces behind the Fed. At the time of passage, Congressman Charles Lindbergh, Sr. warned:

> This Act establishes the most gigantic trust on earth. When the President (Wilson) signs this bill, *the invisible government of the Monetary Power will be legalized...* the worst legislative crime of the ages is perpetrated by this banking and currency bill![29]

Essentially, *whoever controls the Federal Reserve Bank of New York controls the Federal Reserve System.* "Article 1, Section 8 of the U.S. Constitution prohibits private interests from issuing money or regulating the value thereof. This power belongs only to Congress."

The foregoing has been a brief sketch of some of the powerful, concealed forces at work today. The public's lack of knowledge is the biggest factor working on behalf of this drive toward world government. It is difficult to get the average man behind an issue if the media does not cover it.

Decent people find it hard to believe that there could be a core of individuals with enough money and power to accomplish such a mind-boggling task. Nevertheless God's word has forewarned us! A One World Order will manifest in due time. Some men con-

---

28.   Ibid., p.13
29.   Ibid., p. 16

ceive trouble, give birth to evil, and hatch the eggs of vipers (Isaiah 59:4f).

Reemergence of Russia and A Unified Germany

Extraordinary events, hitherto thought remote, have moved at an accelerated speed. Lightning events that stunned the world between 1989 and 1991 were: the destruction of the Berlin Wall, the collapse of Soviet regimes in Eastern Europe, the unification of Germany, the collapse of the Soviet Union, and the Persian Gulf War. Ever since the Berlin Wall was taken down and Germany reunited, people have feared the reemergence of a powerful Germany.

Both Germany and Russia will join certain Muslim countries to attack Israel in the days ahead. *All of Germany* bears the responsibility for Jewish genocide, not just a part of the country. This immeasurable crime has not been dealt with by the hand of God yet! A study by the Carnegie Endowment for International Peace identified Germany as a "weak link" in the world's nuclear export control system. German companies helped Iraq build six poison gas plants. Germany and Japan continue to provide credits to Iran, making it easier for Iran to sponsor terrorism and undermine peace.

Russia, *as distinct from the entire ex-U.S.S.R.*, will lead the invasion of Israel. The same Power that unified Germany dissolved the U.S.S.R. a year later, causing Russia to reemerge as a separate entity. These were the nations of the Holocaust and the *pogroms*. In addition to Russia's ongoing arms sales to Iran, Moscow has contracted to complete an $800m nuclear power plant in Iran. The more hardline the Russian course of action has been against Bosnia and Chechnya (with their Muslim populations), the more Russia has sought to compensate by pro-Islamic policies in the Middle East.

A Stabilizing Force in the Middle East?

How do world conditions affect the delicate balance of power in the Middle East? Since the end of the Cold War, some have said that global rule of law should be enforced by the U.N. However, large unpaid bills, low member- contributions and lack of agreement in the Security Council make this prospect doubtful at present.

As the European Union comes closer to unity, individual states are less able to make swift decisions. It is expected that the constraints imposed by the Maastricht Treaty will become even greater after the review of the state of the E.U. in 1996.

It is unlikely that the E.U. would adopt a pro- Israel stance. Oil interests, historical colonial ties, proximity to Arab North Africa, and recent immigration of 15 million Muslims to Europe are contributing factors. Germany has adopted a strong, pro-Muslim line in Albania and Bosnia. German dominance in European decisions has increased since their reunification (1990) and the Maastricht Treaty (1991).[30]

In addition to budget cuts and reduction in the military, the U.S. would have a difficult time fielding a rescue operation of Israel today. During the Gulf War, America was able to station troops in neighboring countries, except Jordan and Iran. NATO-member Turkey's loyalty to the Western alliance would be in question now due to the increasing strength of Turkey's Islamists.

Israeli officers believe that Iran could produce a bomb in less than five years. It is feared that Iran has already achieved a low-level nuclear capability through ex-Soviet nuclear weapons.[31] Terrorist attacks at home would be of grave concern for both America and Europe. An international network of terrorists is

---

30.   Islamic Affairs Analyst, 11-94, p.7f
31.   Ibid., 2-95, p.1

known to exist. If these fanatics gain nuclear access, they could threaten to explode a nuclear bomb in a Western city. This would profoundly affect support for Israel. How can Israel survive in such a hostile environment?

It is *awesome* to see the factors foretold some 2,600 years ago by the Jewish prophets, coming to pass before our eyes today... Those who take God's Word seriously are mandated to comfort Israel tangibly (Isaiah 40:1f). The prophetic Word is a call to action. Israel is not an end-time football, nor an exercise in futility!

God is observing nations and individuals. We must go as far as He leads us. Are we participants or spectators in the battle raging between the forces of God and of Satan? Ultimately, the battle is the LORD's. He alone can and will deliver Israel.

The Israelis will not be able to depend on the arm of flesh, not even their own. God promises to curse those who curse His people and bless those who bless them (Genesis 12:3; 27:29). He will not change His mind (Numbers 23:19).

> *"All who devour you (Israel) will be devoured...The fierce anger of the LORD will not turn back until He fully accomplishes the purposes of His heart. In days to come you will understand this"*   (Jeremiah 30:16,24)

Chapter Four

THE INVASION OF ISRAEL GOD'S FIERY DELIVERANCE!

When Gog attacks the land of Israel, my hot anger will be aroused, declares the Sovereign Lord...all the people on the face of the earth will tremble. (Ezekiel 38:18ff)

The Invasion

The next event on God's schedule (since the establishment of Israel and her unification of Jerusalem) will electrify Israel and the world. After the Babylonian conquest of Israel about 2,600 years ago, Ezekiel prophesied in detail about another invasion of Israel by Magog and other nations (Ezekiel 38 and 39). It would happen *"in that day"* after a remnant of the Jews had been gathered from many nations to their ancient land. Terms like *"in that day"* and *"the latter day"* are used throughout the Old Testament to refer to the years immediately prior to Messiah's arrival in glory.

When Russia leads certain countries against the Jewish nation (Ezekiel 38:1–4; 39:1f), their collective motivation will be:

I will plunder and loot and turn my hand against the resettled ruins and the people gathered from the nations...living at the center of the land ["erez"—earth or world].

(Ezekiel 38:12)

The invaders would intend to seize the huge mineral deposits in the Dead Sea. An example of the wealth in the Dead Sea is the 573 million dollar value of the fertilizers and chemicals exported from Israel in 1985.[1] One of Israel's main industries is the extraction of bitumen as well as calcium, magnesium (for lightweight metal), potassium (for fertilizer), sodium chlorides, and bromides. The purity of the Dead Sea chemicals makes the fertilizer produced extremely effective.

The warm-weather port of Haifa on the Mediterranean Sea and the pipeline from Haifa to the Gulf of Aqaba would also be most useful to Israel's enemies. The driving forces behind the aggression will be Islamic religious hatred and Russian political/economic weakness. The invaders will be (Ezekiel 38:2–7):

Magog	Russia—the area in the far north between *"Meshech"* (Moscow in the west) and *"Tubal"* (Tobolsk in the east).
Persia	Iran—When the prophecy was given just prior to 573 B.C., Persia (Persis) was limited to the eastern side of the Persian Gulf. Present-day Iran changed its name from Persia to "Iran" in 1935 and declared both names acceptable in 1949. Ayatollah Khomeini's dying wish in 1989 was that Iran

---

1.   *The Europa Year Book 1987—A World Survey,* Vol. 1, p. 1,477.

	should be militarily and economically aligned with Russia. The majority of Iran's population adheres to the warlike Shiite sect of Islam.
Cush*	Western Iran—the area immediately north of the Persian Gulf, not Ethiopia (see Note*).
Put	The area of Libya.
Beth Togarmah	The area of south central former U.S.S.R. It is predominantly Moslem.
Gomer	The area of Germany. The Talmud identifies this as "Germania."[2,3]

*Note: "Cush" is the area through which the Gihon River flowed. The latter was one of the four rivers (Gihon, Pishon, Tigris, and Euphrates) that all came together before entering the Garden of Eden (Genesis 2:10–14). The King James Bible rendered "Cush" as "Ethiopia," which has caused misunderstandings ever since. Of course, Ethiopia is in Africa, far removed from the area where the Tigris and Euphrates rivers meet.

Archaeologist Dr. Juris Zarins of Southwest Missouri State University (in Springfield, Missouri) studied satellite photography of the area. This made clear that four rivers did converge close to the confluence of the Tigris and Euphrates, before flowing into the Persian Gulf. His conclusion is that the Garden of Eden was located between the northern end of the Gulf and the area where the river divided into four.

The Pishon was identified as a dry river bed (Wadi Rimah and Wadi Batin) coming from the southwest through Saudi Arabia. The Gihon (called the Ulai in the Bible and now the Karun) of "Cush" was a perennial river until it was dammed. It flows from an area

2.   *Yoma* 10a, p. 42.
3.   Lindsey, pp. 52–59 citing the Septuagint Bible, Josephus, Pliny, Dr. Gesenius, and Dr. Young.

due north of the Persian Gulf. *Therefore, "Cush" was directly north of the Persian Gulf and is not Ethiopia.*[4] (In Ezekiel's day, Cush was called Elam or Susiana.) Since "Persia" (Persis) was located along the eastern shore of the Gulf, both Cush and Persia would be located in modern-day Iran.

God says He brings the nations down against Israel to punish them all together in one place. Those who have murdered the Jews and attempted to destroy their tiny homeland will experience the vengeance of the God of Israel. It is preordained that there will be a Jewish nation on earth at Messiah's coming.

> *Set your face against Gog* [the leader] *of the land of Magog the chief prince of Meshech and Tubal. Prophesy against him...I am against you, O Gog...I will turn you around, put hooks in your jaws and bring you out with your whole army...I will drag you along. I will bring you from the far north and send you against the mountains of Israel.*
>
> (Ezekiel 38:2f; 39:1f)

> *But they* [Israel's enemies] *do not know the thoughts of the Lord; they do not understand his plan, he who gathers them like sheaves to the threshing floor.*   (Micah 4:12)

The chief prince of Russia will *"devise an evil scheme"* with the other nations. He will lead his whole army and a well-equipped horde by land and air against Israel. The focus of the invasion will be upon *"the mountains."* This is also where the invaders will fall (Ezekiel 38:21; 39:2, 4, 17).

Jerusalem—The Target

Why do the invaders head east for *"the mountains"* instead of west toward the coastal plain, where two-thirds of the population live in the Tel Aviv area (near the airport) and in Haifa (with

---

4.   *Smithsonian,* May 1987, p. 132.

harbor)? Militarily, the high hills, running like a north-south spine through the center of Israel, overlook and control the plains. But it is Jerusalem with the Temple Mount that is the place of significance in *"the mountains."* Why should Islam care about Jerusalem, since they already have two holy cities for which no one is fighting them? Jerusalem, the city of peace, will not gain peace until Messiah arrives.

> *I am going to make Jerusalem a cup that sends all the surrounding peoples reeling...On that day, when all the nations of the earth are gathered against her, I will make Jerusalem an immovable rock for all the nations. All who try to move it will injure themselves.* (Zechariah 12:2f)

When did Jerusalem begin to assume significance for Islam? Jerusalem is never mentioned once in the Koran, the Muslim holy book. The prophet and founder of Islam was Mohammed (570?–632 A.D.). His flight (*hegira*) was from Mecca to Medina in 622 A.D., not Jerusalem. So important was this trip that the Moslem era and calendar begin with that year.

In 624 Mohammed set the direction of prayers (*qibla*) toward Mecca (Koran, Sura 2.136–145). Moslem tradition reports that he had originally faced Jerusalem when praying. This change was one of the most important steps in the independence of the new religion.[5] (By contrast, churches have been built facing Jerusalem for prayer throughout Christian history.) So central is Mecca to Islam, non-Muslims may never enter it.

It was not until six years after Mohammed's death that Moslem troops took Jerusalem (*al-Quds*) in 638 A.D. Nevertheless, Moslems closely connect Jerusalem with resurrection on the Judgment Day in their *Book of the Phases of Resurrection.* Thus, Islam claims Mecca, Medina, and Jerusalem, in that order, as their

---

5.   *Encyclopaedia Judaica,* Vol. 10, p. 1,198.

holy cities, whereas Jerusalem is the only focus of Judaism and Christianity.

Every story in the Koran relating to Mohammed has a definite location. The only exception to this was the night he was sleeping near the mosque of Mecca. The Koran (Sura 17.1) says that Mohammed made a night journey from the mosque to an unspecified "outer mosque" from which he was raised up to heaven.

There is controversy among Moslems about the location of the "outer mosque." Some think it was in Medina. Others consider it to be in heaven. The official opinion is that it was the Temple Mount, in Jerusalem, not the mosque that was built there later and called *Al Aqsa.*[6]

Due to the development of the Omayyad Empire in the area of Syria and Palestine with Damascus as the capital, the Omayyad caliphs needed to create a religious center in their region after 660 A.D. The new center would not replace Mecca and Medina, but supplement them. The location of the "outer mosque" was then determined to be in Jerusalem, already established as the holy city for the Jews and Christians.

Al Aqsa Mosque (Arabic for "the outer") and the Dome of the Rock were built on the deserted Temple Mount. The Dome of the Rock bears the inscription: "seventy of the *hegira* or Moslem era" (691 A.D.) as the year of completion. A wooden Al Aqsa was in place by 680 A.D.[7]

The late King Faisal of Saudi Arabia said repeatedly that Jerusalem, not the West Bank, the Golan Heights, or the Gaza Strip was the real heart of the Arab-Israeli conflict. The Rabat Conference of Arab nations in 1974 affirmed this view.[8]

---

6.   *Encyclopaedia Judaica,* Vol. 9, p. 1,575.
7.   Ben-Dov, pp. 278–280.
8.   Lambert, p. 55.

And why would the modern-day invaders want to capture this unstrategic holy area first? They want to regain Jerusalem, the heart of Judaism, to prevent the construction of the Lord's Temple there. Needless to say, there will be a Temple, because sacrifices are being offered there three-and-a-half years before the true Messiah comes (Daniel 9:27).

The Lord has chosen Zion, he has desired it for his dwelling: This is my resting place for ever and ever; here I will sit enthroned, for I have desired it. (Psalm 132:13f)

Jewish history has always centered around Mount Moriah (the Temple Mount) beginning with Abraham. The Bible states that this was the place to which God sent Abraham nearly four millennia ago (Genesis 22:2). There, the Lord tested Abraham by asking him to sacrifice his son, Isaac. Instead, God Himself provided the sacrifice.

It was, of course, the location of both Temples, one built on the foundation of the other. Jerusalem became David's capital c. 1000 B.C. Jerusalem has hardly ever been without a Jewish presence. In the time of Christ, it had a population of 150,000–200,000.[9] The Jews have constituted its largest single group of inhabitants since 1840.

Jerusalem's Population[10]

Year	Jews	Moslems	Christians	Source
1844	7,120	5,000	3,390	Encyclopaedia Britannica, quoting Turkish census.
1876	12,000	7,560	5,470	The Living Guide Indicator de la Terre-Sainte, (France—1876)
1896	28,112	8,560	8,748	Calendar of Palestine (1895-1896)
1922	33,971	13,413	14,699	Reports and General Abstracts of the Census of 1922 by British Mandate (Jerusalem, Government Printer, 1922)

9.   Ben-Dov, p. 75.
10.   Davis, p. 203.

Year	Jews	Moslems	Christians	Source
1931	51,222	19,894	19,335	E. Mills, Census of Palestine 1931 (Jerusalem, 1932)
1948	100,000	40,000	25,000	Z. Vilnay, Jerusalem—The Old City (1962)
1967	195,700	54,963	12,646	Israel Central Bureau of Statistics
1970	215,000	61,600	11,500	Jerusalem Municipality
1985	306,000	108,500	13,700	Israel Central Bureau of Statistics
1987	340,000	121,000	14,000	Israel Central Bureau of Statistics

At the time of the invasion, God will no longer restrain the murderous hatred that comes to a boiling point against the Jews. As indicated, He himself will put hooks in the jaws of the invaders and bring them down against Israel. God will not permit any other nation to come to Israel's rescue. This is a rendezvous, that He alone will keep.

> *"Sheba and Dedan* [the Arabian peninsula] *and the merchants of Tarshish with all the young lions thereof* [the West: Spain and Britain and the areas they colonized] *shall say unto thee: Art thou come to take a spoil? Has thou gathered thy company* [army] *to take a prey? To carry away silver and gold, to take away cattle and goods, to take a great spoil?"* (Ezekiel 38:13, KJV)

This feeble protest is voiced from a neighboring area and the West. Apparently, the Arabian peninsula does not join other Islamic forces in the invasion. The United States does not appear to come to Israel's aid in this terrible hour.

From the Lord's perspective, the invading countries have fought Jewish return to Israel and caused war in His land. He calls Israel "His" land nine times in the Old Testament. The Lord has not forgotten the anti-Semitism that masterminded the German ovens and gas chambers, which reduced one-third of all Jews to ashes and skeletons, to say nothing of the many Russian *pogroms* which destroyed entire Jewish villages. Judgment will come in God's appointed time. No longer will people say:

Where is their God?   (Joel 2:17)

Very soon my anger against you [the Jews] *will end and my wrath will be directed to their destruction.*   (Isaiah 10:25)

In my burning zeal I have spoken against the rest of the nations...for with glee and with malice in their hearts they made my land their own possession...I swear with uplifted hand that the nations around you [Israel] *will also suffer scorn.*   (Ezekiel 36:5–7)

You will advance against my people Israel like a cloud that covers the land. In days to come, O Gog, I will bring you against my land, so that the nations may know me when I show myself holy through you before their eyes.
(Ezekiel 38:16)

God's Fiery Deliverance

He will bare His right arm of power and hurl His *"fiery wrath"* upon the invaders as they sweep down upon their prey, Israel. The mighty God will respond with a terrible earthquake:

When Gog attacks the land of Israel, my hot anger will be aroused...In my zeal and fiery wrath I declare that at that time there shall be **a great earthquake** *in the land of Israel. The fish...the birds...the beasts...every creature...and all the people on the face of the earth will tremble at my presence. The mountains will be overturned, the cliffs will crumble and every wall fall to the ground.*
(Ezekiel 38:20)

Note: It would be quite feasible for a major earthquake to occur in Israel. As mentioned previously, the world's longest, deepest rift valley, the trough between two major geologic faults, extends from northern Israel down into East Africa. The Dead Sea lies in this rift valley and is 1,306 feet below sea level. It is the lowest place on earth. (How symbolic that this should be located in the Holy Land. God's love will restore the lowest sinner on earth, if that person will turn to the Lord.)

Most of Israel's earthquake epicenters are in or near the Jordan rift valley. In recent times, destructive earthquakes occurred near Safed (1837) and Jericho (1927). Since Jerusalem is built on solid rock, it has remained "relatively undamaged by earthquakes during its history."[11] Nevertheless, if Jerusalem and the Temple Mount are affected by this great earthquake, buildings could be brought down in a moment. This may be God's signal to Israel that the time has come to erect His Temple.

An earthquake can cause a tsunami, a fast-moving seismic seawave. This would affect even *"the fish"* of the area (Ezekiel 38:20). In addition to the terrible earthquake,

I will execute judgment upon him with plague and bloodshed. I will pour down torrents of rain, hailstones, and burning sulfur on him and his troops and on the many nations with him. (Ezekiel 38:22)

After a cataclysm of such magnitude, the ravages of fire will pose a great danger to life. Natural resources exist near the Dead Sea that could provide a deadly display from the sky. There are vast beds of black petroleum on both sides of the Dead Sea. For this reason, the Romans called it "Lacus Asphaltitis." The highly flammable asphalt has risen to the surface during earthquakes.

In addition, a layer of marl (a soft, crumbly soil) impregnated with free sulfur covers a 150-foot stratum of salt at the southern end of the Dead Sea. This was discovered by archaeologists Dr. W.F. Albright and Dr. M.G. Kyle in 1924.[12] Earthquake forces often cause sediments to lose their former strength, liquefy and

11.   *Encyclopaedia Judaica,* Vol. 6, p. 341.
12.   Halley, p. 99.

erupt. Escaping gases from fissures could ignite and explode red-hot chunks of marl, sulfur and salt into the sky.

Note: Albright and Kyle found a striking quantity of artifacts at the southeast end of the Dead Sea near five oases. There was a dense, prosperous population there, which ended abruptly around 2000 B.C. This indicates destruction by a sudden cataclysm. It is thought that this desolate area was the location of Sodom and Gomorrah.[13] All the physical elements are present today to cause burning sulfur to rain down from the sky (Genesis 19:24f) in the future.

On the wicked He will rain fiery coals and burning sulfur. A scorching wind will be their lot.   (Psalm 11:6)

This prediction was made by King David about 1,000 years after Sodom and Gomorrah. It has not been fulfilled yet. God will strike the invaders' weapons down as the men try to release them.

Then, I will strike your bow from your left hand and make your arrows drop from your right hand.   (Ezekiel 39:3)

The invasion will be a time of unprecedented terror. Fear will paralyze the invaders when they realize they are under the ferocious wrath of the God of Israel. Clothed in panic, they will blame and turn on each other.

Every man's sword will be against his brother.
(Ezekiel 38:21)

They will fall on *"the mountains of Israel"* and *"in the open field."* As with Pharaoh and his army, no survivors will be left, not even "a sixth part" (Ezekiel 39:2—RSV; NIV; Interlinear Hebrew-Aramaic Old Testament, Vol. III).

---

13.   *Ibid.*, p. 834.

The Lord fought for Moses, Joshua, Gideon, Jehoshaphat, Hezekiah and others, causing Israel's enemies to kill each other. He will defend Israel again. People will understand that the Bible is no myth.

> *Oh, that you would rend the heavens and come down, that the mountains would tremble before you!...Come down to make your name known among your enemies, and cause the nations to quake before you!*   (Isaiah 64:1f)

> *I will send fire on Magog* [Russia] *and on those who live in safety in the coastlands, and they will know that I am the Lord.*   (Ezekiel 39:6)

It is unknown what area *"the coastlands"* include, but *"fire"* certainly means destruction. God will convulse the attackers with His judgment, which awaits them.

> *I will display my glory among the nations, and all the nations will see the punishment I inflict and the hand I lay upon them* [Israel's enemies].   (Ezekiel 39:21)

> *When your judgments come upon the earth, the people of the world learn righteousness.*   (Isaiah 26:9)

The obliteration of *"the northern army"* between the Dead and the Mediterranean Seas, just prior to *"the day of the Lord,"* is further described:

> *Blow the trumpet in Zion...Spare your people, O Lord...I will drive the northern army from you, pushing it into a parched and barren land, with its front columns going into the eastern* [Dead] *sea and those in the rear into the western* [Mediterranean] *sea. And its stench* [of death] *will go up; and its smell will rise. Surely, he has done great things.*

Be not afraid, O land; be glad and rejoice...Then you will
know that I am in Israel, that I am the Lord your God.
(Joel 2:15, 17, 20ff, 27)

The Lord already has set aside an area near the Dead Sea for
the burial of the invaders, so final is the outcome.

On that day, I will give Gog a burial place in Israel, the
valley of those who travel east toward the [Dead] Sea. It
will block the way of travelers, because Gog and all his
hordes will be buried there. So it will be called the valley of
Hamon Gog [hordes of Gog]. For seven months the house
of Israel will be burying them in order to cleanse the land.
All the people of the land will bury them.   (Ezekiel 39:11f)

Because I [Israel] have sinned against him, I will bear the
Lord's wrath, until he pleads my case and establishes my
right. He will bring me out into the light...My eyes will see
my enemy's downfall.   (Micah 7:9f)

This invasion may be as brief as the Six-Day War in 1967 in
Israel. That war started on Monday, June 5th, *Iyyar* 26—the same
day that Jesus Christ ascended to heaven in 30 A.D. The cease-fire
was on Saturday, June 10th.

God's retaliation will be so intense that it will clear the stage of
a part of Satan's hierarchy and will force the devil to concentrate
his authority and power in one final kingpin. The invasion is the
preview of Armageddon, when all nations will come against
Jerusalem seven years later.

To the Israelis it must appear that:

The Lord awoke as from a long sleep...He beat back his
enemies.   (Psalm 78:65)

Actually, it is Israel and the nations who awaken to the presence, power, and justice of the Holy One of Israel. There will be no

question. Almighty God will have blown the trumpet for all to
hear.

The phrase, the nations (or Israel) will know that I am the Lord,
is repeated exactly 70 times by the prophet Ezekiel until the prophecy of invasion, and never again afterwards. Why is this? The
world will now be alert to God, because of His unbelievable preservation of Israel. This supernatural action will speak to many
Jews in dispersion. Many will desire to move to Israel to prepare
for their Messiah's arrival.

The dimensions of the deliverance are mind-boggling. The
people of Israel will still be alive when they should all be dead!
The staggering number of bodies and war materiel strewn over the
landscape will be somber testimony to the reality that God will
have fulfilled His ancient Word in detail.

To get the full impact of the Lord's intervention upon the
Jewish psyche, His deliverance must be set against 20 centuries of
God's *"hiding his face"* from them. The Jewish heart will be
profoundly moved, and unimaginable joy breaks forth. Their God
will have saved them from utter destruction.

From that day forward the house of Israel will know that I
am the Lord their God.   (Ezekiel 39:22)

As their rejection of God started on the spiritual level first and
ended with their ejection from the land; so their restoration is in
reverse order: agriculture, the nation, their capital, and finally,
their spirit. At last, the Lord will begin His spiritual restoration of
the nation as a whole. This will happen after the committed
Christians are removed.

Israel has experienced a hardening in part until the full
number of the Gentiles has come in [to God's kingdom].
                    (Romans 11:25)

The reality of the God of Israel settles upon each one personally. Many unbelieving Jews repent and experience the God of

their fathers—personally. Thus, the Lord awakens them, before He sends Messiah to them.

I will gather them to their own land, not leaving any behind. I will no longer hide my face from them, for I will pour out my Spirit on the house of Israel.   (Ezekiel 39:28f)

Until the Lord releases His Spirit, there can be little real growth or lasting improvement (Isaiah 32:15; 44:3). He will give the Jews a new spirit (Ezekiel 36:27). The Spirit of the Lord shall rest upon them.

God's Holy Spirit possesses six major attributes: wisdom, understanding, counsel, power, knowledge, and the fear of the Lord (Isaiah 11:1f). The symbol of Israel, the seven-branched candlestick (*menorah*), is a perfect picture of God's Spirit. The central stem represents the Holy Spirit and the branches, His six qualities.

God's Seven-Year Transition

We know that of the 70 "sevens" (490 years) decreed for the Jews as a national entity, the last seven-year period remains on God's timeline for them (Daniel 9:24–27). With the founding of the first village in 1878 and the evolving of the new *yishuv* (community) from 1880, the observable emphasis in the Holy Land has been on reclaiming the land and regathering the people. Since none of the prophesied events of the seven-year interval have happened to date, that time capsule must be reserved for their spiritual revival.

There are two events, one immediately precedes and the other initiates the concluding "seven years" of the Jewish era. The first action is the invasion of Israel, and the second is the confirmation of the covenant in Israel.

This is the day I have spoken of. Then, those who live in the towns of Israel will go out and use the weapons for fuel and

*burn them up...For seven years they will use them for fuel.
They will not need to gather wood from the fields...because
they will use the weapons for fuel.*

(Ezekiel 39:9f)

And he shall confirm the covenant with many [in Israel] *for
one week* [seven years]: *And in the midst of the week he* [this
ruler of Israel] *shall cause the sacrifice and oblation to
cease.* (Daniel 9:27, KJV)

**Since there is only one week of years remaining for
Israel, the seven years of burning the invasion wreckage
must be the same one that starts ticking off when a
beguiling leader** *"shall confirm the covenant"* **with them.**
Accordingly, this leader will do so immediately after the
horrifying attack is over.

Over the millennia, many rabbis have believed that Messiah
will come and mightily deliver the Jewish people from their enemies. **When the Jews see God's supernatural deliverance of
Israel from a FEW nations, many will mistake it for the true
Messiah's future preservation of their homeland from
ALL nations** (Zechariah 12:3; 14:2). Many do not realize
that **two** invasions will occur seven years apart. In their ec-
stasy and euphoria, the Jews will link this leader with God's
awesome intervention and accept him as their long-awaited
Deliverer/Messiah.

Furthermore, his "confirmation" of the covenant, which
follows right after, is most unusual. No ordinary man would have
the authority to confirm an Old Testament covenant given by God
unless he was thought to be divinely appointed. That event will
trigger major prophesied events in rapid succession.

Chapter Five

ISRAEL CROWNS HER KING—HIS FIRST 280 DAYS IN POWER

For unto us a child is born, to us a son is given, and the government will be on his shoulders. And he will be called Wonderful Counselor, Mighty God, Everlasting Father, Prince of Peace. Of the increase of his government and peace there will be no end. (Isaiah 9:6f)

Messianic Figures in History

Thus the Jews worship and thank God for deliverance, but they look to a human leader to guide them through the aftermath of the invasion. Many today do not know the Old Testament well. Therefore, they will fall into the most tragic deception before they realize the truth about their new leader. The hope for a deliverer is buried deep in the Jewish soul, and comes forth in times of national crisis. A study of past messianic figures will shed light on the mood and expectations during this turbulent time in Israel.

There are only three types of messianic figures: the genuine, the fraudulent, and the deranged. Major examples are Jesus of Nazareth (1st century), Simon Bar Kokhba (1st century), David Alroy (12th century), David Reubeni (16th century), Shabbetai Zevi (17th century), and Jacob Frank (18th century).

(1) JESUS OF NAZARETH

Jesus, born in Bethlehem c. 5 B.C., grew up in Nazareth in Galilee of the Gentiles. For a brief time prior to Jesus' ministry, the prophet, John the Baptist, called people to repent and prepare their hearts for the coming of their King and His kingdom. Since John was beheaded just before Jesus started the work He came to do, John did not assist the Nazarene. Some Jews of that day were awaiting the King, the consolation of Israel (John 1:49; Luke 2:25, 38).

Since Jesus began His ministry at the start of His 30th year (Luke 3:23) and ministered for three-and-a-half years, He would have started in the fall, in *Tishri* 26 A.D. In the synagogue of Nazareth, He read about a person whom God would anoint and send *"to proclaim freedom for the captives and release...for the prisoners."* Then He proclaimed:

Today, this scripture is fulfilled in your hearing.
(Luke 4:16-21; Isaiah 61:1f)

He came to fulfill *"the time of God's favor"* (2 Corinthians 6:2). The area of His ministry would be:

In the past he humbled the land of Zebulun and the land of Naphtali, but in the future he will honor Galilee of the Gentiles by the way of the sea, along [beyond] *the Jordan.*
(Isaiah 9:1)

The Via Maris (Way by the Sea), the major highway between Egypt and Damascus, no longer exists as it did 2,000 years ago.

Jesus spent most of His public ministry in Capernaum near that busy thoroughfare. A Via Maris milestone, found close to that former town, is on display there today. Nazareth and Capernaum were located in the land of Zebulun and Naphtali.

This Jesus did many mighty works and miracles in God's name, such as healing the multitudes, casting out demons, feeding several thousand people, and raising Lazarus (who had been dead four days) and two others. However, the Jewish leadership looked for a deliverer who would bring freedom from Rome, as Moses had brought them out of Egyptian bondage. Although Jesus said His kingdom was a spiritual one, the leaders considered that His popularity with the people threatened their authority.

Jesus enraged them further by claiming to be the Son of God, by forgiving sins, and by healing people on the sacred Sabbath. After a ministry of three-and-a-half years, Jesus was judged by the Sanhedrin, the Jewish Supreme Court, to be a blasphemer and worthy of death. At the request of the high court and a crowd, the Romans nailed Him to a cross on Passover, *Nisan* 14, c. 30 A.D. The charge that the Roman governor placed above His head on the cross was *"The King of the Jews"* (Matthew 27:37; Mark 15:26; Luke 23:38).

Jesus came to lay His life down for mankind. Humanity was held in the vice of sin from which we could never free ourselves. **It required the intervention of God Himself to break the power of sin and release mankind.** Jesus could have avoided death at any point, but this was not His Father's will. **The sins of every person who has ever lived caused His death, not just the actions of the people of His day.**

The reason my Father loves me is that I lay down my life— only to take it up again. No one takes it from me, but I lay it down of my own accord. I have authority to lay it down and authority to take it up again. This command I received from my Father.   (John 10:17ff; see Hebrews 12:2)

On the first Passover in Egypt, the Hebrews had to put some of the Passover lamb's blood over the doorway to their homes. That night the angel of death saw that the penalty of death had already been paid. He could legally pass over that house.

Jesus Christ became the sinless Passover lamb, our substitute. Only God Himself could pay the penalty to take away the sins of the whole human race and make us acceptable to enter God's presence again.

When I accept Jesus' blood sacrifice to pay for my sins and continue in trust and obedience to Him, I will escape the second death (Revelation 20:6). That death is the state of eternal separation from God.

He resurrected before dawn on the third day, *Nisan* 16. Jesus was seen on earth during the next 40 days. He ascended to heaven on *Iyyar* 26, or ten days before Pentecost (*Shavuot*).

Since 30 A.D., millions of people have accepted Him as their Messiah, who delivers those who come to Him from their bondage to sin. A deliverer who effects a military victory, however stunning, offers temporary peace. He creates no permanent improvement in the human condition. Man must first be set free from his desire to sin, his sins, and the guilt that follows such actions before he can experience true peace.

All of us have become like one who is unclean, and all our righteous acts are like filthy rags.   (Isaiah 64:6)

He bore the sins of many, and made intercession for the transgressors.   (Isaiah 53:12)

It is interesting that the preceding verse is found in the Old, not the New Testament. The name, Jesus, is Greek for *"Yeshua,"* which means "salvation" in Hebrew.

Note: The word, *yeshua* appears 64 times in the Old Testament and is defined as deliverance, victory, prosperity, and health. It comes from *yasha*, which means to be open, free, safe, or rescued. This word appears most often in Exodus, Psalms and Isaiah.

The title, Christ, means "Anointed One" or Messiah (*Mashiah*). Jesus was also called a Nazarene (Matthew 2:23; Acts 24:5). It was a derogatory term meaning "despised one." Actually, His home town, Nazareth, comes from *"netzer,"* which means branch. So, in calling Him the Nazarene, people were saying *"the Branch,"* a messianic title repeated in Isaiah, Jeremiah, and Zechariah.

Throughout His ministry, Jesus repeatedly referred to the fact that His actions fulfilled Scripture. This will again be the case at the coming of Messiah.

There are unmistakable similarities among Jesus, Joseph (Genesis 37ff), and the Jewish nation.

(1) All went down into Egypt at a young age and left Egypt.

(2) Both Jesus and Joseph were thrown into a pit and sold for silver by their brother(s).

(3) Most of the brothers of Joseph, Jesus, and the Jewish nation were not concerned about their fate: Joseph—his own brothers; Jesus—most Jewish people; the Jewish nation—the other nations.

(4) Jesus was flogged prior to death by the Romans who had no legal limit (Matthew 27:26; John 19:1). He said He would be mocked, spit upon, and scourged (Matthew 20:19; Mark 10:34) in fulfillment of Scripture (Isaiah 50:6; 53:5). Israel received 39 lashes (*malkot*) from the Iraqi Scud missiles in 1991. (This number is the limit set by Jewish law for a flogging: 40 less one in case of a miscount - Deuteronomy 25:3; 2 Corinthians 11:24).

(5) Jesus was the scapegoat (Leviticus 16:8) and upon Him was laid *"the iniquity of us all"* (Isaiah 53:6; cf. 2 Corinthians 5:21; 1 Peter 2:24). Many countries have made the Jews their scapegoat and blamed the latter for social ills.

(6) Before crucifixion, Jesus was deserted by all His disciples (Matthew 26:31, 56; cf. Zechariah 13:7). Israel will be abandoned and left alone when the armies of *all* nations assemble against her at Armageddon (Zechariah 12:3; 14:2; Revelation 16:14ff).

(7) When Jesus took mankind's sins upon Himself, Father God turned His face away from the sin and forsook Christ briefly (Matthew 27:46; cf. Psalm 22:1). God *"hid His face"* from His Jewish nation and *"handed them over to their enemies"* (Ezekiel 39:23f).

(8) Jesus' body was dead and in the grave for three days. He rose by dawn on the third day. The Jewish body politic, which has been non-existent for two millennia, is being brought to life and will be restored fully on the third (Hosea 6:2).

(9) Joseph was sent into Gentile Egypt (a symbol of the world) ahead of his brothers. After 20 years had passed, they entered Egypt due to famine and found Joseph to be the second-in-command to the Pharaoh. Joseph provided them with food (see p. 223). Jesus also has been with the Gentiles for 20 centuries. He is second-in-command to His Father and will revive His Jewish brethren at the end of the 20 centuries (two days - Hosea 6:2).

In 532 A.D., a Christian monk, Dionysius Exiguus, introduced the present system of counting time by starting with the birth of Christ. "Exiguus miscalculated the event four to six years later than the actual date. This method came into general use in Christian countries by about 1400."[1] Thus, the birth of Jesus started a new era.

Isaiah 53, a graphic description of the sufferings of Messiah, was given 700 years before the birth of Jesus. Even though it is not found in the daily synagogue readings, it is in the approved Jewish

---

1.   *The World Book Encylopedia,* Vol. 3, p. 405.

Scriptures. Who is the Son who is born to us, whose name is *"Mighty God...Prince of Peace?"* (Isaiah 9:6)

Who has gone up to heaven and come down?
Who has gathered up the wind in the hollow of his hands?
Who has wrapped up the waters in his cloak?
Who has established all the ends of the earth?
What is his name, and the name of his son?
Tell me if you know.   (Proverbs 30:4)

(2) SIMEON BAR KOKHBA OF KOZIBA

Bar Kokhba, from the town of Koziba, was hailed by Rabbi Akiva and other sages as "King Messiah."[2] The name, "Bar Kokhba," was given him because of the messianic verse:

There shall come a star [kokhav] *out of Jacob, and a scepter shall rise out of Israel.*   (Numbers 24:17, KJV)

This movement grew out of anguish in the Jewish heart against Rome's intolerable cruelty and oppression, pagan culture, and emperor worship. The final affront came when Emperor Publium Aelius Hadrian began to build a temple to Jupiter on the sacred Temple Mount and establish a Roman colony in Jerusalem in 130 A.D., 100 years after the death of Jesus Christ.

To stamp out the memory of the Jews, Hadrian renamed Judea, "Palestine," and called Jerusalem, "Aelia Capitolina," to honor himself and the Roman god, Jupiter Capitolinus. A Jew was only allowed to enter Jerusalem to mourn on the 9th of *Av,* the day both Temples had been destroyed, 656 years apart!

Bar Kokhba captured Jerusalem for a short time. He led the Jews in a series of violent revolts for three-and-a-half years between 132–135 A.D. His letters, found in the caves near the Dead Sea, reflect a harsh, stern, powerful leader. The Jewish

---

2.   TJ. *Taanith* 4:8, Lam. R.2.2, No. 4, quoted by *Encyclopaedia Judaica,*
      Vol. 4, p. 230.

Aggadah (Talmudic narration) depicts him as depending on his own powers rather than upon divine help. "When Bar Kokhba went forth to battle, he said (to God), 'Neither assist nor discourage us.' "[3]

In contrast to the destruction of Jerusalem in 70 A.D., the Jews were now unified under a single military ruler. Their suffering and yearning for freedom were the background for their ready acceptance of the authority of one strong leader.

Bar Kokhba did not sign himself as "King," but used the title of "Nasi (Prince) of Israel," as found in documents and on the coins of the revolt. It appears that a High Court (Sanhedrin), meeting in Betar, took part in his rule. Bar Kokhba was killed on the ninth of *Av* in 135 A.D., defending Betar, the last fortress. Some then called him "Bar Kozivah" (*"kazav"* means lie), due to their bitter disappointment.[4]

During the revolt, the Jews who believed Jesus to be the real Messiah would not fight under a pretender to the title, no matter how worthy the cause. The rest of the Jews considered the former group to be traitors. This resulted in an irreconcilable breach between Judaism and Christianity.

(3) SHABBETAI ZEVI OF SMYRNA (IZMIR, TURKEY)

Another tempestuous movement sprang from religious, not military fervor, and issued from study of the *Kabbala,* Jewish mysticism. The focal point, Shabbetai Zevi, was born in 1626 on the ninth of *Av.* It is well-documented that throughout his life, Zevi experienced "periods of profound depression, euphoria, and normality. In his home town, he was considered partly a lunatic and partly a fool, but he had a very pleasant appearance and was highly musical."[5]

---

3.   *Encyclopaedia Judaica,* Vol. 4, p. 231.
4.   *Ibid.,* Vol. 4, p. 231.
5.   *Ibid.,* Vol. 14, pp. 1,222–1,223.

He appointed the brilliant scholar, Nathan of Gaza, as his prophet. Together, they convinced many Jews worldwide that Zevi was their promised deliverer. Majestically riding around on horseback at age 38, Zevi proclaimed himself Messiah on May 31, 1665. This was contrary to the prophecy depicting Messiah's arrival on a donkey's colt (Zechariah 9:9). Donkeys suggested humility and peace. A spirited horse connoted Gentile rulers with their military power, pomp, and vainglory.

The greatest number of believers were far removed from the two men and depended upon letters for information. These communications said that neither Zevi nor Nathan needed to show proof of the Messianic claim by performing miracles. Rather, the Jews should simply have pure faith. Many stories and myths started to circulate.

Nathan called for repentance before the coming "redemption." Jewish mystics believed that the Messiah would appear in 1666 to start the Messianic Era. Zevi fixed the date for the restoration of Israel as June 18, 1666 (*Sivan* 15).

Note: This is a singular year in light of the number of "666" of the coming world dictator (Revelation 13:18). The number "666" symbolizes man's genius and prowess employed to the highest degree in the three major arenas of life: religious, socio-political and economic. In the same way that the number six is deficient from the complete seven, so also are the efforts of men who depend on themselves to the exclusion of God.

There is only one place in the New Testament with a sixth chapter and a 66th verse. Notice its content:

From this time many of his [Jesus'] *disciples turned back and no longer followed him.*   (John 6:66)

Some of the reasons for the phenomenal success of this messianic frenzy in 1666 were: It originated in the Holy Land. The emphasis on repentance appealed to the best in people and lent a sincere ring to the movement. The concept of the restoration of everything to its proper order was most appealing to a persecuted, hounded people.

Jews from all levels of society became involved. Some claimed to see the prophet, Elijah, who is to return just prior to Messiah. Others fell into trances. Commerce came to a halt and was replaced with festivities, processions with Zevi's portrait, and religious services of repentance.

The atmosphere was one of great joy and exhilaration. Many sold their property and rented ships to go to Palestine. Boundless enthusiasm prevailed. "No opposition from the rabbinical side is recorded."[6] "A mounting wave of messianic terrorism threatened those who spoke derisively of Zevi or refused to take part in the excitement."[7]

Zevi distributed the kingdom of earth among his faithful. He signed his letters with grand phrases like: "I am the Lord your God, Shabbetai Zevi." People called him "Amirah," an abbreviation for "our Lord and King, may his majesty be exalted." Although Zevi appointed a group to represent the 12 tribes of Israel, apparently a Sanhedrin was not installed.

He proclaimed a new era by which publications were dated as the "first year" of the renewal of prophecy and the kingdom. From ancient times, events were dated from the beginning of a new monarch's reign (see Nehemiah 2:1).

"Hundreds of prophets arose and excitement reached a fever pitch."[8] However, true prophets will arise before Messiah comes:

I will pour out my Spirit on all people. Your sons and daughters will prophesy; your old men will dream dreams; your young men will see visions.
                    (Joel 2:28; cf. 1 Samuel 19:20; Zechariah 13:2f;
                                        Matthew 24:4, 11, 24)

6.   *Encyclopaedia Judaica,* Vol. 14, p. 1,235.
7.   *Ibid.,* p. 1,233.
8.   *Ibid.,* Vol. 14, p. 1,235.

Zevi tried to change "appointed times" by abolishing fast days and instituted new festivals, e.g., the 17th of *Tammuz* (the revival of his spirit), the ninth of *Av* (his birthday), and the 10th of *Tevet.* This was an attempt to fulfill the turning of fasts into happy occasions (Zechariah 8:19).

Three months after the date set for the restoration of Israel, Zevi faced death by the Turkish Sultan, and converted to Islam on September 15, 1666. He continued to confirm his messianic mission and persuaded Jews to follow him into Islam. He died on the Day of Atonement, *Yom Kippur,* 1676.

Nathan defended Zevi after death as the epitome of the struggle against evil. This legitimizing of an apostate messiah survived for the next 100 years.[9]

Israel's imposter ruler will also try to change appointed religious days of the year when he comes.

Another king will arise...and try to change the set times and the [religious] *laws.*   (Daniel 7:25)

This is the prerogative of God alone.

Praise be to the name of God forever and ever; wisdom and power are his. He changes times and seasons.
                    (Daniel 2:20f)

As recently as 50 years ago, Adolf Hitler demonstrated this same grandiose control. He quickly established his own "glittering calendar of feast days," mixed with old holidays in Germany. They were calculated to create feelings of tradition, normalcy, and well-being among the populace. These dramatic rituals blazed with the primitive symbol of fire on the summer solstice, the fall equinox, his birthday, and other days.

Hitler relished the pagan appeal of his spectacles and preferred that they be held at night, because "In the evening the people's will

---

9.   *Encyclopaedia Judaica,* Vol. 14, pp. 1,229, 1,235, 1,238.

power more easily succumbs to the dominating force of a stronger will."[10]

Messianic Traditions

Jews who look for a literal Messiah today are unanimous in the belief that He will be a human being, who is divinely appointed. However, the Bible describes His throne as being established *"forever"* and His government as having *"no end"* (1 Chronicles 17:12; 2 Samuel 7:12; Isaiah 9:7). The Midrash on Proverbs 8:9 (Ed. Lemb. p. 7a) mentions Him as one of seven things created before the world: the Throne of Glory, Messiah the King, the Torah (ideal), Israel, the Temple, repentance, and Gehenna (hell).[11]

Messiah's pre-existence to the world is also discussed in *Pesikta Rabbati* 36.161; Targum on Isaiah 9:6; and Targum on Micah 5:2. In the Talmud, it is implied that Messiah is already among the living.[12] "In general, the idea of Messiah's appearance and concealment is familiar to Jewish tradition." [13]

"One Talmudic source attributes immortality to Messiah (*Sukkah* 52a) and the Midrash singles Him out among the immortals of paradise."[14]

Even though Rabbi Akiva gave the title of Messiah to Bar Kokhba, "Akiva also declared that Messiah would occupy a throne alongside God!"[15] The following is said to mean the light of the Messiah:

Arise, shine for your light has come and the glory of the Lord rises upon you.   (Isaiah 60:1)

---

10. Elson, pp. 178–182.
11. Edersheim, *The Life and Times of Jesus the Messiah,* Book 1, p. 175.
12. Jerusalem Berakhoth 2.4, p. 5a; *Sanhedrin* 98a; Jerusalem Targum on Exodus 12:42; *Encyclopaedia Judaica,* Vol. 11, p. 1,411.
13. *Pesiqta,* ed. Buber, p. 49b; Edersheim, p. 175.
14. *Encyclopaedia Judaica,* Vol. 11, p. 1,412.
15. *Ibid.,* p. 1,412.

In your light we see light.   (Psalm 36:9)

When Satan asked for whom this glorious light was reserved, he was told that it was destined for Messiah who would destroy Satan. Upon seeing Messiah, the devil "fell on his face and owned that Messiah would in the future cast him into Gehenna [hell]."[16]

A Messiah that is pre-existent, in the Light or Presence of God, and destined to cast Satan into hell is no ordinary man.[17]

Even the most ideal society can do no more than enforce peace, because hatreds and conflict remain. In the Messianic Age, spoken of by the prophets, an inner harmony will exist in people and govern the environment. Even so, Messiah will rule the nations with an iron scepter (Psalm 2:9; Revelation 19:15).

The Dead Sea Scrolls mention three messianic figures: a priest of righteousness, a king, and a prophet of the last days. These are also the three functions of the ideal Jewish state (*The Apocrypha,* 1 Maccabees 14:41).

In addition to these major roles, a scion of Jesse (David's father) (Isaiah 11:1) will be a warrior, statesman, judge, and teacher. As King, He will redeem and rule Israel at the climax of human history. God will establish His kingdom through Him. Reminiscent of Solomon, He will be known for His justice and His sense of right and wrong of a case. He will be versed in the Torah (the first five books of the Bible).

He is expected to defeat the enemies of Israel, cause the Jews to return to Israel, reconcile them with God, and convert the Gentiles to the God of Israel. Some Jews believe that Messiah will reign in Jerusalem, rebuild the Temple, reinstate the sacrificial system, and introduce the Messianic Age (*yemot ha-mashi'ah*).[18]

---

16.   *Yalkut* ii, p. 56c; Edersheim, p. 175f.
17.   Edersheim, p. 176.
18.   *Encyclopaedia Judaica,* Vol. 11, pp. 1,409–1,411.

Talmudic writing contains many different views. One tradition in the Middle Ages was found in the pseudepigraphal Book of Zerubbabel: "Messiah will be preceded by a satanic king of Rome, who will be the spiritual son of Satan."[19] This emperor would conquer and unify the whole world under his religion and kill the Messiah, son of Joseph. However, Messiah, son of David, would arise and vanquish the demonic dictator and his strong, united Roman empire.[20]

Another variation is that the Messiah, son of Joseph, will be killed or "pierced" waging war against Gog and Magog. Then, the real Messiah, son of David, will come.[21]

The term, son of Joseph, is taken from "house of Joseph" in Obadiah 18 (*Baba Bathra*, 123 b). It came into existence after the failure of Bar Kokhba's revolt in 135 A.D.[22] However, no "Messiah, Son of Joseph," is mentioned anywhere in the Old Testament.

The concept of killing or "piercing" the Messiah came from:

They will look on me, the one they have pierced, and they will mourn for him as one mourns for an only child and grieve bitterly for him. (Zechariah 12:10; Sukkah 52.a)

"The appeal of this apocalyptic literature became universal to all Jews, in all countries, in both medieval and early modern times." It contained many elements from the Bible and the Talmud.[23]

Messiah was described as *"despised and rejected by men"* (Isaiah 53:3). In contrast, the end-time false "king" will exalt and magnify himself above God and be worshiped until the time of wrath is completed (Daniel 11:36; Revelation 13:4).

---

19. *Ibid.,* p. 1,412.
20. *Ibid.,* Vol. 11, p. 1,412f.
21. Bridger, ed., p. 317.
22. Cohen, p. 348.
23. *Encyclopaedia Judaica,* Vol. 11, p. 1,413.

He [the Messiah] *had no beauty nor majesty to attract us to him, nothing in his appearance that we should desire him. He was despised and rejected by men, a man of sorrows, and familiar with suffering. Like one from whom men hide their faces, he was despised, and we esteemed him not.*

Surely, he took our infirmities, and carried our sorrows; yet we considered him stricken by God, smitten by him and afflicted. But he was pierced for our transgressions, he was crushed for our iniquities. The punishment that brought us peace was upon him, and by his wounds we are healed.

We all, like sheep have gone astray, each of us has turned to his own way. And the Lord laid on him the iniquity of us all. He was oppressed and afflicted, yet he did not open his mouth; he was led like a lamb to the slaughter.

(Isaiah 53:2-7)

In recognition of this suffering, a third century Talmudic name for Him is "the leperous or stricken one."[24] Later, it is said that "his suffering atones for Israel."[25]

Moses Maimonides, the famous 12th century Jewish Talmudic authority, saw the coming of Messiah as "a political deliverance of the Jews from Gentile rule, without any upheaval in world order or apocalyptic elements."[26] The last two of the scholar's *Thirteen Articles of Creed* were Messiah's certain coming and the resurrection of the dead.

Maimonides presented the Messianic Age in commonplace, mundane terms to avert the possibility of people being swept up by emotion into the acceptance of a false messiah and the shattering disillusionment which would result. His fears were justified with the likes of David Reubeni and Shabbetai Zevi.

24.   *Ibid.*, p. 1,412.
25.   *Ibid.*, p. 1,412, citing *Sanhedrin*, 98b, PR 37:162b.
26.   *Ibid.*, p. 1,414.

Maimonides outlined these criteria for the recognition of Messiah:

> If there arises a ruler from the House of David, who is immersed in Torah and *Mitzvos* [duties] like David, his ancestor: following both the Written and Oral Law, who leads Israel back to the Torah, strengthening its laws and fighting G-d's battles, then we may assume that he is the Messiah. If he is further successful in rebuilding the Temple on its original site and gathering the dispersed of Israel, then his identity as the Messiah is a certainty.[27]

"Messianic speculations and attempts to find dates were a constant feature of Jewish culture in the Middle Ages and early modern times."[28] Dates set for redemption often coincided with terrible persecutions of the Jews. When the date was not fulfilled, the explanation was always that the Jews were not sufficiently righteous to accept the Messiah. "Among the masses of the people, belief in the apocalyptic redemption did not diminish."[29] Nevertheless, after the Second Temple was destroyed, a personal Messiah is lacking in some writings.

During the 19th century, Jewish socialists replaced the belief in a human Messiah with a Messianic age, brought about through political action, economic reforms, and cultural revival. Since the establishment of Israel, the rabbinate looks upon "the State as *Athalta di-Geullah,*" the Beginning of Ultimate and Universal Redemption.[30]

Today, Lubavitch is the largest group of the ultra-Orthodox Jewish movement called *Hasidism* (Pious Ones). Their venerated rabbi, Menachem M. Schneerson, was the spiritual leader of as many as 500,000 Jews. He was "one of the most powerful men of

---

27.   Kaplan, p. 93f, citing *Yad, Melachim* 11:4.
28.   *Encyclopaedia Judaica,* Vol. 11, p. 1,414.
29.   *Ibid.,* p. 1,414.
30.   Bridger, p. 318.

the world Jewish community" and held great influence over Israeli politics, even though he had never been there for religious reasons. Many of his followers believed that the rabbi, was the Messiah.[31] He died on June 12, 1994.

Israel Crowns King-Messiah

The preceding messianic figures and traditions are an indication of what expectations will be in post-invasion Israel. The invasion will be brief since the Lord will disarm the invaders before they can use their weapons (Ezekiel 39:3). During such a national emergency, people can come forth as great heroes overnight.

The Israeli need for strong leadership during the chaos and crisis of the time will provide fertile soil for the rapid rise of a brilliant man who is without equal. This person will appear on the scene at precisely the right moment. He will capitalize upon the spiritual revival and euphoria, created by God's deliverance. This impressive figure will quickly capture the popular imagination and inspire their allegiance. He far surpasses the impediments that political party opposition would normally impose. This man's bearing and extraordinary abilities will unify Israel and create unbridled hope. He will seem to be the "star" who will cause the law to go out from Zion (Isaiah 2:3; 60:10, 11; Zechariah 14:17).

Israelis will choose this outstanding man upon whom to heap their elation and accolades. Wearing such a mantle, he will be in a position to deceive and betray many (Daniel 9:27). He will experience a meteoric rise to power and will falsely claim to be the promised king:

I will make them one nation in the land, on the mountains of Israel. There will be one king over all of them...
                                                                            (Ezekiel 37:22)

---

31.   *The Washington Post*, September 18, 1991, p. A-3.

If not immediately, he will receive the title of *"king"* (Daniel 11:36).

The first act of this pivotal figure will be to enter into a covenant (*b'rit*) with Israel. He will present this agreement as the *"new covenant with the house of Israel"* (Jeremiah 31:31f) and *"the covenant of peace"* (Ezekiel 34:25).

Shortly before death, Joshua made a covenant for the people. He recorded the people's agreement and God's decrees in the Book of the Law of God (Joshua 24:25f). When King David of Judah (the two southern tribes) accepted leadership over all the tribes, he first signed an agreement with the elders of Israel, establishing his authority over them.

And the Lord said to you, you will shepherd my people Israel [10 northern tribes], *and you will become their ruler. When all the elders of Israel had come to King David at Hebron, the king made a compact with them...and they anointed David king over Israel. David was thirty years old when he became king.*   (2 Samuel 5:2f)

For the Old Testament to prophesy the confirmation of the covenant between Israel and one person indicates the importance of the man and the event. A covenant bound the parties in an inalterable and permanent fashion. It was a matter of the utmost solemnity, as people placed themselves under penalty of divine retribution if they later tried to break their agreement.

He will confirm the covenant with many [not all] *for one week* [seven years].   (Daniel 9:27, KJV)

From a study of the covenants (see p. 31), it is apparent that the one being referred to is the land grant with Abraham. Israel's boundaries have caused so much warfare in the Middle East. This covenant will set the boundaries in accord with the Biblical mandate for the future (Ezekiel 47:15–23). These differ somewhat from the ones settled by Joshua, the Judges, Ezra, and Nehemiah.

There is no neighbor who will protest after God's mighty intervention on Israel's behalf.

The leader will project himself as the bearer of peace, the long-awaited king whom God promised David (2 Samuel 7:12f). He will claim to function like the Lord's *"signet ring,"* the seal or guarantee of Israel's promised inheritance (Haggai 2:23). Notwithstanding all appearances, Jews familiar with Scripture will be forewarned that an impostor will come before the Messiah.

People question whether the man who confirms the covenant will be Jewish or Gentile. What does the evidence suggest?

> *In the middle of the "seven,"* [years] *he will put an end to sacrifice and offering. And on a wing* [of the temple] *he will set up an abomination that causes desolation, until the end that is decreed is poured out on him.*   (Daniel 9:27)

By the middle of the covenant confirmer's seven-year tenure, the Temple will have risen, because the sacrifices and offerings are being made. These can only be offered at the Temple.

The Orthodox Jews will absolutely not permit anyone but a man they believe to be Messiah to build the Temple. Three times a day, these men pray "May it be thy will that the Temple be speedily rebuilt in our days." They believe that Messiah will come and show them where and how to build it.

What did the Lord say to David about this Son of his who would reign forever?

> *I will raise up your offspring to succeed you,* **one of your own sons***...He is the one who will build a house for me, and I will establish his throne forever...I will set him over my house and my kingdom forever; his throne will be established* **forever.**
>   (1 Chronicles 17:11ff; cf. 2 Samuel 7:12ff)

> *I will make a covenant of peace with them; it will be an everlasting covenant. I will establish them and increase*

their numbers and I will put my sanctuary among them forever. My dwelling place will be with them; I will be their God, and they will be my people. Then, the nations will know that I the Lord make Israel holy, when my sanctuary is among them **forever.**   (Ezekiel 37:26f)

Tell him this is what the Lord Almighty says: Here is the man whose name is the Branch, and he will branch out from his place and build the temple of the Lord. It is he who will build the temple of the Lord, and he will be clothed with majesty and will sit and rule on his throne...Those who are far away will come help to build the temple of the Lord, and you will know that the Lord Almighty has sent me to you.   (Zechariah 6:12f; cf. 3:8)

Gentiles will have absolutely no part in the erection of the Temple. For example, when the Turkish Sultan, Suleiman I, offered to rebuild the Temple in the mid-16th century, the Jews firmly refused. (Note the similarity of Suleiman's name to that of "Solomon," the original Temple builder.) Suleiman only rebuilt the walls and gates of Jerusalem.

You [Gentiles] *have no part with us in building a Temple to our God. We alone will build it for the Lord.*   (Ezra 4:3)

Contributions to Temple preparations today can only come from Jews.[32]

Therefore, a person they believe to be Messiah must be present in Israel for the Temple to be built. We know for certain that a messianic pretender will arise before the real Messiah (Daniel 9:27). A Gentile could not deceive anyone into believing him to be the Messiah. Furthermore, it is inconceivable that the real Messiah would allow the sacrifices to be started, then stopped in the middle of the seven years if He were present on earth. The sacrificial

---

32.   *Time,* October 16, 1989, p. 65.

system was the very core of Old Testament worship, set forth by the Lord Himself.

An image of the king will be set up in the Temple (Daniel 9:27). The Jews will have to flee for their lives, because they refuse to worship it (Matthew 24:15ff; 2 Thessalonians 2:4; Revelation 13:14f). What kind of an impotent Messiah would stand by in Israel and let this happen? This does not fit the picture the Bible gives of the triumphant Messiah, who comes to earth in power and great glory with the armies of heaven following Him to deliver the Jews (Daniel 7:13ff; Zechariah 12:9; 14:3; Luke 21:27; Revelation 19:14).

Some believe the coming king will be a "Roman:"

The people of the ruler who will come will destroy the city and the sanctuary [the Roman Titus did so in 70 A.D.]...
                                                          (Daniel 9:26)

This individual will begin to rule over the revived Roman Empire about 280 days (the average human gestation period—see Revelation 12:1–5) after he confirms the covenant with Israel. However, this does not automatically mean that he himself originates from that area.

The only conclusion left is that the covenant-confirmer and a Jewish messianic usurper are one and the same person. As mentioned before, those Jews who look for Messiah are definitely expecting a mere mortal. This, of course, was one of the major Jewish reasons for rejecting Jesus: His claim to divinity.

To qualify legally and eliminate pretenders, the Messiah has to prove through the genealogical charts that He is of the royal lineage of King David. Because of their extreme economic and historic significance, these charts were safeguarded in the Temple. They were also the only means by which the returning exiles could prove legal ownership to their land in Israel. Since everything burned in the Temple in 70 A.D., no Jew has had the legal evidence to prove his genealogy since then. How then will the false messiah prove his?

This legality may be avoided as there are families today who claim to be descendents of King David through the Maharal of Prague, the famous 16th-century rabbi. That rabbi was able to trace his lineage to the Gaonic line of Rav Ha'ai and Rav Sherira, who traditionally were descendents of David.[33]

The opening words of the New Testament declare the genealogy of Jesus' legal guardian, Joseph, back to Abraham, the father of the Hebrew nation. The names of Jesus' forefathers on his maternal side extend to Adam, the father of the human race (Luke 3). Both Joseph and Mary were descendants of David. That the Messiah would be the seed of a woman, instead of a man, was specified from the start to Adam and Eve (Genesis 3:15, KJV). Since women do not bear "seed," but the egg, the indication was there would be no father involved.

In the Bible, names were often changed when one attained a new status in life, for example: Abram to "Abraham" (Genesis 17:5); Jacob to "Israel" (Genesis 32:28); Hoshea to "Joshua" (Numbers 13:16); and Simon to "Peter" (John 1:42). The taking of a Hebrew name is done in Israel today.

Among innumerable possibilities, the covenant confirmer may assume a name like "Judas Netzer." "Judas" would suggest the hero, Judas Maccabeus, who recaptured the Temple from the cruel Syrian king, Antiochus Epiphanes, in 164 B.C. In actual fact, the present-day figure will have the nature of Judas Iscariot. (The latter is the only person in the entire Bible whom we are specifically told that **Satan entered.** This happened right before Judas betrayed Jesus [Luke 22:3; John 13:27]).

"Netzer" (a green branch or sprout, a root out of dry ground) is a messianic title (Isaiah 4:2; 11:1, 10; Jeremiah 23:5; 33:15; Revelation 22:16).

---

33.   Kaplan, p. 99 (Gaon means "Excellency.").

This is what the Lord Almighty says: 'Here is the man whose name is the Branch...It is he who will build the temple of the Lord.'   (Zechariah 6:12)

It is no coincidence that a description of a king follows immediately after one of the rare depictions of Satan in Scripture. On one hand (in Isaiah 14:16–19), this king's power is so extensive that he shook the earth and caused worldwide desolation. Yet in the end, his body is not even considered worthy of burial and is compared to *"a rejected branch."* However, the following describes the true Messiah:

The days are coming...when I will raise up to David a righteous Branch, a King who will reign wisely and do what is just and right in the land. In his days, Judah will be saved and Israel will live in safety.   (Jeremiah 23:5f)

Speaking of the promised Son of David:

I will place over them one shepherd, my servant David,... I the Lord will be their God, and my servant David will be prince among them...I will make a covenant of peace with them.   (Ezekiel 34:23f)

With overwhelming popular support, Israel's ruler could re-establish the Sanhedrin in keeping with:

I will restore your judges as in days of old, your counselors as at the beginning.   (Isaiah 1:26)

This body would then be able to recognize him formally as the messiah.[34]

The impostor may come to power at 30 years of age, as did Joseph in Egypt (Genesis 41:41–46) and David over Judah

---

34.   Cf. *Tosefta Sanhedrin* 3.2, *Yad, Sanhedrin* 5:1, *Melachim* 1:3. (Quoted by Kaplan, p. 93).

(2 Samuel 5:4). In sharp contrast, David loved to be in God's presence and distinguished himself for bravery and leadership from the time he was a lad. He was an eminently tried and tested servant of the Lord, which this man will not be. Thirty was the age at which the Levite undertook his full service in the Temple (Numbers 4:3, 23).

Thirty is not too young an age for a brilliant individual to gain recognition. For example, the great Jewish scholar, the Gaon of Vilna (18th century) was already famous for his phenomenal knowledge at age 20. His counsel was sought by leading rabbis of his day.[35] Alexander the Great had conquered vast territory extending from Greece to India before his death at 32. Napoleon seized power and became dictator of France by age 30.

In our day, it is unlikely that Messiah could fulfill Scripture by being born in Bethlehem of Judah, since it is a wholly Arab town.

> *But you, Bethlehem "Ephrathah"* [this is the old name for Bethelem in Judah - see Genesis 35:19], *though you are small among the clans of Judah, out of you will come for me one who will be ruler over Israel, whose origins are from of old, from ancient times.* (Micah 5:2)

Shortly after the birth of Jesus, Herod asked the chief priests and all the teachers of the law where the King of the Jews would be born. They answered, "Bethlehem" (Matthew 2:4f). It was also common knowledge among the people of the day that Messiah would come from Bethlehem (John 7:42). From whence will this arrogant impostor arise?

The False Messiah and the Tribe of Dan

There has been a Jewish tradition that links the end-time king of Israel to the tribe of Dan (judgment) instead of David's tribe of Judah (praise). Although it may be impossible to trace the king's

---

35. Bridger, ed., p. 161.

lineage to the tribe of Dan, his family could have lived in the area of Dan (northern Israel) for a long time. Dr. Chaim Weizmann, the first President of Israel, observed in 1907 that there were descendants of Jews who had never left the Holy Land.[36] This would be especially true in the north.

An example of this linkage is in "The Testaments of the Twelve Patriarchs" in *The Old Testament Pseudepigrapha*.[37] The *Pseudepigrapha* is a part of Jewish literature written in the second century B.C. and preserved through the Christian churches. Fragments of it were also found among the first-century Jewish Dead Sea Scrolls and in the medieval Geniza (synagogue storeroom) in Cairo. The "Testaments of the Twelve Patriarchs" are the solemn words of the 12 sons of Jacob to their own sons before death.[38] We read in *The Old Testament Pseudepigrapha* Vol. 1, The Testament of Dan 5:4, 6:

> For I know that in the last days you will defect from the Lord. You will be offended at Levi [the priests] and revolt against Judah [Messiah's tribe]; but you will not prevail over them. An angel of the Lord guides them both; because by them Israel shall stand...You are motivated to all wickedness by the spirits of deceit among you...For I read...that your prince is Satan...[39]

What were the final words of Dan's father, Jacob, to his son?

I will tell you what will happen to you in the days to come...Dan shall judge his people, as one of the tribes of Israel. Let Dan be a serpent on the way [cart rut or track], *a horned snake on the path, that bites the horses heels; and*

---

36.   Zagoren, p. 72.
37.   *Encyclopaedia Judaica,* Vol. 3, p. 62.
38.   *Ibid.,* Vol. 14, p. 811.
39.   Charlesworth, ed., pp. 809–810.

its rider falls backwards. **I have waited for your salvation, O Jehovah.**   (Genesis 49:16ff, The Interlinear Bible)

Why did his father call him *"a serpent,"* another name for
Satan from the first to the last book of the Bible? What was God
showing Jacob that caused the man immediately to implore the
Lord for deliverance? The very first time this word, "salvation" or
yeshua (*yshuwah*), is used in the Bible, it is in relation to Dan, "a
serpent…a horned snake".

Was Jacob prophetically seeing Dan's apostasy? They appear
to have been the first tribe to worship idols instead of the true God
(Judges 18:30). After Solomon's death, a golden calf, Egypt's
pagan symbol of vitality and strength, was set up for the people to
worship at Dan and at Bethel (1 Kings 12:28ff). Excavations have
uncovered the platform for this calf at Tel Dan. Dan remained a
center for idolatrous worship (2 Kings 10:29). Even the Greek
writer, Homer, used the word "Danites," to refer to the Greeks, so
worldly had Dan become.

The first part of Jacob's prophecy was fulfilled by Samson, a
Danite judge of Israel. He single-handedly destroyed many of the
Philistines (Judges 14–16). Will any son of Dan fulfill the figure of
the serpent? Notice that Jacob prophesied that Dan *"shall"* judge,
but did not declare ahead of time that Dan must be a snake. Rather
Jacob said *"let"* Dan be a serpent. This demonstrates this future
man's access to free will.

The Danite territory, described in Jacob's prophecy to Dan,
appears to be their original location in Israel, adjacent to the
Mediterranean Sea and to a major caravan route. Jacob said that
they would attack travelers like a serpent, or gain advantage by
cunning, surprise, and speed. The expression, "a serpent striking
the heel," is first used in the Garden of Eden, where God told
Satan:

And I will put enmity between you and the woman, and between your seed and her seed. He [Messiah] *will bruise* [crush] *your head, and you shall bruise his heel.*
(Genesis 3:15, The Interlinear Bible)

Moses' last words about the tribe of Dan, prior to his death seem devoid of blessing. However, the statement holds profound meaning:

Dan is a lion's whelp [cub]. *He shall leap from Bashan.*
(Deuteronomy 33:22, KJV)

This tribe was unable to occupy the area they were allotted. They attacked Laish in the north and took over that land east of the Jordan River (Judges 18). It was a part of Bashan, which contained hills with fierce lions and bulls. It included about half of the area now known as the Golan Heights.

Will a future young king spring from the area of the Golan Heights as a lion, king of the beasts, would do? If this happens, both he and Antiochus IV would originate from Syria. The Golan belonged to Syria until 1967, when it was occupied by Israel. If the king is 30 years of age when he comes to power, he could have been born in the 1960s when the Golan still belonged to Syria. This area is distinctly not the town of Bethlehem, the prophesied birthplace of Messiah (Micah 5:2).

Note: Psalm 22 opens with words that Jesus uttered from the cross. The psalm depicts the scene of His crucifixion in detail. He is surrounded by His enemies, whose vigor and ferocity are compared to strong, wild bulls of Bashan, roaring lions and dogs.

What about the tribe of Dan's original size or strength? Moses was told by God to take a census of the men at the beginning and again at the end of their 40 years in the wilderness (Numbers 1 and 26). The tribe of Dan increased in number, and on both occasions was second only to Judah (Messiah's tribe) in size. Nevertheless, Dan was the only tribe that had only one clan of descendants (Genesis 46:23; Numbers 26:42).

Dan and Zebulun are entirely omitted from the genealogical lists, which conclude by stating:

> *All Israel was listed in the genealogies recorded in the book of the kings of Israel.*   (1 Chronicles 2:3–9:1)

Judah went first in the marching order of the tribes and Dan was *"the rear guard for all the units"* (Numbers 10:14, 25). Judah received the first allotment and the last lot came out for Dan, when the tribes received the Promised Land (Joshua 19:40ff).

When the area of Dan is mentioned later, it again involves venomous snakes, biting vipers, and horses.

> *We hoped for peace but no good has come, for a time of healing but there was only terror...horses...from Dan...the whole land trembles...Vipers...Is the Lord not in Zion? Is her King no longer there?...***The harvest is past, the summer has ended, and we are not saved...****I mourn and horror grips me. Is there no balm in Gilead? Is there no physician there? Why, then, is there no healing for the wound of my people?*   (Jeremiah 8:15–22)

> *Every brother is a deceiver...and no one speaks the truth...*
>
> (Jeremiah 9:4)

Will this picture find its final fulfillment at the time in which Israel's eyes are riveted upon her (false) messiah? Their hope will vanish into a quicksand of terror when he commands them to worship him as God. No peace, only horror...

Dan is also the only tribe missing from the original 12 tribes of Israel from whom the 144,000 *"servants of our God"* will come (Revelation 7:4ff). (Dan is replaced by Manasseh.) The implication is that the Danites are significantly out of favor with God.

The Danite banner was white and red with an eagle. This would synchronize well with the eagle of the old Roman Empire, over which the false messiah will also rule. (The Romans erected their golden eagle over the great gate of the Temple. This represented Rome's subjugation of the Jewish people.)[40]

To recapitulate, it seems illogical to believe that the Jewish people would choose a Gentile to be their *"king"* (Daniel 11:36). A divine requirement for a Jewish king is that *"he must be from among your own brothers"* (Deuteronomy 17:15).

And, he would need to be a Jew to convince anyone that he is the Messiah. Whoever this man is, his terrible arrogance is similar to the ruler described here:

In the pride of your heart you say, "I am a god; I sit on the throne of a god..." But you are a man and not a god.
(Ezekiel 28:2)

Even though the 12 apostles were in the presence of Jesus' sinless character for three-and-half years, one of them still found it possible to betray Him with the help of Satan. High treason will be committed against Israel as well. The miracle of it all is that because of God's amazing mercy, the tribe of Dan will find forgiveness and reinstatement in the millennial reign of Messiah (Ezekiel 48:1).

Final Ingathering to Israel

To return to the post-invasion period, early Jewish scholars have ruled that the rebuilding of the Temple must await Messiah. Maimonides said the Temple would not be built until a majority of the Jewish people live in Israel. Rabbis also say that the Jubilee year cannot be celebrated in Israel until *"all"* the Jews are back in the land (Leviticus 25:10). Only about 5.20 million of the world's 18 million Jews (29%) are there now.[41]

---

40.   Josephus, p. 468.
41.   1993-Houghton Mifflin Almanac., pp. 209, 408.

In May 1991, Israel completed the rescue of 14,500 Ethiopian Jews in less than 30 hours, before rebel forces attacked the capital. Operation "Moses" originally took 7,000 of them to Israel in May 1985. They left Judea in the second century B.C. These people want to be in Israel. For them it fulfills God's promise to take them back to Zion before Messiah comes.

The Ethiopians have lived by the rules of the first five books of the Old Testament.

> The writings of the rabbis from the second century onward, the foundation of modern Jewish theology, were either unknown or ignored...The religion they practice differs from the Orthodox Judaism practiced in Israel.[42]

During the seven months after the coming invasion when the Israelis are interring the dead troops (Ezekiel 39:12, 14), Jewry will be simultaneously burying their own alienation and "dead" attitudes toward their God forever. The effect of the divine intervention will be so far-reaching that it will galvanize the Jews who are still in dispersion.

Many will gather in Israel to take part in the unequalled messianic fervor, hope, and excitement. God's direct intervention is His stirring alarm, His sounding of the ram's horn (*shofar*) to call His people back to Israel. The impact of this call does not register on us now from our present, unawakened vantage point.

> *In that day, the Lord will thresh from the flowing Euphrates to the Wadi of Egypt, and you, O Israelites, will be gathered up one by one. And in that day a great trumpet will sound.*   (Isaiah 27:12f)

Then, the Jews will know that this is the final ingathering to the Messiah—God's last call to come into their ark—Israel. There will

---

42.   *The Washington Post* pp. C-6, 7.

be no time to delay. Also, Israel will be a far safer place for Jews to live once the armed forces of her hostile neighbors have been destroyed by God. Therefore, the element of danger will appear to have subsided.

Joseph's dying words to his brothers in Egypt still apply to the Jews in dispersion today.

But God will surely come to your aid and take you up out of this land [the Gentile nations] *to the land he promised on oath to Abraham, Isaac, and Jacob.*   (Genesis 50:24)

They will follow the Lord; he will roar like a lion. When he roars, his children will come trembling from the west.
(Hosea 11:10)

Thou shalt arise and have mercy upon Zion; for the time to favour her, yea, the appointed time is come...when the Lord shall build up Zion, He shall appear in his glory...This shall be written for the [Jewish] *generation* [dor] *to come* [acharown]. (*Acharown* means late or last to come from the west as you face east!)
(Psalm 102:13, 16, 18, KJV)

This anticipates the fact that some of the last Jewish people in dispersion who will immigrate to join their brothers in Israel are those from the west.

I will have compassion on all the people of Israel...When I have brought them back from the nations and have gathered them from the countries of their enemies, **I will show myself holy through them in the sight of many nations**...*I will gather them to their land, not leaving any behind.*   (Ezekiel 39:25ff)

I will establish them and increase their numbers, and I will put my sanctuary among them forever.   (Ezekiel 37:26)

*I will surely gather all of you, O Jacob; I will surely bring
together the remnant of Israel. I will bring them together
like sheep in a pen...the place will throng with people.*

(Micah 2:12)

The days are coming when people will no longer speak about
the great exodus from Egypt, but about their release from *"the
land of the north"* (Jeremiah 23:7f; 16:15; 31:8). This is happening today with the release of the Russian Jews.

*I will say, bring my sons from afar, and my daughters from
the ends of the earth—everyone who is called by my name.*

(Isaiah 43:6)

There is another powerful stimulus. God will remove the
committed Church, in whose charge He placed the kingdom nearly
2,000 years ago (Matthew 21:43), He will commission 144,000
Jews themselves to spread the gospel of Jesus Christ. Their
gestation period (280 days) will begin the day the covenant is
confirmed in Israel. They will appear and *"the rest"* of Messiah's
brothers still in dispersion will understand the urgency of the hour
and will return to Israel (see p. 154).

*Therefore, Israel will be abandoned until the time when she
who is in labor* [Israel] **gives birth** *and the rest of his* [Mes-
siah's] *brothers return to join the Israelites.*

(Micah 5:3)

Some Jews appear to remain outside Israel during the king's
seven-year rule.

I will send some of those who survive [God's wrath]...*and
they will bring all your brothers from all the nations to my
holy mountain in Jerusalem.*

(Isaiah 66:19f; see also Zephaniah 3:20)

The Magnificent Third Temple

Even now, the Jews are preparing for their sacred Temple. Nearly 500 students are learning how to rebuild the Temple and perform the services. A convention was planned in 1990 for those of priestly descent (surnamed Cohen). Since 1983, the Temple Institute has been making implements for the offering of sacrifices, musical instruments, vestments of handspun flax, and blueprints for a miniature Temple replica. "Historian David Solomon insists that a new Temple is essential: It was the essence of our Jewish being, the unifying force of our people."[43] The Israeli government is also sponsoring the first Conference of Temple Research.

After intensive investigation of the Temple Mount since 1967, Asher Kaufman has made a most exciting and important discovery. Using existing archaeological remains, information from the Talmud and Josephus he seems to have identified the exact location of both Temples.[44]

Not only will the Jews build the Temple on the foundations of the two prior Temples, they will adhere to the Biblical specifications (Ezekiel 40–46) for this Sanctuary which will reign over Jerusalem and finally, the world. It must surpass the magnificent Second Temple that Herod rebuilt.

The closed eastern gate to the Temple Mount is built immediately over the prior gate. This gate is lined up due east of a small, unimposing cupola. The Arabic names of this structure are the "Dome of the Spirits" or the "Dome of the Tablets." This lends recognition to the Holy Spirit and the Tablets of the Law which must have resided there.

The cupola shelters a large, flat bedrock, the "Foundation Stone." Otherwise, the surrounding area is all paved with

43.   *Time,* October 16, 1989, p. 65.
44.   Kaufman, pp. 40–61.

flagstones. The ancient rabbis wrote that upon entering the Holy of Holies every *Yom Kippur*, the High Priest would place his censer of burning coals in front of the Ark of the Covenant on the "Foundation Stone," the *"Even Shetiyah."*[45]

It may be that the glory of God once dwelt above this very bedrock in the Holy of Holies and will return to the Temple when Messiah comes (Ezekiel 43:7). There are no tool marks upon the bedrock's surface in keeping with God's instructions (Exodus 20:25; Deuteronomy 27:5; 1 Kings 6:7).

The "Foundation Stone" protruded three fingerbreadths (2 inches or 5.4 cm) above the level of the Temple floor.[46] The Inner Court was 8.6 feet (2.62 m) below that same floor (*Middoth* 3:6). These three levels agree "well-nigh perfectly" with the different levels established by the rock and cistern surfaces existing at the site.[47]

Note: One may wonder what the purpose was of *"as- Sakhra,"* the huge irregular rock formation nearby under the present Dome of the Rock. It is thought to have been the Stone of Claimants from which lost and found announcements were made.[48] The main center of activity in the Temple area was on the southern side.[49] There may have been other usages, as it has a large hole cut through it.

There was a steep ascent to Herod's Temple, which rose about 150 feet into the air.[50] The Temple was a spectacular sight of dazzling splendor, which shone like a jewel in the sunlight. The Sanctuary was constructed of white marble, richly adorned with gold. It

---

45.   *Tosefta-Yom Ha-kipurim* 3.6; *Yoma* 21b, p. 94; 53b, p. 251.
46.   *Yoma,* 53b, p. 251.
47.   Kaufman, p. 53f.
48.   *Taanith* 3:8.
49.   *Middoth* 2:1; Kaufman, p. 53.
50.   Jerusalem, p. 35.

was amazing to see the excellent workmanship and the vast number of materials used. Immense wealth had been devoted to it.[51]

The Temple was the site of the Divine Presence, the *Shekinah* glory (1 Kings 8:10–12). Therefore, it was the center of the nation and the preferred place for prayer (2 Kings 19:14ff; 1 Kings 8:44, 48). People would assemble there in times of distress, and the priests would weep between the Temple porch and the altar (Joel 2:15ff).

The Third Temple will crown Mount Moriah, which all believers will ultimately ascend with joy.

"The glory of this present house will be greater than the glory of former house...And in this place I will grant peace."   (Haggai 2:9)

Construction of the Temple must wait for at least seven months after the invasion, since all the Israelis will be occupied cleansing the land by burying the dead (Ezekiel 39:12ff). Even if Jewish priests were available to build it, it would be unthinkable for the Jews to undertake such a sacred task, while the land was defiled by unburied bodies. If the invasion occurs on *Rosh Hashanah* and the burying is over by the end of *Nisan,* they could begin building the Temple in the month of *Iyyar.* This was the month in which both the First and the Second Temples were started (1 Kings 6:37; 2 Chronicles 3:2; Ezra 3:8).

Solomon required seven-and-a-half years to build the First Temple from the laying of the foundation. Zerubbabel's Temple took a little less than half that time (Haggai 1:14f; Ezra 6:15). If the Third Temple follows this pattern, it will be completed about a year-and-a-half later in the month of *Tishri.* This is a reasonable amount of time for its erection.

---

51.   Josephus, pp. 335, 581.

Note: Herod's Temple may shed much light upon the construction of the Third Temple. When Herod rebuilt Zerubbabel's Temple, it retained the name "Second Temple." King Herod was not ordained by God to undertake this work. The king considered the perfecting of the Temple as the project that would be "an everlasting memorial of himself."[52]

When King Herod rebuilt Zerubbabel's Temple, the king promised the people that it would not be torn down until everything was prepared. The priests were trained as stonecutters and carpenters; 10,000 of the most skillful workmen were chosen; and 1,000 wagons were constructed. The actual Temple itself was completed by the priests in 18 months.[53]

> It is also reported that during the time the Temple was building, it did not rain in the daytime, but that the showers fell in the nights, so that the work was not hindered. And this our fathers have delivered to us; nor is it incredible, if any have regard to the manifestations of God.[54]

Josephus was alive during the lifetime of many who built or saw Herod's Temple under construction; and would have spoken with them directly in order to offer these facts.

The Talmud also reports that at dawn:

> The wind blew, and the clouds dispersed, the sun shone so that the people were able to go out to their work, and then they knew they were engaged in a sacred work.[55]

In our day, Meir Ben-Dov, leader of the Temple Mount archaeological team, said that he considered these descriptions to be exaggerations before starting the dig in 1968. However, after 14 years of work on the Temple Mount, he found they "lost an

---

52.   Josephus, p. 334.
53.   *Ibid.,* pp. 334, 336.
54.   *Ibid.,* p. 336.
55.   *The Jerusalem Talmud,* Berachoth 1:8 and *Babylonian Talmud,* Taanith 23:71.

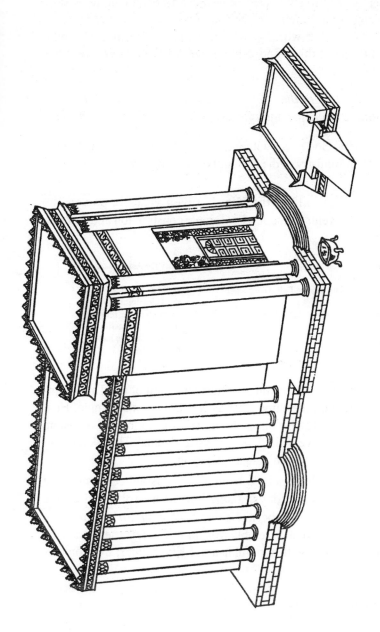

A Rendition of Herod's Temple

Then suddenly the Lord you are seeking will come to his temple (Malachi 3:1)

average of only five workdays a year due to rain or snow, as most of the precipitation fell at night."[56]

We know that worship will be taking place in the Temple before the first three-and-a-half years of the leader's rule has transpired:

In the middle of the "seven" [years], *he* [the king] *will put an end to sacrifice and offering.*   (Daniel 9:27)

Secondly, God's two witnesses are told to measure the Temple during their ministry in the first half of the king's reign (Revelation 11:1).

In the first half of the King's seven years in power, the sequence of events of the Jewish Temple construction and worship may be:

1/2 year	(Seven Months:) Fall, *Tishri* - Spring, *Nisan*	Bury the dead invaders.
1-1/2 years	Spring, *Iyyar* - Fall, *Tishri*	Build and dedicate the Third Temple.
1-1/2 years	Fall, *Tishri* - Spring, *Nisan*	Worship in the Temple until Temple sacrifice and offering are halted by the king.

It would be highly fitting for the dedication of the Third Temple to be held on the same feast as was Solomon's Temple. How better could the Jewish nation honor this most glorious occasion, for which they have waited nearly two millennia? This would also be the king's second anniversary in power.

Solomon and the people from all over Israel celebrated the dedication for seven days (*Tishri* 8th–14th), followed by the seven-day Feast of Tabernacles or *Sukkot* (*Tishri* 15th–21st). *Tishri* 22 was the final assembly (*Shemini Azeret*), after which the people went home with a joyful heart (1 Kings 8:65f; 2 Chronicles 7:8f).

56.   Ben-Dov, pp. 28, 84.

Josephus described the timing of the celebration of Herod's Temple.

For at the same time of this celebration of the work on the Temple, fell also the day of the king's inauguration, which he kept of an old custom as a festival. And the inauguration now coincided with the other [celebration], which coincidence of them both made the festival more illustrious.[57]

The wilderness Tabernacle and the less imposing Temple of Zerubbabel were both completed and dedicated before Passover (Exodus 40:17; Ezra 6:15–19).

The Zadokites—Priests of the Temple

Since the high priest Zadok (of the lineage of Aaron and Phinehas – 1 Chronicles 6:3, 4, 8) was faithful to Solomon, Zadok gained for himself the privilege of serving in the Temple. This fulfilled God's covenant with Phinehas for a lasting priesthood (Numbers 25:13). Solomon removed Abiathar of the house of Eli from sharing that position (1 Kings 2:27). Though the Zadokites were later put out of office, the Qumran religious community continued to be loyal to them.[58]

The Zadokites alone will enter the Lord's sanctuary and be the priests in the Millennial Temple (Ezekiel 40:46; 43:19; 44:15). They will be given *"a special gift"* of the most holy portion of the land surrounding the Temple (Ezekiel 48:12).

...the Zadokites, who were faithful in serving me and did not go astray as the Levites did when the Israelites went astray.

(Ezekiel 48:11)

---

57. Josephus, p. 336.
58. *The NIV Study Bible*, Note 44:15, p. 1,290.

Chapter Six

CHURCH CALLS THE WORLD TO ESCAPE GOD'S COMING WRATH

Many will be purified, made spotless and refined, but the wicked will continue to be wicked.   (Daniel 12:10)

God's Final Call to Safety before His Coming Wrath

What will happen with God's forces following the invasion? Israel will be extremely occupied: cleansing the land for the first seven months by burying the dead invaders and engaging in mounting messianic exhilaration.

The prophecies will not only be coming to pass, they will be impacting on us! God's predictions will have moved off the pages of Scripture onto the ever-clamoring television which commands our attention. People will see that God's Word is altogether accurate down to the last detail.

This will be the Church's finest hour since the first century. The invasion may constitute God's *"shout"* to let the believers in Christ know that their Bridegroom's arrival is very near (Matthew

25:6). The invasion **and** Israel's confirming the covenant with a man will cause informed Christians to know without a doubt that there are only seven years until Jesus returns to earth. Christians will go forth immediately after the invasion to call people to repent and turn to the Messiah.

This would be the interval between the cry that rings out at the midnight hour announcing that the Bridegroom is on His way, and His actual arrival (Matthew 25:6–12). Tragically, only half of the Church will have *"oil for their lamps"* to enable them to light the way for others to see. In other words, only 50 percent of the Christians will be equipped, through a godly life and the understanding of God's Word, to tell others what is taking place. Jewish leaders rejected entrance into the Kingdom of God because they thought they were already there. Many churchgoers who practice dead, religious rituals, but have no personal relationship with Jesus, are making the same mistake.

…having a form of godliness, but denying its power.
(2 Timothy 3:5)

At that time the kingdom of heaven will be like ten virgins who took their lamps and went out to meet the Bridegroom. Five of them were foolish and five were wise. The foolish ones took their lamps but did not take any oil with them. The wise, however, took oil in jars along with their lamps…The foolish ones said to the wise, "Give us some of your oil. Our lamps are going out." " 'No,' they replied, 'There may not be enough for both us and you. Instead, go to those who sell oil and buy some for yourselves.' "
(Matthew 25:1ff)

Christians will tell people that the only way to be acceptable to God is through accepting the righteousness that Jesus Christ offers them. God will confirm their words with powerful signs, wonders, and healings. Multitudes will repent utterly. Myriads of believers, not just church leaders, will carry the message. Christians will bring life to the spiritually "dead" worldwide through the "good news" of Jesus Christ, while the Israelis are interring the dead. Many Jews will also bury their old views about their God and draw closer to Him.

People will come into relationship with God. He will give mankind one last opportunity to come into His kingdom through His Son before He removes His followers from earth.

For He will finish the work and cut it short in righteousness; because a short work will the Lord make upon the earth.   (Romans 9:28, KJV; see also Isaiah 10:22f; 28:22)

The Holy Spirit will pour down upon people as *"the latter rain"* (Joel 2:23).

And afterward, I will pour out my Spirit on all people. Your sons and daughters will prophesy, your old men will dream dreams, your young men will see visions. Even on my servants, both men and women, I will pour out my Spirit in those days.   (Joel 2:28f)

The Holy Spirit will move upon the hearts of backsliding Christians, unbelievers, and hardened sinners. The Spirit will bring renewal right into Satan's territory. God will rescue those who love God but are enslaved to sin. They will be like *"a burning stick snatched from the fire"* (Amos 4:11). The Lord will recharge the spirit of many.

Many will understand that Jesus is coming to rescue His followers as He promised to do, before God releases His wrath on earth:

I will also keep you from the hour of trial that is coming upon the whole world to test those who live on earth.
(Revelation 3:10)

For God did not appoint us to suffer wrath but to receive salvation through our Lord Jesus Christ.
(1 Thessalonians 5:9)

Jesus, who rescues us from the coming wrath.
(1 Thessalonians 1:10)

Since we have now been justified by his blood, how much more shall we be saved from God's wrath through him!
(Romans 5:9)

His Spirit will break our idols and melt the arrogance of the rebellious. A strong sense of God's holiness will be felt throughout entire communities as in the American Revivals of 1856 and 1906 and the Welsh Revivals of 1859 and 1904. True revival is spontaneous and sovereign. It does not bring excitement, but an awakening, a severe conviction of sin, repentance, and a turning to God. People will cover themselves in righteousness that only Jesus offers and accept God's forgiveness and His gift of eternal life.

One of the most striking characteristics of the 1859 Welsh Revival was its effect on young people, and even on children. All ages and classes possessed the spirit of prayer.[1]

The same purity and power that was the hallmark of the first century Christians will once again be evident among true believers. God will anoint His servants, so that it will be known that God is with them. The world will see miracle after miracle wrought by the Almighty.

The apostles performed many miraculous signs and wonders among the people. And all the believers used to meet together in Solomon's Colonnade. No one else dared join them, even though they were highly regarded by the people. Nevertheless, more and more men and women believed in the Lord and were added to their number.

(Acts 5:12f)

---

1.   Phillips, pp. 21, 67.

*And everyone who calls on the name of the Lord will be
saved.*   (Joel 2:32; Acts 2:21)

You may ask, "What will happen to those in remote places who
have never heard of Jesus and His righteousness?" Our Maker knows
our heart and our actions. God can find a way to reveal Jesus to the
person whose heart is open. Time and space present no limitation to
our Creator. The Lord holds us responsible for obeying what we do
know in our minds and hearts (Romans 2:12–16).

We can be assured that God's evaluation of each of us will be
entirely righteous. None will be able to complain of unfairness, as
God's judgment will be *"based on truth,"* on all the facts (Romans
2:2). Therefore, every mouth will be silenced (Romans 3:19).

The Bridegroom and His Bride

Jesus and His believers are described in the New Testament as
betrothed. He is called the *"Bridegroom"* and the committed
followers, His *"Bride."*

*In my Father's house are many rooms...I am going there to
prepare a place for you...I will come back and take you to
be with me that you also may be where I am.*   (John 14:2f)

In ancient times, the Jewish marriage consisted of two parts: Betrothal (*erusin*), followed a while later by marriage (*nissu'in*). At
the betrothal, the young man made the covenant for his bride, drank
the cup to signify agreement, and paid the bridal price. He would then
return to his father's home to prepare a place for his future wife.

Only when his father gave approval of the new quarters was
the groom free to claim his bride. In accord with tradition, his arrival would totally surprise the bride and might happen while she
was asleep.[2]

2.   Levitt, *A Christian Love Story,* p. 18ff; Landman, Vol. 10, p. 480ff;
      Schneid, pp. 10, 37, 48.

The bride would quickly put on her wedding garments and veil (cf. Genesis 24:65). In ancient times, she was escorted to the groom's home by a procession of people, some of whom carried lamps or torches. In those days, the bridal canopy (*huppah*) was a tent or a room where the union took place.

After the ceremony was over, the friend of the bridegroom waited outside the chamber for word that the union had been completed (cf. John 3:29). The "wedding week" celebrations concluded with the final feast, enjoyed by the family and guests (cf. Revelation 19:7-9).

People who make up the Bride of Christ do not merely "believe" that Jesus existed in history. Similar to any bride, the believers have developed a loving, intimate relationship with Him. They not only watch for Him; they long for His return. The only people He can call up to Himself are those who are waiting for Him.

He will appear a second time, not to bear sin, but to bring salvation to those who are waiting for him.

(Hebrews 9:28)

...the crown of righteousness which the Lord, the righteous Judge, will award...to all who have longed for his appearing. (2 Timothy 4:8)

...the blessed hope—the glorious appearing of our great God and Savior, Jesus Christ. (Titus 2:13)

...as you eagerly wait for our Lord Jesus Christ to be revealed. (1 Corinthians 1:7)

True love is expressed by the person who will leave his own interests for those of the beloved. When the Bridegroom comes for His Bride, she will be about his business. She will be in *the vineyards*, bringing the harvest of lost souls into the kingdom of God. This is where the *"bride"* (Song of Solomon or Canticles

4:8) is met by the lover of her soul when He comes (Song of Solomon 7:12).

Rebekah's willingness to leave her home immediately to go and marry Isaac, whom she had never seen (Genesis 24:55f), is a picture of the true Church leaving right away to go to her beloved Lord when He comes for her. He will present her to Himself as a radiant, unblemished Church (Ephesians 5:27).

How does the Holy Spirit describe this Messiah who has given His life to redeem all men?

He is the image of the invisible God, the firstborn over all creation. For by him all things were created: things in heaven and on earth, visible and invisible, whether thrones or powers or rulers or authorities. All things were created by him and for him. He is before all things, and in him all things hold together. (Colossians 1:15ff)

The Son is the radiance of God's glory and the exact representation of his being, sustaining all things by his powerful word. (Hebrews 1:3)

For in Christ all the fullness of the Deity lives in bodily form, and you have been given that fullness in Christ. (Colossians 2:9f)

My purpose is that they may be encouraged in heart and united in love, so that they may have the full riches of complete understanding, in order that they may know the mystery of God, namely Christ, in whom are hidden all the treasures of wisdom and knowledge. (Colossians 2:2f)

Previous Rescues by God

At the same time that the Jews are going home to Israel, committed Christians know that Jesus is coming to call them home to heaven. Jesus does not meet His true Church on earth but in the air.

This *"catching up"* of believers is known as the "Rapture." The word comes from the Latin *"rapio"* (Greek - *harpazo*) which means to seize, take by force, to catch up.

The concept of the Rapture was providentially reawakened in the Church by the book, *Jesus Is Coming,* by William E. Blackstone in 1878. Numerous editions followed in 25 different languages.

There are only two precedents in the Old Testament of people being taken up to heaven alive. These are:

1. Enoch, the Gentile (Genesis 5:24) who foreshadowed the Rapture of the Church.

2. Elijah, the Jew (2 Kings 2:11) who symbolized the catching up of the male progeny, the 144,000 *"first-fruits"* of Israel.

In the first century A.D., Paul and John both reported being taken up to heaven temporarily (2 Corinthians 12:2f; Revelation 4:1f).

Biblical examples of the removal of believers from the scene immediately before God brought destruction were:

1. Noah and his family were told to get into the ark seven days before the door to the ark was closed and the Flood started (Genesis 7: 4, 10, 16; cf. Matthew 24:37ff).

2. Lot and his family (except his wife who agonized over leaving) were taken out at dawn before Sodom and Gomorrah were destroyed (Genesis 19; cf. Luke 17:28).

3. Rahab and her family were spared when Joshua and his men destroyed Jericho (Joshua 6:23).

4. Jesus was careful to forewarn the Jewish believers to escape when they saw armies surround Jerusalem (Luke 21:20ff). Thus, they fled to Pella when General Titus brought the 5th, 10th, 12th and 15th Legions of Rome (almost 80,000 men) against Jerusalem, in the spring of 70 A.D.[3]

---

3.   Keller, p. 408.

5. In the future, post-Rapture Christians are instructed to flee from Judea when the false messiah sets up *"the abomination that causes desolation"* in the Holy Place (Matthew 24:15f).

"Caught Up"

We are instructed that three different groups will be caught or called up to heaven in the future. The first two will be withdrawn before God begins His wrath upon earth (see p. 127f).

1. The Bride of Christ (1 Thessalonians 4:17) is *"caught up."*
2. The Jewish male progeny (the 144,000) is *"caught up"* (Revelation 12:5, KJV).
3. The two witnesses are *"called up"* (Revelation 11:12).

"Firstfruits"

The first two groups listed, the Bride of Christ and the 144,000 Jewish men, are **the only groups** called *"firstfruits"* in the New Testament. Jesus is called *"the firstfruits of those who have fallen asleep"* (died) (1 Corinthians 15: 20, 23).

His Church (Jewish and Gentile believers) are called *"a kind of firstfruits of all he created"* (James 1:18). The 144,000 Jewish *"servants of our God"* are *"offered as firstfruits to God and to the Lamb"* (Revelation 14:4).

In Israel, the firstfruits of the crop were waved before God as a sample of more harvest to come. These groups, one from the Church and one from Israel, will be the first people who will be offered to God from among men. Therefore, this special name, "firstfruits" *may refer to TWO RAPTURES.*

The "Catching Up" of the Bride of Christ

At midnight, when there is great spiritual darkness and the Church has fallen asleep, the cry will ring out that the Bridegroom is coming. **There will be an interval between the shout and His arrival.** In Jesus' own words:

> *The kingdom of heaven will be like ten virgins who took their lamps and went out to meet the Bridegroom. Five of them were foolish and five of them were wise. The foolish ones took their lamps but did not take any oil* [the understanding of God's Word] *with them. The wise, however, took oil in jars along with their lamps…*
>
> *At midnight the cry rang out: "Here's the Bridegroom! Come out to meet him!" … But while they* [the professing Church] *were on their way to buy the oil, the Bridegroom arrived. The virgins who were ready, went in with him to the wedding banquet. And the door was shut. Later, the others came. "Sir, sir," they said. "Open the door* [to heaven] *for us!" But He replied, "I tell you the truth, I don't know you." Therefore, keep watch, because you do not know the day or the hour.*   (Matthew 25:1–13)

Notice that only half of the virgins were ready to go with the Bridegroom into the wedding. At formal banquets, once the company was assembled and the door shut, no one else was allowed to enter, no matter how great the entreaty.

> *According to the Lord's own word, we tell you that we who are still alive, who are left till the coming of the Lord, will certainly not precede those who have fallen asleep* [died]. *For the Lord himself will come down from heaven, with a loud command, with the voice of the archangel and with the trumpet call of God, and the dead in Christ will rise first. After that, we who are still alive and are left will be caught up together with them in the clouds to meet the Lord in the air. And so we will be with the Lord forever.*
>   (1 Thessalonians 4:15–17)

Listen, I tell you a mystery; we will not all sleep [die]; *but we will all be changed—in a flash, in the twinkling of an eye, at the last trumpet. For the dead will be raised imperishable, and we will be changed. For the perishable must clothe itself with the imperishable and the mortal with immortality.*   (1 Corinthians 15:51ff)

After the Bridegroom's shout awakens the committed Church, "the Bride of Christ," the Rapture can take place at any moment. Since God prepares us through precedents, we should remember the short duration of John the Baptist's ministry.

John was six months older than his cousin, Jesus. Jesus' mother became pregnant when John's mother was in her sixth month (Luke 1:26). John was a priest because he was the son of the priest Zechariah (Luke 1:5).

In accord with the Levitical requirement (Numbers 4:3, 23), Jesus and John would have begun their service for God at 30 years of age. Thus, John would have started six months ahead of Jesus to prepare the way for Messiah by preaching repentance to Israel.

As soon as Jesus was baptized in the Jordan River at *"about 30 years old"* (Luke 3:23), He:

...was led by the Holy Spirit in the desert, where for 40 days he was tempted by the devil.   (Luke 4:1f)

After the temptation, Jesus heard that John had been imprisoned; and Jesus returned to Galilee (Matthew 4:12; Mark 1:14; Luke 4:14ff). Imprisonment ended John's ministry as he was beheaded soon after. Thus, the duration of John's exhortation to Israel appears to have been **about** six months and 40 days or 220 days. (A Biblical prophetic month has 30 days.)

God gave Noah's generation one final seven-day period to repent and get aboard with Noah before God shut *"the door"* to the ark (Genesis 7:16). After the Lord gives the world one more chance to come to His Son, He will *"catch up"* all who respond and close *"the door"* to heaven (Matthew 25:10; Luke 13:25). In other words, there will come one specific day when the open *"door"* to heaven (Revelation 4:1), the escape hatch from God's wrath, will be closed to mankind in general.

It is astounding that the ratio between God's final call to *safety* **and His wrath may be identical in both His first and His second** *worldwide* **judgments.**

We know that the door of the ark remained open for seven (7) days before the 40 days that the Flood waters increased (Genesis 7:17). If God follows the precedent He set with John the Baptist, the true Christians may be allotted **about** 220 days to call the world to the Saviour of mankind just prior to the Rapture of the Bride. The length of the Lord's coming wrath will be **exactly** 1,260 days (Daniel 7:25; 12:7; Revelation 12:6, 14; 13:5). Therefore:

The Ratio in Noah's Day:

7 days last call to safety (before door to ark was closed): 40 days wrath = **0.175**

Possible Ratio in This Era:

220 days last call to safety (before door to heaven will be closed): 1,260 days wrath (the Great Tribulation) = 0.1746 = **0.175**

It is reasonable to hope that God's rescue of the Bride of Christ will take place in the first year of the seven, due to the Biblical precedent of "the bridal week" celebration observed by:

Jacob and Leah and Rachel   Genesis 29:27, 28

Samson and his bride   Judges 14:10, 12, 17

In Jewish tradition, the wedding festivities for a virgin must last a full week,[4] during which time the groom may not leave his bride to go to work.[5]

---

4.   *Landman,* Vol. 5, p. 504; Vol. 10, p. 480.
5.   Schneid, p. 47.

In summary, marriage involved: the contract (covenant), the drinking of the cup, the bridal price, the groom's departure to build a home, his unspecified return for his bride, the bridal chamber, and the marriage supper.[6] The couple celebrated the first seven days in the groom's father's home before going to their own residence.[7] Thus far, Jesus has closely followed the Jewish marriage tradition and will return for His Bride.

Jacob worked for Rachel's father for seven years before gaining her hand in marriage. If Messiah's actual bridal week consists of seven years (not seven days) in His Father's house, the believers would have to be caught up to heaven sometime during the first year of the seven transitional years. (The Old Testament Jewish measurement of time would consider a partial year still to be a year.) Then, Messiah and His Bride will return to rule on earth (Psalm 2:9; Revelation 19:15; 3:21; 2:26f).

Jesus clearly expected us to *"know how to interpret this present time"* (Luke 12:56). However, He said, **there is no way to know the *"day or hour"* of the removal from the earth of those who believe in Jesus, the Jewish Messiah** (Matthew 24:36–41; Mark 13:32). So sudden will it be that He declared:

Two men will be in the field; one will be taken and the other left. Two women will be grinding with a hand mill; one will be taken and the other left. Therefore keep watch, because you do not know on what day your Lord will come.

(Matthew 24:40–42)

We see the same proportion in this example as in Jesus' parable, in which only half of the virgins entered the wedding banquet (Matthew 25:1f). Whatever the day, true Christians will want to live in a manner pleasing to their Lord, so they will be able to go with Him at a moment's notice.

---

6.   Levitt, *A Christian Love Story,* pp. 1–30.
7.   *Ibid.,* pp. 5–6.

At the actual moment when Jesus will evacuate His Bride, He has urgently warned us not to *"go back for anything. Remember Lot's wife!"* (Luke 17:31f) Desire for anything may cause a person to get left behind at the last moment like Lot's wife, who was in the midst of being rescued! (Genesis 19:26)

The historic rejection of Jesus by the Jewish people as a whole may not have changed much before the Bride of Christ is removed. Israel may be too preoccupied with the immediate task of the burial of the dead after the invasion (Ezekiel 39:12, 14) and euphoria over her brilliant new ruler to respond to the urgent call from the followers of Jesus. Though individuals will respond, Israel as a nation will realize too late:

> *The harvest is past, the summer is ended, and we are not saved.*   (Jeremiah 8:20)

> *Israel has experienced a hardening in part until the full number of the Gentiles has come in* [to the kingdom of God].   (Romans 11:25)

> *Devout men are taken away, and no one understands that the righteous are taken away to be spared from evil.*
>   (Isaiah 57:1)

Once the Rapture has happened, a person's eternal spirit can still be saved, but he will have no physical way to escape the evil conditions on earth. In the last three-and-a-half years of the king's regime, people will get beheaded for their belief in Jesus Christ (Revelation 20:4; 6:9). Masses will still come into God's kingdom, but they will endure terrible tribulation. Death will be their only form of release. The saints will be defeated by the world dictator (Daniel 7:21; Revelation 20:4b).

There appears to be a brief transition or overlap at the end of the Church Age. Both the true Church and God's "two witnesses" may be on earth simultaneously at the start of the reign of Israel's ruler. Since both Israel and the Church embrace the Old Testament, the two men will be welcomed by both groups.

The Two Witnesses

God will send two of Israel's greatest spiritual leaders to earth to bring about revival. **The two witnesses will come forth the same day that the leader confirms the covenant with Israel,** because they will testify to the truth of God's Word for 1,260 days (Revelation 11:3).

Their 1,260 days on earth will be the first half of the seven transitional years. Immediately after these two men are called up to heaven, it is stated:

> *The second woe has passed; the third woe* [of seven] *is coming soon.*   (Revelation 11:14)

They cannot be on earth during the second 1,260-day period, as there will be no more *"woes"* following the end of the seven years. God's wrath will be over.

Moreover, there will be no additional three-and-a-half days for their two dead bodies to remain unburied if they are killed at the end of the second set of 1,260 days. Messiah will come precisely at the end of the second 1,260-day period (Daniel 9:27; 12:7; Revelation 12:6, 14; 13:5). God's two witnesses will start their powerful ministry on the day Israel signs the covenant with her impressive leader. If this is on *Yom Kippur, Tishri* 10, the two men will finish their 1,260 days on *Nisan* 10.

Note: The added month of *Adar* II every two or three years is ignored in the Biblical prophetic count of the 1,260 days. (The insertion of the extra month is periodically required to reconcile the modern Jewish lunar calendar to our solar one.)

Who are these men who will stand against the ruler as Moses and Aaron did against Pharaoh? (Exodus 6 to 12) The body of opinion is that they are Jewish, because they are referred to as *"prophets"* and the *"two olive trees."* These are Old Testament terms relating to the Jewish people.

The Lord will return the kingdom to the Jews in their final seven years after *"the full number of the Gentiles has come in"* (Romans 11:25b). Since Gentiles are still getting saved throughout the entire seven years (Revelation 7:9; 16:15), the arbitrary cutoff point referred to in *Romans* can only be the Rapture of the Bride of Christ.

The two men are dressed in *"sackcloth"* (Revelation 11:3). This garb signifies mourning, wailing, and crying out to the Lord (Joel 1:13ff). They are introduced as *"witnesses"* because their primary job is to testify to the fact that Messiah has already come, not to prophesy about the future, as they did when they originally lived on earth.

Though they also prophesy, the title of *"prophet"* is not employed until after they lie dead. Temple worship is again taking place at some point during their 1,260 days of ministry, because they *"measure the Temple of God and the altar"* (Revelation 11:1f).

These men have power to shut up the sky, so that it will not rain during the time they are prophesying. They have power to turn the waters into blood and to strike the earth with every kind of plague as often as they want.

(Revelation 11:6)

These were the same powers given to Moses in Egypt. And Elijah caused there to be no rain for three-and-a-half years during the time of King Ahab (1 Kings 17:1; 18:1; Luke 4:25; James 5:17). It was Moses and Elijah who were chosen to appear and speak to Jesus at His glorious transfiguration in appearance before Jesus' departure (Matthew 17:3). It is logical that they will be the ones to represent Him before His return.

We know for certain Elijah will return before *"that great and dreadful day of the Lord comes"* (Malachi 4:5; cf. Matthew 17:11). He represents "the Prophets," and his goal is restoration. *He will turn the hearts of the fathers to their children, and the hearts of the children to their fathers* (Malachi 4:6). John the Baptist also offered a clear picture of Elijah's future ministry.

And he [John] *will go before the Lord, in the spirit and power of Elijah, to turn the hearts of the fathers to their children and the disobedient to the wisdom of the right-eous—to make ready a people for the Lord.*

(Luke 1:17)

Elijah never died, but was taken to heaven (2 Kings 2:11).

Moses may be the second witness, representing "the Law." His goal will be to lead his people again out of bondage to sin and back to God. Of course, he was the first leader of the Israelite nation. After guiding his people out of slavery in Egypt and through the Red Sea, he received the Law from God on Mount Sinai. The Bible pinpoints why this man was such an extraordinary leader:

Now, Moses was a very humble man, more humble than anyone else on the face of the earth.   (Numbers 12:3)

Because Moses was so yielded to God, the Lord could use him mightily.

During the time of their assignment, anyone who tries to harm these two servants of the Lord will die. The precedent for this was the destruction by fire of 100 men who tried to arrest Elijah (2 Kings 1:10ff). Many in Israel will be brought back to their God through them.

Since we know that these two witnesses will be killed after 1,260 days, one could argue that the second personage could not be Moses. How could he die a second time since he already expired on Mount Nebo? (Deuteronomy 34:5) However, these two men will not remain dead long, as they are resurrected within days. Biblically speaking, it is not impossible to pass through the state of death twice. Examples of this are the three people Jesus raised from the dead and others.

In summary, people who do not respond to Christ until after the Rapture, will live through "hell on earth" that they could have avoided. Although they will enter the kingdom of God, such people will lose the inestimable honor to be part of the Bride of Christ. Only the Bride will enjoy intimate UNION with Jesus throughout eternity.

What we partake of today will determine our stature in heaven. Our daily intake determines our degree of peace, wisdom and revelation. These factors enable us *to gain victory* over our problems.

With God's help, we die to our self-nature (with its loud demands and complaints) by trusting in Christ's provision every step of the way. It is a Christian's *peace of mind* that will attract others.

Some of the factors that keep us from being overcomers are: sin, unbelief, no spiritual vision, lack of discipline and "busy" works. Let us not sell our birthright for a mess of pottage (Genesis 25:33).

The next bench mark in the onward move of events is that Israel's ruler will gain leadership of the European Union as well. Let us consider the background for this.

Chapter Seven

THE EUROPEAN UNION HAILS THE KING HIS NEXT 980 DAYS IN POWER

Behold a red dragon, having seven heads and ten horns.
(Revelation 12:3)

The Club of Rome

There is an influential, non-political organization called the Club of Rome, which first met in Rome in 1968. Thus, it came into being the year after Jerusalem came under Jewish control. It consists of 100 scientists, humanists, economists, educators, political leaders, industrialists, and civil servants of 51 countries. They consider the complex world problems resulting from the threat of nuclear war, industrialization, global pollution, depletion of resources, and the like. The Club conducts research and "seeks to act as a catalyst in affecting (social) change."[1]

---

1. Estell, p. 852.

Backed by scientific data and statistics, this high ranking group foresees the total collapse of the world system by early to mid-21st century if nothing is done about the problems society now faces. The Club of Rome is headquartered in Paris with a Washington office.

All the world problems working together have more impact than each would have separately. The conclusion of The Club of Rome is that without global unity, it is impossible to address the overwhelming needs of the world. They recommend:

1. A new form of thinking leading to a fundamental change in human behavior and society. (Albert Einstein said, "We shall require a substantially new manner of thinking if mankind is to survive.")
2. Control and redistribution of population growth.
3. Redistribution of wealth and technology of the developed nations.
4. Substantial material sacrifices by this generation for the future generations.
5. **Division of the world into 10 economically interdependent regions,** which all make global problems their first priority.
6. "A rational master plan" or One World Government with the resources and power to enforce that plan.[2]

The European Union (E.U.)

These are world problems that the E.U. will inherit. European leaders have worked for a single market for economic survival since 1949. A common European Currency Unit (ECU) and Central Bank are planned as part of the Eurospirit. The collapse of the Soviet system has lessened the Communist threat to peace. This clears the way for the E.U. to focus more attention on political and economic union.

---

2.   Goetz, p. 26.

The E.U. set a 1992 deadline for the elimination of all the internal boundaries, thus permitting the free movement of persons, goods, and services. One indication of this was the construction of the Channel Tunnel, the first fixed link between England and Europe, which was opened in 1993. This had been suggested in the past, but never approved, due to British security reasons.

The resignation of England's Prime Minister Margaret Thatcher, on November 2, 1990, removed the main voice urging restraint and caution to the unification process. Both she and her predecessor, Edward Heath, had been longtime opponents of a European superstate. The unification that both Napoleon and Hitler wanted to accomplish by force is coming to pass at a headlong rate of its own momentum!

The Assembly, the European Parliament, is already in place and has been elected by direct suffrage in June 1979, 1984, 1989, and 1994. This is presided over by a rotating six-month president from within the E.U. They will be faced with the even more basic issue, global environmental survival. Nations will be compelled to preserve our environment through enforceable laws across national boundaries. No single nation can solve world problems alone.

Hail Caesar!

After the ruler of Israel takes office, his fame will spread like wildfire. This leader, an extraordinary political orator, will captivate audiences through his irresistible eloquence. God's Word stresses both his eyes and boastful mouth (Daniel 7:20, 25; 11:36; Revelation 13:5). Contrast this with Jesus Christ who *"did not open his mouth"* when He was afflicted and was *"led like a lamb to the slaughter"* (Isaiah 53:7).

In his thirst for power, the leader will not be satisfied to rule only Israel. In the same length of time as it takes to bring forth a baby (280 days average) (cf. Revelation 12:1–5), this man will expand his power base to encompass the flourishing European arena. The E.U. will need leadership and will recognize this man's vast genius, statesmanship, and efficiency.

Like Charlemagne, the leader will preach that if the strength of the Roman Empire is restored, it could unite the world and bring peace (*Pax Romana*). The urgency of the situation demands immediate attention. He will be hailed as the prince of peace, and the one most equipped to address the overwhelming problems threatening mankind and the environment.

You [Christians] *know very well that the day of the Lord will come like a thief in the night. While people are saying, "Peace and safety," destruction will come on them suddenly.* (1 Thessalonians 5:1f)

Three European rulers will oppose him and fall from power. *"He will subdue three kings"* (Daniel 7:24). However, their countries will continue as part of the E.U. The remaining heads of state will not discern the man's real nature and will support him. The ruler will then be in control of the new political bloc, united Europe with ten nations under his control.

Can it be! Will one man actually forge Israel's alignment with this superpower at its inception and in the very area where Jews have been persecuted for so long? Needless to say, his renown will expand both at home and abroad. No doubt, he will be riding a phenomenal tide of popularity.

God will seemingly pick up where He left off with the Jews c. 30 A.D. and revitalize the first-century Roman Empire. Though Turkey applied for membership in the E.U. in 1987, neither the North African nor Asian sections of the original Roman Empire will be present. As discussed, the troops from the areas of Put and Beth Togarmah will have been decimated in the invasion (see p. 71).

The Roman Empire never did include Denmark, Sweden, Finland, Ireland, or Germany, which are among the fifteen present E.U. members. In fact, Rome built stone walls 20 feet high to

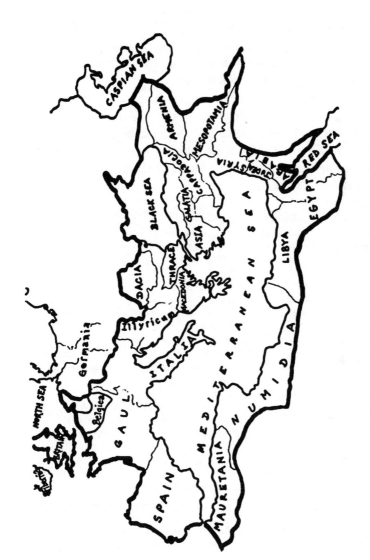

THE ROMAN EMPIRE AT THE TIME OF CHRIST
Map copyright © Hammond Incorporated, Maplewood, N.J.

protect its provinces from the northern barbarians. These barriers are still standing in Scotland, Germany, and Romania.

The ten countries under this powerful ruler may include the present E.U. nations of Belgium, France, Greece, Italy, Luxembourg, the Netherlands, Portugal, Spain, Britain and Austria. The revision of the Maastricht Treaty in 1996 should consolidate the European Union further.

The extension over centuries and re-emergence of the Roman Empire at the close of this epoch was foretold by Daniel. God gave His prophet the interpretation of King Nebuchadnezzar's dream of the statue of a man. It symbolized man's rulership on earth from that time forward. The four sections of the statue represent successive world empires.

THE FOUR MAJOR EMPIRES

Empire	Body Part	Dates of Empire
Babylonian	Gold head	626 to 539 B.C.
Medo-Persian	Silver chest and arms	539 to 331 B.C.
Greek	Bronze belly and thighs	331 to 63 B.C. Alexander the Great's empire was divided among his generals: Cassander, Lysimachus, Seleucus I and Ptolemy. 164 to 63 B.C. Jewish Maccabees (Hasmoneans) rule Judah Until General Pompey captured Jerusalem for Rome in 63 B.C.
Roman	Two iron legs	27 B.C. (First Roman Emperor... ...Western Empire existed until 476 A.D. ...Eastern Empire existed until 1453 A.D. The Empire was revived in German area as the Holy Roman Empire (800A.D. - 1806 A.D.)
Revived Roman	10-toed feet of iron and clay	Begins with 10 nations in area of Old Roman Empire, but expands to include the entire world divided into 10 regions.

(See Daniel 2:32-45; 8:19-25; 11:2-4)

God made clear that as the quality of the statue's metal decreased in value (Daniel 2:36f; 7:19), the metal's strength would increase. So the four empires would be characterized by the deterioration of the quality of leadership and the increased use of strength to govern the people. The iron of the last kingdom represents the tyranny and strength of dictatorship. (Notice that the wall of separation around the ex-Soviet Union was referred to as the "Iron Curtain.")

The Roman Empire did extend in a two-legged form for many centuries in the West until 476 and in the East until 1453. The Holy Roman Empire was established in the area of Germany and lasted until 1806. The titles "Czar" and "Kaiser," both of which mean Caesar, were used until 1917 in Russia and 1918 in Germany, respectively.

In Nebuchadnezzar's dream of a man, the 10-toed feet represent the revitalization of a 10-nation European confederacy in the area of the old Roman Empire. The dominion of the dictator (the Anti-Christ) will then expand to encompass the entire world, divided into 10 regions.

[Note: There is a connection between the name Caesar and Satan. Caesar, the name of ruler of the Roman world system, is Latin for "the hairy one." Satyr is a Greek deity which is part-man and part-goat and has a hairy body and horns on his head. This is a frequent representation of Satan. In Hebrew, *"Sair"* means "he-goat" or "hairy one." The Arabic, *"sha'r"* also means "hair." The name of the godless "Esau" (Hebrews 12:16) also means "hairy" (Genesis 25:25; 27:11). He sold and despised his godly birthright for fleeting, fleshly gratification (Genesis 25:33f).

Moses was told that the Israelites must no longer offer sacrifices to male goat idols (demons) (Leviticus 17:7). Such worship was re-established among the 10 northern tribes when the kingdom was divided after Solomon's death (2 Chronicles 11:15).

Jesus said He will judge the nations upon His return. He will separate the people one from another as a shepherd separates the sheep from the goats and send the "goats" to eternal punishment (Matthew 25:31ff)]...

At the rise of the false messiah, the Scriptural promise that peace and justice will ultimately flow from Jerusalem for all mankind seems to be within reach at last in Israel.

The law will go out from Zion, the word of the Lord from Jerusalem. He will judge between the nations and will settle disputes for many peoples...   (Isaiah 1:3f)

Arise, shine, for your light has come, and the glory of the Lord rises upon you. See, darkness covers the earth and thick darkness is over the peoples, but the Lord rises upon you and his glory appears over you. Nations will come to your light, and kings to the brightness of your dawn. Lift up your eyes and look about you. All assemble and come to you. Your sons come from afar, and your daughters are carried on the arm. Then, you will look and be radiant. Your heart will throb and swell with joy.   (Isaiah 60:1f)

Many Jews and Gentiles are not aware that before this glorious state can materialize, evil must be judged. A hypnotic demagogue will arise and deceive those who do not love God's truth.

My people are destroyed from lack of knowledge.
(Hosea 4:6)

The ox knows his master...but Israel does not know, my people do not understand.   (Isaiah 1:3)

They perish because they refused to love the truth and so be saved.   (2 Thessalonians 2:10)

I have come in my Father's name, and you do not accept me; but if someone else comes in his own name, you will accept him.   (John 5:43)

Many believe that men can solve the problems of humanity unaided. Here is the opportunity, par excellence, to prove this. All elements will emerge simultaneously: the need, the unity, the "prince" and the power. The ruler is the epitome of human ability. He also provides the consummate expression for those who rebel against God. In the end, they will have to submit to the Lord; but it will be through force, rather than by free will.

Due to the E.U.'s inexperience in functioning as a union, there may be inadequate restraints upon the new leader's power. In addition, a political vacuum will exist, as the counter-balancing force of Russia and her invasion allies will have been destroyed in the blitzkrieg of Israel.

This proud colossus of a man will seize his shining moment to rebuild the empire that once was Rome. As he organizes Europe, he will become more politically entrenched with every passing day.

Unity and leadership come at a high price. In less than three years after the ruler takes the helm, the nations of the E.U. will find that the sovereignty they sacrificed to achieve political and economic strength will have bought them tyranny instead.

Chapter Eight

GOD'S 144,000 JEWISH SONS GO FORTH (DURING THE 980 DAYS)

Thou shalt arise and have mercy upon Zion: for the set time to favor her yea, the set time is come.

(Psalm 102:13 KJV)

A great and wonderous SIGN appeared in heaven: a woman clothed with the sun...She gave birth to a son, a male child.

(Revelation 12:1,5)

The 144,000 Jewish Servants

Jesus said the kingdom of God would be taken away from the Jews of His day and given to a people who would produce its fruit (Matthew 21:43). When the true Church is removed, the Church era is officially over. The Lord will resume with Israel where He left off at the end of the 69 *"sevens"* just after Messiah was *"cut off"* (Daniel 9:24–26) (see p. 228).

Did they [the Jews] *stumble so as to fall beyond recovery? Not at all! Rather, because of their transgression, salvation has come to the Gentiles to make Israel envious...if their loss means riches for the Gentiles, how much greater riches will their fullness bring!... For if their rejection is the reconciliation of the world, what will their acceptance be but life from the dead?*   (Romans 11:11ff)

Who are God's Jewish spokesmen during the first half of the seven years? They will be the 144,000 *"servants of our God"* (Revelation 7:3ff). "Servant of the Lord" is a special title the Most High uses for those who carry out His purposes. As the Jewish forefathers are called the "early" fruit (Hosea 9:10), so the fig tree of Israel will bear "late" fruit as well.

The Lord will have Jewish sons who preach the good news of salvation from our sins and from hell through Jesus Christ. The 144,000 come from the 12 tribes (Revelation 7:1–8).

A great and wondrous sign appeared in heaven: a woman clothed with the sun...She was pregnant and cried out in pain as she was about to give birth...She gave birth to a son, a male child...   (Revelation 12:1ff)

Up to now, this "woman" has pictured the true Church travailing to bring forth her children. However after the Bride has been raptured, Jewish people will bring forth strong male progeny.

This Jewish *"son"* and the *"two witnesses"* will be God's final *human* agents on earth before His wrath begins! Multitudes will gain eternal life through them. The 144,000 Jews are also a sign in heaven that Satan and his angels will be hurled out of heaven shortly.

The word "son" (*huios*) implies a son's continuation of the family line and family leadership. Indeed, this "son" *will "rule the nations with an iron scepter"* (Rev. 12:5) with Christ (Psalm 2:9) and His Bride (Rev. 2:27)

When the "woman" gives birth, it is with pain and torment (*basanizo*). Why then does Isaiah say, "before she travailed, ...before the pains come upon her, she delivers a son "(66:7)? When Jesus arrives on the Mount of Olives, Jews will behold the One who was "pierced" (Zech. 12:10). Israel will receive this "Son" immediately–without any more torment

Sing, O barren woman, you who never bore a child...shout for joy, you who were never in labor (Isaiah 54:1)

Though the first Christians were all Jews, the Jewish nation has never recognized her children who stood for Jesus as the Messiah of Israel. At last the time will have come that God's own Jewish sons will be preaching the truth to Israel and the world that Jesus Christ is coming and He is the long-awaited Jewish Messiah.

As mentioned, these Jewish scions will probably come forth about 280 days (40 weeks - gestation period) after Israel confirms a covenant with a leader. Israel will no longer *"be abandoned"* by God.

Therefore Israel will be abandoned until the time when she who is in labor gives birth and the rest of his [Messiah's] brothers return to join the Israelites.

(Micah 5:3)

These men are sealed, protected, and empowered by the Holy Spirit (Revelation 7:3). In the midst of all manner of corruption and pressure, these 144,000 are not defiled. Since they accept the true Messiah, *"the lie"* (that Israel's false ruler is the Messiah) is not in them (Revelation 14:5; 2 Thessalonians 2:11). The Lamb's name and the Father's name are written on their foreheads (Revelation 14:1).

They will go forth preaching that people must repent and believe in the Messiah, who is coming at the end of the seven-year period. They will teach Israel that Jesus Christ fulfilled the law and the prophets and is the unblemished Lamb of God, sacrificed for mankind. The Holy Spirit will confirm their ministry with

miracles, signs and wonders. Many Jews will believe, repent and
be saved. God guided the Israelites by signs and wonders long ago,
and He will do so again.

According to God's original design, these men come from all
the tribes (Exodus 19:6; Isaiah 61:6), not just from the Levites
(Exodus 32:26–29). As we have seen, the tribe of Dan will be
replaced by his nephew Manasseh. (The tribe of Dan was a major
promoter of idolatry. Judges 18:30; Hosea 4:17; 1 Kings 12:29;
Amos 8:14).

Gentiles will be profoundly moved to repentance as well.
God's Jewish servants bring an untold multitude of *"every nation,
tribe, people, and language"* (Revelation 7:9) into God's kingdom. Since the estimate of the Jews worldwide is over 18 million,[1]
God's servants will represent less than 1% of the Jewish people
and about 0.003% of the world's 5.6 billion people. God only uses
this infinitesimal number of men to finish His call to people everywhere.

Departure of the Two Witnesses and the 144,000 Jews

The midpoint of the seven years is a day of eternal significance. It will be the day the 144,000 are *"caught up unto God"*
(KJV); the two witnesses finish their testimony and are killed; the
king's real identity as the beast is recognized; and the wrath of God
begins on earth.

> *The secret power of lawlessness is already at work; but the
> one* [the Holy Spirit—impersonal pronoun] *who holds it
> back will continue to do so till he* [the Holy Spirit in the
> believer—personal pronoun] *is taken out of the way. And
> then the lawless one will be revealed, whom the Lord Jesus
> will overthrow with the breath of his mouth and destroy by
> the splendor of his coming.*   (2 Thessalonians 2:7f)

---

1.   Hoffman, p. 591.

Of course, the Holy Spirit is omnipresent. So, the only sense in which He could be *"taken out of the way"* is as He resides in His active agents on earth, the believers.

Do you not know that your body is a temple of the Holy Spirit, who is in you, whom you have received from God?
(1 Corinthians 6:19)

The Bride of Christ has the *"seal"* of the Holy Spirit (2 Corinthians 1:22; Ephesians 1:13; 4:30), but so do the 144,000 (Revelation 7:3f)! ***"Lawlessness"* will be restrained until both groups, the Bride and the 144,000 Jews, are taken out of the way and the two witnesses killed.** Then, *"the lawless one"* will know no bounds and his bestial nature will be fully revealed (2: Thessalonians 2:7f).

The messianic community flees immediately after her progeny is *"caught up to God and to His throne"* (Revelation 12:5f). Because God will take care of her for 1,260 days (Revelation 12:6, 14) we know that her sons must be *"caught up"* at the exact midpoint of the seven-year period (1,260 days before the coming of Messiah).

Since the ministry of the two witnesses will end after 1,260 days (see p. 139), they will be killed on the same day that the 144,000 are *"caught up."* If the covenant is confirmed on *Tishri* 10 (*Yom Kippur*), 1,260 days later logically appears to be *Nisan* 10, four days before Passover. The two are killed by the beast from the Abyss (Revelation 11:7).

The bodies of the two witnesses lie on the street in Jerusalem and are refused burial. Jews consider this to be the greatest dishonor. It was one of the curses for disobedience to God's law (Deuteronomy 28:26).

Their bodies will be viewed by the entire world. So important is their death to the forces of Anti-Christ (the beast) that the event is given world coverage. Due to the dictator's control, satellite television will carry the news nonstop for three-and-a- half days of the beast's victory over his two arch enemies.

For three-and-a-half days men from every people, tribe, language and nation will gaze on their bodies and refuse them burial. The inhabitants of the earth will gloat over them and will celebrate by sending each other gifts...
(Revelation 11:9f)

For these three-and-a-half days, people in remote places, who might not otherwise have heard, will be able to see and discuss the two supernaturally empowered men of God. Thus, even in death, the two will draw attention to their Messiah, who died to take the penalty of death for all of us.

As indicated, the Jews taught that by the fourth day, the soul took its leave beyond recall from the body (see p. 214). Victory should come at dawn on *Nisan* 14, which is Passover. God's breath of life enters the two dead witnesses after three-and-one-half days!

...they stood on their feet, and terror struck those who saw them. Then they heard a loud voice from heaven saying to them, "Come up here." And they went up to heaven in a cloud, while their enemies looked on. (Revelation 11:11f)

Since the bodies of the two will be shown on television for the entire time they lie on the street (perhaps from *Nisan* 10 to 14), the cameras will be focused on them at the time of their actual resurrection as well. Unless one reads the Bible, no one will know ahead of time that the men will come back to life. Therefore, they will not know to turn off the cameras! What explanation will the beast give at this point? It will be impossible for him to hide their resurrection from the world. These two witnesses will be the last believers to go up to heaven alive.

What Satan considered victory, the crucifixion of Jesus Christ, turned out to be Satan's defeat. Once again, the devil's triumph will be short-lived. The resurrection of God's two prophets on *Nisan* 14 would underscore the protection-from-death aspect of Passover. On the first Passover, no firstborn was killed in the Jewish households that had the blood of the lamb over the doors.

Within the hour after their ascension, a great earthquake will shake Jerusalem, due to the impact of God's *"breath"* coming into their two dead bodies. The earthquake will cause a tenth of the city to collapse and 7,000 people to die. The terrified survivors will give glory to the God of heaven (Revelation 11:13). At the moment that Jesus gave up His spirit, the earth also shook and the rocks split (Matthew 27:51).

The slow-of-heart will repent, but the wicked will continue to be wicked and will not understand (Daniel 12:10; Revelation 22:11). God's parallels are awesome!

The days between *Nisan* 10 and 14 was the interval God told Moses that Israel must observe the Passover lamb for imperfections before it was sacrificed on *Nisan* 14. *Nisan* 10 was also the day Jesus, the unblemished (sinless) Lamb of God presented Himself as King Messiah of Israel. He was focused upon until His crucifixion on the *Nisan* 14. Thus, during the identical days that Jesus and the Passover lamb were observed, these two men may also be gazed upon by the world.

Flight of Some Post-Rapture Christians

Jesus said the day the beast sets up his image for worship in the Temple in the middle of the seven years, all who are in Judea must flee for their lives to the mountains (Matthew 24:16). The messianic community that brought forth the 144,000 men will fly on *"the two wings of a great eagle"* (airlift?) to a place prepared for her by God in the desert (Revelation 12:6, 14; cf. 1 Kings 17:4–6).

It is noteworthy that Israel's neighbors east of the Jordan River, *"Edom, Moab and the leaders of Ammon will be delivered from his* (the ruler's) *hand."* He will invade the Beautiful Land (Israel), and her southern neighbor, Egypt, will fall under his iron grasp

(Daniel 11:41ff). Thus, it would seem that the place prepared for the families of the 144,000 will be in Edom, Moab, and Ammon. Today, this area would extend from Jordan's southern boundary with Saudi Arabia and the Gulf of Aqaba, northward to the present city of Amman. (Biblical "Ammon" did not go northward to the Sea of Galilee as the nation of Jordan does today.)

(Before Jerusalem was destroyed in 70 A.D., the followers of Christ heeded His instructions (Luke 19:43ff; 21:20ff). They fled east across the Jordan River to Pella.)

The remaining Jews and the post-Rapture Christians will be persecuted by the ruler during the remaining three-and-a-half years of his reign (Daniel 7:21, 25; Matthew 24:21f; Revelation 12:17; 13:7). People are still accepted into God's kingdom throughout this period (Revelation 7:14; 14:13).

Israel's Agricultural Harvests

God's harvest of people into His kingdom seems to parallel the sequence of Israel's agricultural harvest, of which there are three stages.

1. A sheaf of the first harvest, the barley crop, is offered or waved before the Lord on the Feast of First Fruits, *"the day after the Sabbath"* (Leviticus 23:11). It is celebrated on the first Sunday during the week of Unleavened Bread, *Nisan* 14–21 (Exodus 12:18). If the Passover falls on Friday, *Nisan* 14, First Fruits is on Sunday, *Nisan* 16th.

2. The main harvest is the wheat, which comes 50 days after *Nisan* 16 on *Sivan* 6 (May–June), the Feast of Harvest or Pentecost (*Shavuot*) (Leviticus 23:15f). (This celebrates the giving of the Law on Mount Sinai, the birthday of the Israelite nation. It also was the day on which the Jewish Church was born at the coming of the Holy Spirit on Jewish believers in Jerusalem.)

3. The smaller harvest of the orchards and vines took place in the fall at the Feast of Tabernacles, (Ingathering, or Booths [*Sukkot*]) on *Tishri* 15–21.

Finally, there were *"the gleanings"* which were **not harvested**, but left on the field for the poor and alien to gather (Leviticus 23:22).

The three harvests were the three appointed times that the Jewish men were required to appear annually before their Sovereign Lord in Jerusalem (Exodus 23:15ff).

God's Human Harvest

After Jesus was crucified on *Nisan* 14th, He resurrected on Sunday, *Nisan* 16, the day after the Sabbath. He was the sheaf of the first harvest, *"the firstfruits of those who have fallen asleep"* (died) (1 Corinthians 15:20). Many holy people were raised to life and showed themselves in Jerusalem after Jesus' resurrection (Matthew 27:52f).

The second phase will be the main harvest of both dead and living believers in Jesus Christ. They will be resurrected and *"caught up"* at the Rapture.

The third division is the 144,000 servants of our God from twelve tribes of Israel. They are also *"caught up"* (Revelation 12:5). Like the Levites of old, these men with the Spirit of God upon them will not be counted with the other Israelites, but separately (Numbers 2:33). They are offered as firstfruits to God and the Lamb (Revelation 14:4).

The two witnesses are probably not included in phase three, as they will be *"called up"* three-and-a-half days later. Also, the two were previously in heaven.

The idea that God's harvest of souls will occur in **different divisions** is alluded to:

...even so in Christ shall all be made alive. But every man in his own order [turn]: *Christ the firstfruits; afterward they that are Christ's at his coming.*

(1 Corinthians 15:22f, KJV)

The Greek word for "order" is *tagma.* It is a military term meaning a division, battalion, orderly arrangement, series or succession. In the original Exodus of God's people from Egypt, it is reiterated five times that they departed by "divisions." These will also be orderly departures from earth to heaven.

Another parallel is seen in the three people Jesus raised from the dead during His earthly ministry, compared to the three groups He takes to heaven before His return:

The first was Jarius' daughter. This is given great emphasis, as it is reported in three of the gospels (Matthew 9:18ff; Mark 5:22ff; Luke 8:41ff). Does this young girl symbolize the resurrection/rapture of the Bride of Christ?

The raising of the unnamed son of the widow of Nain was second (Luke 7:11ff). (Nain means "pasture.") This may parallel the catching up of the 144,000 sons of "the mother" figure (Revelation 12:1ff).

The third was the raising of Lazarus, Jesus' friend who was dead four days (John 11:1ff). This could point to the friends of God, the two witnesses, who will have entered their fourth day of death before they are raised. The sequence in which Jesus resurrected these three individuals, while He was on earth, is perhaps the same order in which He will raise the three divisions up to heaven.

The godly have been swept from the land; not one upright man remains. All men lie in wait to shed blood...Both hands are skilled in doing evil...[in] *the day God visits you.*
(Micah 7:2ff)

The people who will be left on the earth now are: (1) The families of the 144,000 men, who will be protected by God in the desert for the remaining 1,260 days (Revelation 12:6, 14ff); (2) the unconvinced about Jesus Christ; and (3) the hard core who will never repent. The removal of so many God-fearing people will have a profound impact on the quality of life on earth;

God will not designate any believers to remain on earth as His agents once His wrath starts. Instead, we are told of three angels, flying in mid-air. One will proclaim the eternal gospel: *"Fear God and give him glory, because the hour of his judgment has come. Worship him who made the heavens, earth, sea, and springs."* **Even at that final hour, God will still be giving all people the chance to repent and come to Him.**

The second angel will announce that Babylon, the unbelieving, harlot Church, has fallen and has become *"a home for demons and a haunt for every evil spirit"* (Revelation 14:8; 18:2f).

The third angel will warn people not to worship the beast and his image, and receive his mark on the forehead or hand. If they do, those people *"will drink the wine of God's fury, which has been poured full strength into the cup of his wrath."* Their torment will go on for ever and ever (Revelation 14:6–12).

Life and the environment will have become so unbearable that God will say, *"Blessed are the dead who die* [believing] *in the Lord from now on"* (Revelation 14:13). They will constitute the last phase of the harvest, the *"gleanings."* They did not obey God's call to repent and cover themselves in the righteousness of Jesus before the rescue of the Rapture. They will have waited too late and will be:

> *...beheaded because of their testimony for Jesus and because of the word of God. They had not worshipped the beast or his image and had not received his mark on their foreheads or their hands. They came to life and reigned with Christ a thousand years.*   (Revelation 20:4; also 7:14)

The *"gleanings"* will be made up of individuals living today who could have avoided these terrible conditions on earth, but did not respond soon enough. During the last three- and-a-half years, they will wholeheartedly commit their lives to Jesus, knowing they will be beheaded for such a decision under Anti-Christ's demonic reign of terror. In agricultural terms, the post-Rapture believers are not harvested and removed (*"caught up"* to heaven) but remain in the field (the earth).

Though these post-Rapture believers will become *"priests of God and of Christ and will reign with Him"* (Revelation 20:6b), they are not described as being a part of the "Bride of Christ." The Bride loved Christ and looked for His appearing. The *"first resurrection"* will be complete when this fourth group, the *"gleanings,"* comes to life at the beginning of the 1,000 years (Revelation 20:5f).

Chapter Nine

THE WORLD WORSHIPS THE KING–HIS LAST 1,260 DAYS IN POWER

Satan...was hurled to the earth, and his angels with him...But woe to the earth and the sea, because the devil has gone down to you! He is filled with fury, because he knows his time is short. (Revelation 12:9, 12)

The Satanic Triad

When unrestrained, evil displays its true nature. Rebellion, cruelty and contempt for decency will come to a climax. Though active, Satan is unrecognized. Allurement and deceit have been the devil's major strategy.

He and his angels are *"hurled to the earth"* on the day that the 144,000 men are caught up to heaven, the mother-figure flees, and the beast emerges. For 1,260 days Satan, Anti-Christ, and the false prophet will operate on earth as the demonic trinity. Satan's goal has always been to have men worship him rather than their Creator. God describes him:

How you have fallen from heaven, O morning star ["Lucifer," KJV]...*You have been cast down to earth, you who once laid low the nations!*

You said in your heart... "*I will raise my throne above the stars of God. I will sit enthroned on the Mount of Assembly* [Temple Mount in Jerusalem] *on the utmost heights of the sacred mountain...I will make myself like the Most High.* "
(Isaiah 14:12ff)

(The "morning star" is a bright planet seen in the east directly before the rising sun. The Romans called it "Lucifer" or "Apollo"). Satan indeed will appear (through the Anti-Christ) directly before *"the sun of righteousness"* comes from the east (Malachi 4:2; Ezekiel 43:2) .

The name (signifying the true nature) of the angel of the Abyss or Satan is *"Abaddon"* in Hebrew and *"Apollyon"* in Greek (Revelation 9:11). Both mean "destroyer." Apollyon or Apollo (Roman) was the god representing the epitome of male beauty and charm. In one of the rare descriptions of Satan in the Bible, his original beauty and wisdom are emphasized twice (Ezekiel 28:12, 17).

The man, who personifies "destruction," is also described as coming up out of the Abyss (Revelation 17:8). That a human could cause such vast destruction is beyond comprehension.

They ponder your fate: Is this the man who shook the earth and made kingdoms tremble, **the man who made the world a desert,** *who overthrew its cities, and would not let his captives go home?*   (Isaiah 14:16f)

This person, who Satan has been grooming to deceive the world, will be the demonic masterpiece. The man will be introduced with all kinds of counterfeit miracles, signs, and wonders and with every sort of evil (2 Thessalonians 2:9). These will be performed by the dictator's false prophet. The latter will even call fire down from heaven to earth in front of men (Revelation 13:13).

The zenith of Satan's pride will be the false messiah's proclamation of himself as God in the Temple. This may occur on *Nisan* 10 (p. 264f), the same day that Jesus offered Himself in 30 A.D. as Israel's King-Messiah. Henceforth, everyone who refuses to worship Anti-Christ or his image erected in the Temple will have to flee (Daniel 9:27; Matthew 24:15; 2 Thessalonians 2:4; Revelation 12:17; 13:14f).

Needless to say, there have been other rulers who have deified secular authority and commanded worship in order to increase their power or unite their far-flung empire. They include the Pharaohs who claimed to be the sun-god incarnate, Alexander the Great, the Caesars, and Napoleon of the 19th century.

Note: The equipment exists today by which a dictator could demand worship over a fiber optic transmission network. Because it is a two-way system, whatever is taking place in the room can also be recorded on computers. The pinhead-sized camera lens on the end of the fiber optic "can still see and record everything, even when the television set is not turned on."[1] This makes 24-hour surveillance available now.

By the end of 1991, Time-Warner, the second largest cable television company in the United States (with 6.5 million subscribers), planned to link its New York City customers (750,000) with two-way transmission between viewer and programmer. The prohibitive expense of wiring each home with a separate fiber wire can now be avoided through a new switching system. Video signals are sent from a fiber optic main line to the existing cable connections into the home. Time-Warner wants to

---

1.   Gaverluk and Fisher, p. Introduction.

make "picture phones" with simultaneous reception of voice and video images available.[2]

We can derive a vivid picture of the rise of this demagogue by considering the late Adolf Hitler. The latter claimed Germany would become "lord of the earth" and that the Third Reich would rule 1,000 years. The German people were energized with his propaganda.

He systematically perverted truth to serve his purposes. He wrote in his book, *Mein Kampf,* that "the big lie" must be told often and with bravado, because "the masses more readily fall victim to the big lie than to the small lie." He used levers of power, like the propaganda and the secret police, to complete his deception, and won the support of the German people with startling swiftness. Thereafter, he stifled dissent through terror.

Hitler was determined to unite and use the Church of 45 million Protestants to serve Nazi purposes. Twenty-eight denominations worked toward unification as the German Evangelical Church under a single head. April 1, 1939 was the day of their first national rally and the start of a three-day German boycott of all Jewish businesses.

In June, Nazi officials invaded the church offices and took over administrative positions. A small group of Christians, the Young Reformation Movement, arose to resist governmental control of the Church and were put down with force. A July election was held in the name of German Christians and won 70 percent of the votes.

Adoring masses hailed Hitler at huge rallies, containing pageantry and color. Neither the media, the unions, the political parties, the universities, nor the Church raised a voice in opposition. Only a few Christians, who believed in the authority of Scripture, opposed **his rise to absolute power within six months**.

---

2.   *The Washington Post,* March 7, 1991, p. A-1.

Even as a young child, Hitler was interested in learning how to gain supernatural powers. Hitler believed in the occult and sought to embody demonic energies and to use drugs for mind expansion. He introduced occult teaching and pagan practices into ordinary German life. This dictator established a Bureau of the Occult, *Ahninerne*, as a part of his government and also a separate bureau within the SS (protection squad).[3]

Heinrich Himmler created Hitler's deadly SS. Himmler also believed it was important to harness occult forces to serve the Nazi army.[4] The SS had to undergo mystic group initiations to "the forces" to gain psychic abilities and superhuman strength.[5] They took a "blood oath" of allegiance to Hitler and bound themselves "to carry out all orders conscientiously and without reluctance." This oath was administered at the stroke of midnight, because "In the evening the people's willpower more easily succumbs to the dominating force of a stronger will."[6] The beast will also honor the *"god of forces"* (Daniel 11:38, KJV).

As we have seen, the midpoint of the king's seven-year-rule is also the turning point for the world. After the withdrawal of the Bride of Christ and the 144,000 Jews and the killing of the two witnesses, evil intensifies on all sides. The second period of 1,260 days will be no time to be on earth. From that day forward, the earth will be under God's wrath for the 1,260 days.

Since the bodies of the two witnesses will lie dead for the first three-and-a-half days of the ruler's world power, God does not use them to restrain evil. People who refuse to love God's truth will be deceived by the Anti-Christ. This is Satan's great offensive against God for the souls of men.

---

3.   Cumbey, pp. 100–110.
4.   Wurmbrand, p. 95.
5.   Cumbey, p. 110.
6.   Elson, p. 182.

They [unbelievers] *refused to love the truth and so be saved. For this reason, God sends them a powerful delusion, so that they will believe the lie.*

(2 Thessalonians 2:10ff)

[The great lie is that man of lawlessness is God incarnate— verse 4.]

Satan will give the false messiah power to conquer the saints until the Ancient of Days pronounces judgment in their favor (Daniel 7:21). In fact, the dictator will be given authority over everyone on earth (Revelation 13:2, 7). He will get a fatal wound by a sword and yet survives. This will appear miraculous and will cause many to worship him and Satan (Revelation 13:2–4; 13:12–15). On the other hand, these same people will not glorify God for the resurrection of His Son.

The third member of the triad, the false prophet, employs all the authority of the king on the latter's behalf (Revelation 13:12). The prophet will have the appearance of a lamb, but will speak like a dragon (Revelation 13:11).

All the inhabitants of the earth, will worship the beast—all whose names have not been written in the book of life belonging to the Lamb that was slain from the creation of the world. (Revelation 13:8)

David's prophet was called Nathan as was the one who aided Shabbetai Zevi. The name of David's prophet is used to represent all those Jews who consider themselves prophets at the time of Messiah's return (Zechariah 12:12). It will be interesting to see what name the false prophet will adopt.

He will cause those who will not worship the image of the dictator to be killed. The former will also force every person to receive the mark of the beast on the right hand or forehead in order to buy or sell (Revelation 13:16f). Without a number, no transactions will be possible.

Note: Today, we implant an electronic identification unit just below the surface of the skin on animals. This radio receiver-transmitter is the size of a grain of rice and can be programmed with up to ten digits. Upon activation, it transmits its number. Animals are being tagged and traced for better control.

The development of this beast is:

1. He will confirm a covenant with Israel and appear to be a brilliant leader.
2. About 280 days later, he will be made ruler over the ten-nation E.U. Only seven of the ten heads of state will support him and the other three will fall from power. The area represents much of the old Roman Empire.
3. Three-and-a-half years after confirming a covenant with Israel, this man will be made ruler of the entire world, which will be divided into ten regions with ten kings. (This division has been proposed by the Club of Rome). These ten kings will receive their authority as kings along with the beast. *"They will have one purpose and will give their power and authority to the beast."* Their armies will be gathered to make war against Jesus when He returns with His army (Revelation 17:12–17; 19:19).

The removal of the restraint of evil depends upon God's timetable, and not upon Satan's initiation. As pointed out, Satan's fury will be pitted against those who choose God...but waited too long to do so. Now, they will be caught in a demonic maelstrom of wickedness and destruction.

In the days that follow the removal of the 144,000 Jews and the flight of their families (on the day the dictator takes control of the world), Satan goes after the rest of God's children.

The dragon [Satan] *was enraged with the woman* [Israel's messianic community] *and went off to make war against the*

rest of her offspring—those who obey God's command-
ments and hold to the testimony of Jesus.

(Revelation 12:17)

Since the Anti-Christ and his false prophet are energized by
Satan; rebellion, treachery and oppression have full sway.

Justice is driven back, and righteousness stands at a
distance...Honesty cannot enter. Truth is nowhere to be
found.   (Isaiah 59:14f)

The Prototype for the False King-Messiah

The Bible and history both provide a prototype of the false
king-messiah, who will deceive the Jews. The forerunner was the
Seleucid tyrant, Antiochus IV Epiphanes, the king of Syria in 175–
163 B.C.

Antiochus IV's determined effort to destroy the Jewish faith
and Hellenize the Jews started in the autumn of 169 B.C., when he
massacred the people of Jerusalem and plundered the Temple
treasury. The climax came two years later when he captured the
Temple and halted the sacrifices (Daniel 8:11–14, 24). The Jews
regained the Temple in 164 B.C. Here are several similarities between Antiochus IV (Daniel 8:9–26; 11:21–35) and the cruel,
boastful ruler of the last days (Daniel 7:20–26; 9:27; 11:36–45).
Both:

1. Are contemptible people who are not given the honor of
   royalty.
2. Terminate the Temple sacrifice and offering and erect the
   "abomination" in the Temple.
3. Dedicate the Temple to a false god.
4. Appear when rebels become completely wicked.
5. Become very strong, by the power of a foreign god (Satan).
6. Cause astounding devastation.
7. Are successful until the appointed end.

8. Are masters of intrigue, causing deceit to prosper and truth to be trampled.
9. Greatly honor and reward those who acknowledge them.
10. Wage war against other rulers.
11. Challenge the God of gods.
12. Defeat God's people for a specified time.
13. Are destroyed, but not by human hands.
14. May come from the same area, Syria.

An obvious difference between them is that Antiochus stopped the two daily sacrifices and desecrated the Temple for 2,300 sacrifices. The false messiah will hold the Temple for 2,520 sacrifices. Also, Antiochus was a Gentile and the dictator may be Jewish.

The Beast of the World

At the exact midpoint of his seven years, the king is said to emerge as the beast *"out of the sea"* (Revelation 13:1). This is a picture of his being singled out and identified from among the nameless masses of humanity. The words *"out of the sea"* does not prove him to be a Jew or a Gentile. It merely announces that this person will arise from the common man, rather than from a specific, identifiable lineage as Messiah did. From then on, the beast's true nature will be clearly visible.

So closely identified are Satan and his representative, that they are both described in a similar way. The enormous red dragon (Satan) is symbolically pictured as having seven heads (rulers), ten horns (emblems of strength, kings or kingdoms), and seven crowns (one on each of the seven heads of state) (Revelation 12:3). This refers to the seven leaders and the ten nations of the E.U. that promote and sanction the demagogue (Daniel 7:2, 20, 24).

Subsequently, the beast is introduced as having ten horns, seven heads, and ten crowns on his horns (Daniel 7:7, 24; Revelation 13:1). Though the seven heads are still present, the primary position will now be given to the ten horns (kings) and their respective kingdoms into which the entire world will be divided (Revelation 17:12, 16). Therefore, the number of crowns will increase to ten.

Parallels Between the Second and Third Temples

The first act of the ruler of the world will be to desecrate the Third Temple and demand worship of his image set up there. To better understand this event, one needs to look at the infamous precedent in the Second Temple.

On *Kislev* 25, December 13, 167 B.C., Antiochus ("the opposer") Epiphanes ("God made manifest") erected the *"abomination that causes desolation"* (Daniel 11:31) in the Second Temple area. This was an altar to Zeus upon which Antiochus:

> ...offered swine upon the altar, and sprinkled the Temple with the broth of their flesh, in order to violate the laws of the Jews and the religion they derived from their forefathers.[7]

To the Jews, there could be no greater sacrilege nor insult. A statue to the Greek god, Zeus, was also set up, which resembled Epiphanes. The Jews called him "Epimanes" (madman). He enforced the worship of the pagan Greek gods and outlawed the practice of Judaism under penalty of death. Some of the Jews themselves even built a large gymnasium to practice nude body-building, in keeping with the fashion of nudity in ancient Greece. Some Jews "submitted to uncircumcision and disowned the holy agreement it symbolized" (1 Maccabees 1:14).

As prophesied many years before, it took 2,300 consecutive evenings and mornings (1,150 days) from the day the two daily sacrifices were halted until they were resumed by the Jews (Daniel 8:14). To be told ahead of time how long the Temple would remain in foreign hands inspired the Jews to persevere in their guerilla warfare until they regained their Sanctuary from the Syrians.

---

7.   Josephus, p. 278; cf. 1 Maccabees 1:59.

The 1,150 days equal **over 38 Biblical months**. Is this a reminder of the **over 38 years** that the Israelites wandered in the wilderness after they refused to enter the Promised Land? Their complete restoration from slavery to sin may well take place in the 21st century. That will be **the 38th century** since Jacob and his clan entered Egypt c. 1711 B.C.

Note: This is an example of the exquisite synchronization in God's universe. The number 2,300 is "the most perfect astronomical cycle known." It requires 2,300 solar years to restore the sun and moon exactly to their former position.[8] Is it just a coincidence that God chose this to be the number of sacrifices halted before they were reinstituted?

Since the Second Temple was rededicated by the heroic Maccabees on *Kislev* 25, 164 B.C., the two daily sacrifices were terminated by Antiochus on *Tishri* 15, 167 B.C., or 1,150 days previously. *Tishri* 15 was the first day of the Feast of Tabernacles (*Sukkot*). This date was all the more humiliating, since it was the very feast at which Solomon had dedicated the First Temple (see p. 122).

Why did Antiochus specifically choose the 25th day of the month of *Kislev* to set up his idolatrous worship in the Temple? It was related to a pagan winter holiday, following the shortest day of the year. The Romans also observed December 25 as the birthday of the sun.

The Jewish Feast of Lights on *Kislev* 25 is also called *Hanukkah* ("dedication"). It commemorates the Maccabean victory over the Syrians, the rededication of the Temple, and God's miracle of a day's supply of oil which burned for eight days in the Temple.[9] When the Hebrew word *"Hanukkah"* is divided in

---

8.   Orr, p. 306.
9.   *Shabbat* 21b.

two, it reads "on the 25th, the Jews were able to rest, to be at peace from the enemies they had driven out."[10]

God prepares His people for an important event by foreshadowing it long in advance. His selection of *Kislev* 25 for the rededication is a case in point. Here are important events on that date:

1. God gave the prophet Haggai four messages calling the Jews to rebuild the Second Temple. The final two messages were both given on the eve of *Kislev* 25, 520 B.C. Haggai said Jehovah would shake the heavens, the earth, and the sea. He would overturn thrones and shatter the power of kingdoms. The *"desired of all nations"* would come and guarantee their inheritance like the seal of a signet ring (Haggai 2:7, 21, 23).

2. On *Kislev* 25, 164 B.C., the Maccabees rededicated the Temple precisely three years after its desecration.

3. *Kislev* 25, (December 10), 1917, was the day the British General Edmund Allenby entered Jerusalem and freed it from 400 years of Turkish rule. (He did not fire one shot.)

4. There is reason to believe that *Kislev* 25 will be the date of the rededication of the Third Temple, 1,335 days after it is desecrated by the wicked ruler of Israel (see p. 198, 291).

The Two Babylons Destroyed

The unfaithful, harlot Church, which never loved nor obeyed Jesus Christ, will not be raptured. She is described as sitting on seven hills (Revelation 17:10). Rome originated on the left bank of the Tiber on seven hills. References to Rome as "the city on seven hills" are common among Roman writers, e.g., Virgil, Martial, and Cicero.[11] This term would have been in use around 90 A.D., when Revelation was written.

---

10.   Vainstein, p. 129.
11.   *The NIV Study Bible,* p. 1,944.

This is not a designation of any one church, but rather of a composite, ecclesiastical hierarchy which may be headquartered in Rome, as capital of the beast's empire. It is man's effort to fashion religious unity, and it is not instigated by the Lord. In fact, the Holy Spirit already overcame denominational barriers. He brought a true oneness of spirit among Catholics and Protestants who would receive it ever since the Charismatic Renewal in the 1960s.

The unfaithful body is called *"Babylon the Great, the Mother of Prostitutes."* She prostitutes herself to an opportunistic world and its lack of values. Having discarded righteousness, she is devoid of God's Spirit who alone can inspire repentance and restore people.

The inhabitants of the earth were intoxicated with the wine of her adulteries.   (Revelation 17:2)

People's senses will be stimulated by her worldly trappings, and their thinking distorted by her reprobate teaching. She will speak lies in the name of God.

The beast will turn to her organization for assistance. She will bask in his secular support and ride upon his power and momentum. So identified are they, that both are dressed in scarlet (Revelation 17:3f).

After the beast has exploited her vast influence over the multitudes and built his own hierarchy, he and his ten kings of the whole world will hate, ruin, and *"leave her naked."* Finally, they will *"burn her with fire"* (Revelation 17:16).

The other infrastructure that will collapse is the commercial arena and its city of power, also called "Babylon." This will occur with a worldwide, economic crash. The merchants of the earth and the shipping industry will be terrified and aghast. Both the religious and the commercial Babylon are described in the same manner. There is no observable difference between them:

The woman was dressed in purple and scarlet and was glittering with gold, precious stones, and pearls.

(Revelation 17:4; 18:16)

Chapter Ten

GOD'S JUDGMENT (DURING THE 1,260 DAYS) THEN RESTORATION!

Therefore I will make the heavens tremble. And the earth will shake from its place at the wrath of the Lord Almighty, in the day of his burning anger. (Isaiah 13:13)

The Great Tribulation—The Crucible of God's Wrath

The last half of the seven years, the Great Tribulation, (Matthew 24:21, KJV; Revelation 7:14) is referred to in the Old Testament as *"a time, times, and half a time"* (Daniel 7:25; 12:7). In order to prevent misinterpretation, the New Testament defines it in three ways: *42 months; 1,260 days; or a time, times, and half a time* (Revelation 11:2, 6; 12:6, 14; 13:5). **As with the terrorized Jews under Antiochus Epiphanes in 167 B.C., it will be crucial for Bible believers still on earth to know the precise length of time the ferocious, worldwide conditions will last.**

How awful that day will be! None will be like it. It will be a time of trouble for Jacob, but he will be saved out of it. In

that day I will break the yoke off their necks...They will
serve the Lord and David their king.   (Jeremiah 30:7f)

The spiritual warfare of six millennia will climax. The devil
would have man believe: **there is no God, He is indifferent to
men, or He is impotent against evil.** These are Satan's lies.

Having given men freedom of choice, God allows us to use it
to honor or rebel against Him. Of course, our actions carry
consequences. God has revealed His utmost love for us by sending
His Son to take our penalty of death for sin. And the Lord
continues to reveal Himself to believers through His Word and
Holy Spirit. Many individuals who remain unconvinced by His
mercy will respond to His justice.

When your judgments come upon the earth, the people of
the world learn righteousness.   (Isaiah 26:9)

Jesus read Isaiah 61:2 the day He began His ministry in
Nazareth. He only read the first part of the verse, proclaiming
freedom for the prisoners (of self, sin, and Satan) and the
acceptable year of the Lord. He then announced: *"Today, this
scripture is fulfilled in your hearing"* (Luke 4:21). He stopped
short and did not read the rest of the verse and proclaim:... *"the
day of vengeance of our God"* (Isaiah 61:2).

Indeed, God's seven-year cycle was interrupted. Messiah came
offering forgiveness, salvation, and restoration. He revealed
Himself as the King of the Jews on *Nisan* 10, and was *"cut off"* on
Nisan 14, 30 A.D., after a ministry of precisely three-and-a-half
years.

**God will again offer this Jewish generation (and every-
one else) another three-and-a-half year period to receive the
Jewish Messiah.** This will be done through the Bride of Christ,
the two witnesses, and the 144,000 Jews. However, the two witnesses are the only ones the Bible specifies will minister throughout the entire first half (1,260 days) of the king's seven-year reign.

Then, God's wrath will be poured out upon the unrepentant for an equal length of time. *"The day of vengeance"* will come to pass. God refers to His wrath as *"his strange work...his alien task"* (Isaiah 28:21).

> *The Lord will carry out his sentence on earth with speed and finality.*   (Romans 9:28; cf. Isaiah 10:22f)

> *For then there will be great distress, unequaled from the beginning of the world until now—and never to be equaled again. If those days had not been cut short, no one would survive, but for the sake of the elect those days will be shortened.*   (Matthew 24:21f)

> *Go, my people, enter your rooms and shut the doors behind you. Hide yourselves for a little while until his wrath has passed by. See, the Lord is coming out of his dwelling to punish the people of the earth for their sins.*
> (Isaiah 26:20f; cf. Psalm 57:1)

After the Rapture, man's choices are stark:

1. Worship God and His Messiah, receive His Holy Spirit, be killed by the Anti-Christ, go to heaven, return shortly with Messiah to reign with Him for 1,000 years (Revelation 20:4), and remain in the presence of God for eternity.
2. Worship Satan and his beast, take his mark of identity, try to survive on a tortured earth, die, and remain among the damned for eternity (Revelation 14:9ff).

God's wrath will be directed against those who worship demons and gold and silver idols. These people will not repent of their murders, their witchcraft and drugs (Greek *"pharmakeia"*), their sexual immorality, or their thefts (Revelation 9:21). The unrepentant will cry out, but not to *"the stone the builders rejected"* (Psalm 118:22; Isaiah 8:14b; 1 Peter 2:7f), which is Christ.

They call to the mountains and the rocks, "Fall on us and hide us from the face of him who sits on the throne and from the wrath of the Lamb! For the great day of their wrath has come and who can stand?"

(Revelation 6:16)

Men will flee to caves in the rocks and to holes in the ground from dread of the Lord and the splendor of his majesty, when he rises to shake the earth. In that day men will throw away to the rodents and bats [which are with them in the caves] *their idols of silver and idols of gold.*

(Isaiah 2:19f)

If we deliberately keep on sinning after we have received the knowledge of the truth, no sacrifice for sins is left, but only a fearful expectation of judgment and of raging fire that will consume the enemies of God. Anyone who rejected the law of Moses died without mercy on the testimony of two or three witnesses. How much more severely do you think a man deserves to be punished who has trampled the Son of God under foot, who has treated as an unholy thing the blood of the covenant that sanctified him, and who has insulted the Spirit of grace? For we know him who said, "It is mine to avenge; I will repay"...It is a dreadful thing to fall into the hands of the living God.

(Hebrews 10:26–31)

There will be signs in the sun, moon, and stars. On earth, nations will be in anguish and perplexity at the roaring and tossing of the sea. Men will faint from terror, apprehensive of what is coming on the world, for the heavenly bodies will be shaken. At that time, they will see the Son of Man coming in a cloud with power and great glory. When these things begin to take place, stand up and lift up your heads, because your redemption is drawing near.

(Luke 21:25–28)

If we disbelieve in the idea of judgment in the past, we may for the future as well.

In the last days scoffers will come, scoffing and following their own evil desires. They will say, "Where is this 'coming' he promised? Ever since our fathers died, everything goes on as it has since the beginning of creation."

(2 Peter 3:3f)

During God's punishment of evildoers, a quarter of the world's population will be subject to death by sword, famine, plague, and wild beasts (Revelation 6:8). Then, the four angels who have been kept ready for *"this hour and day and month and year"* will be released from the place where they are bound at the Euphrates River (Revelation 9:14f).

The timing of their release will be that precise. They will kill a third of the remaining three-quarters of those alive (another quarter), using 200 million mounted troops. The top part of the vehicles of the troops will resemble a lion's head and the rear, a serpent's tail. Out of these carriers will issue fire, smoke, and sulfur (Revelation 9:16–19). Adding the two quarters together, we come to the solemn realization that the one half of mankind, who have not already been raptured by God or beheaded by the Anti-Christ (the beast), will meet God's wrath.

Why are we specifically told the location from which the four angels are released? At the southern end of the Euphrates was the Garden of Eden where man lost his position in God through rebellion. Not only was this river valley the site of our original home, but it was also the seat of the first three empires: Nimrod in Shinar, Assyria, and Babylon. The distant northern end of the river was given to Abraham as the northern boundary of the Promised Land. We make our own journey back to God via a life of trust and obedience to the Lord.

God's wrath is not impulsive but is measured out in sets of seven judgments each: seals, trumpets, and bowls (Revelation 6 through 19). The bowl or vial judgments cause:

1. Sores—ugly and painful sores on people who have the mark of the Anti-Christ and worship his image.
2. Sea of blood—everything in the sea dies.
3. Rivers and springs of blood.
4. Sun—extreme heat will scorch and sear people. (Depletion of the ozone layer must be a factor.)
5. Darkness*—darkness over the beast's kingdom.
6. The Euphrates River—dried up to prepare the way for kings from the East to march to Israel.
7. An earthquake—unequalled in the history of man, by which cities collapse, islands and mountains disappear. 100-pound hailstones fall from the sky.

*Note: Darkness was one of the plagues brought upon Egypt. For three days it was so dark, it could *"be felt"* (Exodus 10:21). Stuart Roosa of the Apollo 14 mission described the back of the moon:

> "As you pass through this total darkness, it is so incredibly dark you almost...can feel it. The spacecraft drops in temperature, and with the condensation on the bulkheads, it gets a clammy feeling to it."[1]

God gives us this and other solemn information about His wrath to warn us. His judgment will come upon a corrupt and a violent generation just as surely as it did in Noah's day and Lot's day.

The Lord saw how great man's wickedness on the earth had become, and that every inclination of the thoughts of his heart was only evil all the time. The Lord was grieved that

---

1.   *Eastern Airlines Review,* June 1990, p. 52.

*he had made man on the earth, and his heart was filled with
pain.*
(Genesis 6:5f; cf. Matthew 24:37; Luke 17:26ff)

*Truth has perished...It has vanished from their lips...Take
up a lament...for the Lord has rejected and abandoned this
generation* [of the wicked] *that is under his wrath.*
(Jeremiah 7:28f)

Union in Heaven and the Wedding Supper

After the committed Christians are caught up from earth, the
works of each person raptured will be judged by Jesus in heaven.
The efforts of some will stand the test, while that of others will be
burned up. If the works survive, the person will receive his reward.
If not, he will suffer loss; but he himself will be saved (1
Corinthians 3:12f; Revelation 22:12).

For we must all appear before the judgment seat [bema] *of
Christ, that each one may receive what is due him for the
things done while in the body, whether good or bad.*
(2 Corinthians 5:10)

Before Messiah leaves his *"place"* (Hosea 5:15) in heaven to
come to earth, His marriage to His Bride will be celebrated with
great rejoicing at the wedding supper (Revelation 19:7ff; Matthew
22:2–14; 25:10; Ephesians 5:31f). The union of God with His people has its roots in the Old Testament with Jehovah's marriage to
Israel (Isaiah 54:5–7; Hosea 2:19f; Song of Songs [Canticles]).
Those called to the wedding feast are united with the Son. They
partake of His nature, having escaped the corruption that is in the
world (2 Peter 1:4).

It is difficult to appreciate the union of spirit between God and
His people unless we experience it for ourselves. Love in a happy
marriage is a picture of this mystery. While the Bride is worshiping
her Lord in heaven, many on earth will be deifying the beast.

Armageddon

The beast, the ten kings, and troops from all nations will assemble at Armageddon (Mount of Megiddo) on the spacious Plain of Jezreel in northern Israel.

Note: The ancient city of Megiddo stood at the pass where the route from Egypt to Babylon and Assyria crossed the Carmel Range in Israel. Needless to say, Megiddo became a military stronghold, guarding this pass. Tribute money had to be paid for its use to the ruler who controlled it. For thousands of years, the armies of Africa and Asia marched through or clashed on this famous battlefield, including those of Thutmose III, Joshua, and Pharaoh Necoh. It was one of Solomon's chariot cities for defense. British General Allenby fought the Turks there in 1917. Megiddo again saw combat in 1948.

On that fateful day before Messiah comes…

Then, they gathered the kings together to the place that in Hebrew is called Armageddon.   (Revelation 16:16)

I have decided to assemble the nations, to gather the kingdoms and to pour out my wrath on them—all my fierce anger.   (Zephaniah 3:8)

From Armageddon, the armies will advance south and capture Jerusalem.

A large and mighty army comes, such as never was of old, nor ever will be in ages to come. Before them, fire devours. Behind them, a flame blazes. Before them, the land is like a Garden of Eden. Behind them, a desert waste—nothing escapes them.   (Joel 2:2ff)

They have the appearance of horses…At the sight of them, nations are in anguish, every face turns pale.
(Joel 2:4ff; cf. Revelation 9:7)

I will gather *all the nations to Jerusalem to fight against it. The city will be captured, the houses ransacked, and the women raped. Half of the city will go into exile, but the rest of the people will not be taken from the city.*
(Zechariah 14:2)

Israel's Deliverer-Messiah Arrives

When the times will have reached their fulfillment...
(Ephesians 1:10)

The Deliverer will come to Zion. That day and moment will arrive. People will actually see Messiah coming in the sky. Seated on a white horse, He will bear the name, *"King of Kings and Lord of Lords."* His eyes will be like blazing fire (Revelation 19:11ff).

As we know, when Jesus presented Himself to Israel as her King, He came humbly, riding a lowly donkey's colt (Zechariah 9:9; Mark 11:7). This time, He will be presented on a mighty steed of war.

The Lord thunders at the head of his army. His forces are beyond number, and mighty are those who obey his command. The Day of the Lord is great. It is dreadful. Who can endure it?
(Joel 2:11)

Messiah will arrive on the Mount of Olives, east of the Temple Mount. Both sites, Jesus' agony in Gethsemane the night before His crucifixion and His ascension, are on the Mount of Olives. They are situated east of the closed eastern gate, which was due east of the Temple. The Mount of Olives is separated from the Temple Mount by the deep Kidron Valley.

I saw the glory of the God of Israel coming from the east. His voice was like the roar of rushing waters, and the land was radiant with his glory.
(Ezekiel 43:2)

Then, the Lord will go out [from heaven] *and fight against those nations, as he fights in the day of battle. On that day, his feet will stand on the Mount of Olives, east of Jerusalem, and the Mount of Olives will be split in two from east to west, forming a great valley. Then, the Lord my God will come, and all the holy ones with him.*

(Zechariah 14:2ff)

The hillside will split apart from the sheer power of Messiah's mighty Presence when His feet touch down upon earth. The brilliance of His glory will be like looking directly at the noonday sun (Revelation 1:16).

The glory of the Lord will be revealed, and all mankind together will see it.   (Isaiah 40:5)

The section of the Mount of Olives directly across from the Temple Mount contains Gethsemane, the Ascension Chapel, several Christian churches, and many olive trees. There is also the traditional Palm Sunday road on which Jesus is thought to have made His triumphal entry into the city. This road abruptly divides the Christian part of the hillside from the huge adjacent area to the south, dotted with thousands of white Jewish gravestones. Since the green, Christian area is in line with the closed eastern gate of the Temple Mount, it would seem to be the exact terrain that will cleave under *"the soles"* of Messiah's feet.

As in the Roman siege of Jerusalem in 70 A.D., **the Temple** will become the focus of the whole battle. This is the last place that the forces arrayed against the God of Israel will relinquish in the cosmic struggle, because the Sanctuary is the place to which God's Presence will return. It is the center on earth of God's purposes for mankind. Although the Israelis captured Jerusalem in 1967, God has chosen to leave the Temple Mount in non-Jewish hands until *"the fullness of time."*

THE PLACE OF MESSIAH'S ARRIVAL ON EARTH
THE MOUNT OF OLIVES

Jerusalem from the South. The Valley of Jehoshaphat (Kidron) separates the Temple Mount with buildings (center, rear) from the Mount of Olives (right rear).

Troops led by the false messiah will amass in the Kidron Valley to defend the Temple. Accompanied by His armies, Messiah will come down from heaven from the east. His feet will stand on the Mount of Olives, east of the Temple. He will deliver all those who believe in Him and release creation from the power of evil (see Joel 3:2, 12, 14; Zechariah 14:4; Revelation 19:11–21; Romans 8:19-22).

The way God will deal with evil is to let it consolidate and take its stand. He will then destroy it. As we saw, first a few nations will invade Israel and head for Jerusalem. Seven years later, all nations will assemble in Israel against Jerusalem. Then, at the end of the millennium of peace, multitudes will again gather against Jerusalem for the last time.

Under the command of the beast and the ten kings, soldiers will fill the deep Kidron (Jehoshaphat) Valley which lies between the Temple Mount on the west and the Mount of Olives on the eastern side. Indeed, this is the *"valley of decision"*!

Let the nations be roused. Let them advance into the Valley of Jehoshaphat, for there I will sit to judge all the nations on every side...Multitudes, multitudes in the valley of decision! The sun and the moon will be darkened, and the stars no longer shine. The Lord will roar from Zion and thunder from Jerusalem. The earth and the sky will tremble. But the Lord will be a refuge for his people, a stronghold for the people of Israel.　　　　　　　　　　　(Joel 3:12ff)

I have decided to assemble *the nations, to gather the kingdoms, and to pour out my wrath on them—all my fierce anger.*　　　　　　　　　　　(Zephaniah 3:8)

So the Lord Almighty will come down to do battle on Mount Zion and on its heights. Like birds hovering overhead, the Lord Almighty will shield Jerusalem. He will shield it and deliver it.　　　　　　　　　　　(Isaiah 31:4f)

He will strike the earth with the rod of his mouth; with the breath of his lips will he slay the wicked.　　(Isaiah 11:4)

This is the plague with which the Lord will strike all nations that fought against Jerusalem. Their flesh will rot while they are still standing on their feet. Their eyes will

rot in their sockets, and their tongues will rot in their
mouths. On that day, men will be stricken by the Lord with
great panic.   (Zechariah 14:12f)

The beast and false prophet will be cast alive into the lake of
fire. The kings of the earth and their armies will be slain. Satan will
be bound and imprisoned in the Abyss for 1,000 years (Daniel
7:11; Revelation 19:20f; 20:3).

On that day, there will be no light, no cold or frost. It will
be a unique day, without daytime or nighttime—a day
known to the Lord. When evening comes there will be light.
                                                 (Zechariah 14:6)

God's *shekinah* glory, His brilliant, outshining Presence, will
return to dwell in the Holy of Holies as in the days of Solomon.
Jehovah's purposes will be accomplished in His appointed time
(Ezekiel 43:5, 7; Matthew 24:30).

"The bride" of Christ (made up of Jews and Gentiles) is presented to the world for the first time on the day she comes with the
Messiah (Revelation 17:14; 19:14, 7, 8).

The Resurrection

Upon arrival, Messiah will resurrect the Old Testament saints
and the post-Rapture believers, who were beheaded for their testimony of Jesus and the Word of God.

But at that time, your people—everyone whose name is
found written in the book—will be delivered. Multitudes
who sleep in the dust of the earth will awake: some to ever-
lasting life...   (Daniel 12:1f)

As for you [Daniel], go your way till the end. You will rest,
and then at the end of the days, you will rise to receive your
allotted inheritance.   (Daniel 12:13)

At that time, the sign of the Son of Man will appear in the sky, and all the nations of the earth will mourn. They will see the Son of Man coming on the clouds of the sky with power and great glory. And he will send his angels with a loud trumpet call, and they will gather his elect from the four winds, from one end of the heavens to the other.
(Matthew 24:30ff)

And he will send his angels and gather his elect from the four winds, from the ends of the earth to the ends of the heavens.   (Mark 13:27; cf. Luke 21:27f)

This gathering of His elect includes the Old Testament and the post-Rapture saints who have died as well as all believers who are still alive on earth.

They (the post-Rapture believers) *had not worshipped the beast or his image and had not received his mark on their foreheads or hands. They came to life and reigned with Christ a thousand years. (The rest of the dead did not come to life until the thousand years were ended.) This is* [ends] *the first resurrection. Blessed and holy are those who have part in the first resurrection. The second death has no power over them...*   (Revelation 20:4ff)

You may wonder, who are the Old Testament saints? How can people who lived prior to the death, burial and resurrection of Jesus be saved from going to hell by His sacrifice? Such people followed the only method God had provided thus far: substitution of an innocent animal's life on behalf of the guilty. The people who believed and obeyed God's requirements for their day will be God's Old Testament saints. The sacrifices of the Old Testament were symbolic, but ordained by God until the real Sacrifice was offered.

Note: Sacrifices did not come into being at the time of Moses and the Israelite nation. They started with our very first parents. God killed an innocent animal to cover the nakedness of Adam and Eve (Genesis 3:21). (Prior to their disobedience, they were covered with the radiance which emanated from their bodies.) Their son, Abel, brought an acceptable offering to God. It was not plant life (as was Cain's), but it was portions from the firstborn of Abel's flock (Genesis 4:4).

The very first act Noah did upon leaving the ark was to offer a sacrifice to the Lord (Genesis 8:20). This was *"Job's regular custom"* to do on behalf of his family (Job 1:5). We know that Jacob offered a sacrifice on *Nisan* 14, the day before he entered Egypt (Genesis 46:1; Exodus 12:17, 41; Numbers 33:3).

The Jewish Reunion

Jacob's ancient blessing over Judah may come to pass soon. Messiah is the Lion of the Tribe of Judah.

The scepter will not depart from Judah...until he comes to whom it belongs, and the obedience of the nations is his.
(Genesis 49:10)

Most marvelous is Jesus' reunion with His fellow Jews, after His separation from them for about 20 centuries. A miniature picture of the inexpressible joy of this moment is found in Joseph's revelation of his identity to his brothers after 20 years of being with the Gentiles in Egypt (Genesis 45). The joy of the Jewish people will be bittersweet when they see Messiah's pierced hands and feet (Zechariah 12:10).

Israel will grieve keenly over Messiah. All levels of society will mourn for Him as for an only child, a firstborn son. This includes leaders, prophets, priests, and even those who cursed the Lord's Anointed, as Shimei did (Zechariah 12:10ff; 2 Samuel 16:5). The mourning may last for the traditional 30 days.

[The Jewish Book of Jubilees (second-century B.C.) connects *Tishri* 10 with mourning. It stated that on that day Jacob was told of Joseph's alleged death, over which Jacob mourned greatly.[2]]

In that day, the remnant of Israel, the survivors of the house of Jacob, will no longer rely on him who struck them down; but will truly rely on the Lord, the Holy One of Israel. A remnant will return, a remnant of Jacob will return to the Mighty God. Though your people, O Israel, be like the sand by the sea, only a remnant will return.
(Isaiah 10:20f)

Their bloodguilt which I have not pardoned, I will pardon.
(Joel 3:21)

"All the nations of the earth will mourn" too (Matthew 24:30; Revelation 1:7). Many of those people will have rejected Messiah and will not repent of their sins.

When the Son of Man comes in his glory, and all the angels with him, he will sit on his throne in heavenly glory. All the nations will be gathered before him, and he shall separate the people one from another...I tell you the truth, whatever you did for these brothers of mine, you did for me.
(Matthew 25:31, 32, 40)

The Year of Jubilee

"The Restitution of All Things"
(Leviticus 25 and 27; Numbers 36:4; Ezekiel 46:17; Isaiah 49:8, 61:2; Luke 4:19, 29; Acts 3:21; 2 Corinthians 6:2).

The Jubilee Year holds profound significance and still awaits fulfillment. It may be a watershed year in the annals of human history.

2.   Charlesworth, Vol. 2, p. 121.

The Jubilee Year, the Year of the Lord's Favor (*Yobel*), denotes liberty. Jubilee was inaugurated by the blowing of the ram's horn throughout the land on the Day of Atonement. The Israelites were first required to carry out Jubilee in **the year after they had taken possession of and cultivated the Promised Land for 49 years (7 seven-year periods).**

Consecrate the fiftieth year and proclaim liberty throughout the land to all its inhabitants. It shall be a jubilee for you. Each one of you is to return to his family property and each to his own clan...Even if he is not redeemed in any of these ways, he and his children are to be released in the Year of Jubilee. (Leviticus 25:10, 54)

The blowing of the trumpet on the fiftieth *Yom Kippur* meant restitution for Israel, the release of Hebrew slaves, the return of mortgaged land to its original owner, and a year of rest for the land. Through this periodic correction of economic imbalances, God intended the Israelites to restore their society. The Jubilee gave poor families a new start in life and avoided the concentration of land in the hands of only a few. Their claim to their land was one of possession, not ownership.

The land must not be sold permanently, because the land is mine; and you are but aliens and my tenants...The Israelites are my servants, whom I brought out of Egypt. (Leviticus 25:23, 42)

The Jubilee Year is the only year in which the year begins on the tenth, instead of on the first day of the new year. Notice the specific day on which Ezekiel was given a vision of the glory of the Lord returning to the Temple:

At the beginning [head] *of the year (rosh ha shanah) on the* **tenth of the month**...*on that very day...I saw the glory of the God of Israel coming from the east...The glory of the*

*Lord entered the temple through the gate facing east. Then,
the Spirit lifted me up and brought me into the inner court,
and the glory of the Lord filled the temple...I heard someone speaking to me from inside the temple. He said, "Son
of man, this is the place of my throne and the place for the
soles of my feet. This is where I will live among the Israelites forever."*   (Ezekiel 40:1; 43:2–7)

This vision seems to indicate that the Messiah will enter the
Temple in glory on (*Tishri* 10), the first day of the Jubilee Year.
**One can understand why the Jubilee Year could not start
until *Tishri* 10. True restoration cannot begin until Messiah
comes,** which may be on *Yom Kippur* (see p. 244), the day on
which Israel gains forgiveness.

He must remain in heaven until the time comes for God **to
restore everything,** *as he promised long ago through his
holy prophets.*   (Acts 3:21)

A Talmudic rabbi expressed the importance of Jubilee: "In the
last Jubilee, the Son of David will come."[3]

"It is doubtful whether the Jubilee was ever really observed."[4]
The last reference to the law of redemption of the land in the 50th
year was just before the Jews entered Babylonian exile in the time
of Jeremiah (Jeremiah 32: 6-15; cf. Leviticus 25:23-25; Ruth 4:3)
Today, rabbis hold that the Jubilee must await the return of all the
Jews to their land before the Jubilee can be accomplished.

*Consecrate the fiftieth year and proclaim liberty through-
out the land to* **all** *its inhabitants.*
                                              (Leviticus 25:10, 13)

---

3.   *Sanhedrin*
4.   Winter, *The High Holy Days*, p. 15.

Today, great portions of the land belong to the state of Israel and the Jewish National Fund. The land will finally be divided among the prince, priests, Levites, and tribes (Ezekiel 45, 48).

Is the fiftieth year an extra year added to the 49-year cycle, or simply **the first year of the ensuing seven-year cycle?** The importance of this will be seen later."Both in the tannaitic literature and in the Apocrypha, two different systems of calculation for the Jubilee...are found."[5] There is little reference to the Jubilee in the *halakhah* (Talmudic laws governing all phases of Jewish life) or in documents uncovered by archaeology.[6]

After the destruction of the First Temple, "the Jubilee years were not even calculated, only those of *shemittot*" (seven-year cycles).[7] Josephus frequently refers to the sabbatic year but only twice to the Year of Jubilee.[8]

However, God outlined 70 *shemittot* (490 years) remaining for His nation (Daniel 9:24). This total is divisible by 49 and not by 50. **Astronomy indicates that there was no added 50th year:**

> **This period of 49 solar years was astronomically a period of restitution, for the sun and moon returned nearly to their original positions relative to each other, since 49 solar years are 606 lunar months with an error of only 32 hours.** So that though the Jubilee period is not a perfect lunar cycle, it was quite exact enough to guide the Jewish priests in drawing up their calendar in cases where failure of observation of the moon had given rise to some doubt.[9]

Thus, the Jubilee is tied to the sun and moon. Observation of the *"two great lights"* from one centralized location, Jerusalem,

---

5.   *Encyclopaedia Judaica,* Vol. 14, p. 579.
6.   *Ibid.,* p. 581.
7.   *Ibid.,* p. 579.
8.   Josephus, p. 81.
9.   Orr, p. 305.

worked while the Jews lived in their own land. The sun and moon were given as signals *"to mark the seasons and days and years"* as well as for light (Genesis 1:14ff).

Each month, the start of the agricultural year at *Rosh Hashannah*, and the new 49-year cycle (in the 50th year) were announced by loud blasts on the *shofar* (ram's horn). After the new moon was sighted, a chain of bonfires were lighted on a series of mountains to inform the more distant areas of the new month (*Rosh Hodesh*). These places are still pointed out today.

Note: The Aramaic papyri found at Aswan (Syene, Egypt) indicated that after the Babylonian destruction of Jerusalem, Jewish refugees who fled into Egypt developed an exact luni-solar calendar based on calculation rather than on observation. This was later attributed to Meton, the Athenian.[10]

King's Inauguration and Rededication of the Temple

Messiah may be crowned King during the final Feast as was Solomon! Israel will mourn for Messiah, probably for 30 days. The obscure schedule of 30 days (after *Yom Kippur*) plus 45 days (Daniel 12:11f), brings us to *Kislev* 25! *Hanukkah* must be the day the Temple may be rededicated to God. This was the very day the Maccabees reconsecrated the Second Temple in 164 B.C. after Antiochus Epiphanes desecrated it for three years.

Will the Third Temple in which the Anti-Christ demands worship be destroyed and a new Millennial Temple built? Even though there is an earthquake at the coming of Messiah, it splits the Mount of Olives in an exact way (Zechariah 14:4). The Temple Mount is not mentioned at all. Morever, upon Messiah's arrival, He immediately enters the Temple in glory (Ezekiel 43:1-7).

We are told that the Temple Mount will be exalted above the surrounding hills (Isaiah 2:2). All the land north and south of

10.   *Ibid.*, p. 305.

Jerusalem will be leveled like a plain. The city will rise above it and *"remain in its place"* from its northern to its southern boundaries (Zechariah 14:10).

Therefore, we will assume that the Temple Mount will be undisturbed as the spiritual center of the earth and that the Tribulation Temple will be rededicated on the same day of the year as the Second Temple was.

Conditions in the Seventh Millennium

Life on earth during the seventh millennium will be dramatically different from anything we now experience. Messiah will rule with an iron scepter (Psalm 2:9; Revelation 2:26f; 19:15).

What is the nature of those around God's throne? They are symbolized as being a "lion" in the sense of majesty and rulership, but also an "ox," indicating servitude. Their third projection is that of a "man," therefore approachable. And finally, there is the mighty "eagle," which is not earth-bound, but can soar in the heavens (Ezekiel 1:10; Revelation 4:7).

The saints will be given authority over the nations (Revelation 2:26) and administer cities (Luke 19:17ff). They will eventually judge the world and even fallen angels (1 Corinthians 6:2f). *"Truth, humility, and righteousness"* (Psalm 45:4) will be the hallmark of Messiah's reign.

Blessed are the meek for they will inherit the earth.
(Matthew 5:5)

Though God's wrath will shake both the earth and the heavens (Haggai 2:6f; Hebrews 12:26), it appears that the environment will be restored to a state of balance and perfection in which longevity is possible again (Isaiah 65:17–20). Conditions may be similar to pre-Flood times, as the Deluge altered the earth's atmosphere tremendously. How does Genesis describe the pre-Flood heavens?

So God made the expanse (sky) *and separated the water under the expanse from the water above it.*   (Genesis 1:7)

This gives rise to the theory that the earth was originally enveloped in a thick vapor canopy.[11] (Venus has a dense cloud cover that has been difficult to pierce until the radar eyes of the spacecraft Magellan.[12]) In such an enclosure, the earth would have had a much higher atmospheric pressure.

Note: In diving experiments, four men lived for several weeks in a diving bell at about 200 pounds per square inch without any ill effects.

In fact, they found if you cut your finger, it would usually heal in one day. Some experiments where surgery has been performed under increased room pressure have produced less damage to tissue and more rapid healing.[13]

For the creation was subjected to frustration...the creation itself will be liberated from its bondage to decay and brought into the glorious freedom of the children of God.
(Romans 8:20f)

Such a heavy cloud cover would have produced a terrarium-like environment with a warm, tropical climate which was watered by a *"mist"* (Genesis 2:6, KJV). This would explain the evidence of tropical conditions prevailing in our northern regions, such as:

(1) Fossil impressions of palm fronds have been found in northern Vancouver Island in Canada.

(2) Explorers reported seeing entire fruit trees with the fruit still on them inside immense gravel mounds on the New Siberian Islands and the Spitzbergen Islands inside the Arctic circle.

---

11.   Morris, pp. 277–282.
12.   *The Washington Post,* July 1, 1991, p. A-3.
13.   Anderson film.

(3) Redwood forests are found buried under ice deposits at the South Polar region. They require special climates, like that of northern California near the coast.[14]

Apparently, it did not rain until the Flood (Genesis 2:5; 7:4). We are also told that *"on that day all the springs of the great days burst forth"* (Genesis 7:11). Such eruptions could have been volcanic in nature.

Simultaneous volcanic action would produce sulfur aerosols which reflect sunlight back into space (as with acid rain). This could have caused the temperature of the earth's atmosphere to drop several degrees and made the entire vapor canopy condense and fall as rain. "A heavy layer of volcanic ash has been found beneath the polar ice cap."[15] The water level on earth would have increased by many feet (Genesis 7:20).

One of the most significant results of the new atmospheric conditions after the Flood was a shortened human lifespan. Longevity will be restored in the millennium.

He who dies at a hundred will be thought a mere youth. He who fails to reach a hundred will be considered accursed.
(Isaiah 65:20)

Damaging ultraviolet rays may again be shielded from reaching earth. These "short rays harm the skin and tissues of the body...and can also delay, and even change, the growth of cells"[16] This radiation contributes greatly to the aging process.

Do not dismiss the possibility of longevity too hastily, due to our lack of experience. About 60,000 Hunzas of the Himalayas are not the only community famous for living to advanced ages in supreme health with full mental and physical vigor.

Most importantly, the people who are allowed to enter the millennium will seek after God and have a peaceful spirit.

---

14.   Petersen, p. 29.
15.   Anderson film.
16.   *The World Book Encyclopedia,* Vol. 20, p. 8.

*They will neither harm nor destroy on all my holy moun-
tain, for the earth will be full of the knowledge of the Lord
as the waters cover the sea.*   (Isaiah 11:9)

*He will teach us his ways, so that we may walk in his paths.
The law will go out from Zion, the word of the Lord from
Jerusalem.*   (Micah 4:2)

He [Messiah] *will judge between many peoples and will
settle disputes for strong nations, far and wide. They will
beat their swords into plowshares and their spears into
pruning hooks. Nation will not take up sword against nation, nor will they train for war anymore.*
                                    (Micah 4:3; Isaiah 2:3)

The wild spirit will also have departed from the animal
kingdom. The serpent will be harmless, and formerly carnivorous
animals will eat straw.

The infant will play near the hole of the cobra.
                                                (Isaiah 11:8)

*The wolf and the lamb will feed together, and the lion will
eat straw like the ox.*   (Isaiah 65:25)

The survivors of God's wrath and the beast's reign of terror
will populate the earth during the millennium.

*The remnant of my people will plunder them. The survivors
of my nation will inherit their land. This is what they*
[Israel's enemies] *will get in return for their pride, for
insulting and mocking the people of the Lord Almighty. The
Lord will be awesome to them when He destroys all of the
gods of the land. The nations on every shore will worship
him, every one in its own land.*   (Zephaniah 2:10)

The survivors from all the nations that have attacked Jerusalem will go up year after year to worship the King, the Lord Almighty and to celebrate the Feast of Tabernacles [the seventh Feast]. *If any of the peoples of the earth do not go up to Jerusalem to worship the King, the Lord Almighty, they will have no rain.*   (Zechariah 14:16f)

And many peoples and powerful nations will come to Jerusalem to seek the Lord Almighty and to entreat Him...In those days, ten men from all the languages and nations will take firm hold of one Jew by the hem of his robe and say, "Let us go with you, because we have heard that God is with you." (Zechariah 8:22f)

In spite of Messiah's righteous rule, peace in men and animals, and the restored ecology, there will still be some who will reject Messiah. At the end of the thousand years, the devil will be released from the Abyss. He will go out worldwide to deceive the people who are born during that period (Revelation 20:7). These individuals will still have the freedom to choose whom they will serve. A large number will come from all over the world against Jerusalem. Fire will come down from heaven and devour them. Satan will be cast into the lake of fire, prepared for him and his demons (Revelation 20:10; Matthew 25:41).

Final Judgment and Restoration

After the end of Messiah's millennial reign of peace, all the wicked dead will be raised and *"the dead were judged according to what they had done."* They had not taken refuge in the righteousness Messiah offered them. Those not found in God's Book of Life at the Great White Throne Judgment will be cast into the lake of fire (Revelation 20:11ff).

But the day of the Lord will come like a thief. The heavens will disappear with a roar; the elements will be destroyed

by fire, and the earth and everything in it will be laid
bare…That day will bring about the destruction of the
heavens by fire, and the elements will melt in the heat. But
in keeping with his promise, we are looking forward to a
new heaven and a new earth, the home of righteousness.
(2 Peter 3:10–13)

This may refer to the end, not the start of the seventh millennium because at the time of the final judgment, it is stated:

Earth and sky fled from his presence, and there was no
place for them.   (Revelation 20:11)

Then follows a description of life in the new heavens, the new earth, and the new Jerusalem (Revelation 21 and 22). This begins the eighth millennium.

Now the dwelling of God is with men, and he will live with
them. They will be his people, and God himself will be with
them and be their God. He will wipe every tear from their
eyes. There will be no more death or mourning or crying or
pain, for the old order of things has passed away. He who
was seated on the throne said, "I am making everything
new!"   (Revelation 21:3–5)

No longer will there be any curse.   (Revelation 22:3)

Then, the end will come, when he [Jesus] hands over the
kingdom to God the Father after he [Jesus] has destroyed
all dominion, authority and power. For he must reign until
he has put all his enemies under his feet. The last enemy to
be destroyed is death.   (1 Corinthians 15:24ff)

The Father is the head, and the Son executes the Father's will. The Spirit is sent by the Father and the Son to bring conviction, repentance, and renewal to people who want to know God (Joel 2:28f; John 16:7f; Acts 2:16ff, 33).

Chapter Eleven

GOD'S HISTORIC PRECEDENTS AND PARALLELS

And God blessed the seventh day.　　　　　(Genesis 2:3)

Seven—The Complete Cycle

Throughout the Bible, the cycle of seven is God's expression of completed action. In nature, this unit of seven is manifested in the musical scale and the colors of the rainbow. God insists that every seventh day, year, or multiples thereof, should be one of rest and restoration.

> *By the seventh day, God had finished the work he had been doing; so on the seventh day, he rested from all his work. And God blessed the seventh day and made it holy...*
>
> 　　　　　　　　　　　　　　　　　　　(Genesis 2:2f)

> *Six days you shall labor, but on the seventh day you shall rest, even during the plowing season and harvest you must rest.*　　　　　　　　　　　　　　(Exodus 34:21)

God says about the Sabbath:

*This will be a sign between me and you for the generations
to come, so that you may know that I am the Lord, who
makes you holy.*   (Exodus 31:12f)

So significant is the seventh day, that it is listed fourth in the
Commandments, preceded only by those regarding the Almighty,
false gods, and the Lord's name (Exodus 20; Deuteronomy 5). It
was based on God's own great day of rest (Genesis 2:2). This basic
pattern of seven is seen in:

Week of Days	Seven days
Week of Weeks	Followed by the 50th day, Pentecost, *(Shavuot)* (Leviticus 23:15f).
Week of Months	The Atonement, *(Yom Kippur)* in the seventh month (Leviticus 16; Numbers 29:7f).
Seven-Day Feast	Unleavened Bread and Tabernacles, *(Sukkot)* (Leviticus 23:6f, 34f).
Week of Years	The Sabbatic year *(Shemittah)* (Exodus 21:2f; Leviticus 25:2f; Deuteronomy 15:1f).
Seven Weeks of Years	49 years before liberty in the 50th year (Leviticus 25:8f).
Week of 70 Years	Restoration will come (Daniel 9:24–27).
Week of Eras	Innocence, Conscience, Government, Promise, Law, Grace, and Messiah's Reign of Peace on earth.

The sacred seven is God's manifest pattern for the religious
Feasts, the daily life and the agriculture of God's chosen people.

Another seven is found in God's law that a Hebrew servant was
to serve for six years and then be set free in the seventh year
without paying anything (Exodus 21:2; Deuteronomy 15:12f).

Will creation be liberated from its bondage to decay (Romans 8:21) after the sixth millennium? People who belong to God will not have to pay for their sins since they repent and place themselves under the righteousness of the Messiah.

God also insisted that the Hebrews were to cancel debts every seven years (Deuteronomy 15:1, 2, 9). It seems reasonable to believe that He will follow His own pattern. Even the land was to lie fallow every seventh year.

Notice that it was not until the people had walked around Jericho once on six consecutive days that God gave them their first victory in the Promised Land **at daybreak of the seventh day** (Joshua 6:15, 16).

And consider Enoch who walked so closely with God that the Lord took him off the earth alive (Genesis 5:24). He was the only example of this prior to Elijah. Equally significant is Enoch's genealogical placement. He was the seventh from Adam through Seth (Genesis 5:18–24; 1 Chronicles 1:1–3; Jude 14). This points to completion and perfection in man's seventh cycle. In a sense, God Himself will not rest until His fallen creation is restored; and His kingdom of righteousness has been established on earth in His "appointed time."

Upon this undergirding principle, one concludes that after six millennia of man's efforts, the seventh may be the millennium of restoration of righteousness and justice under Messiah's reign (Revelation 20:2–7). Truth will triumph over deception, and love over selfishness.

Therefore will the Lord wait that he may be gracious unto you.   (Isaiah 30:18, KJV)

There remains then, a Sabbath-rest for the people of God.
(Hebrews 4:9)

For a thousand years in your sight are like a day that has just gone by.   (Psalm 90:4)

But do not forget this one thing, dear friends: With the Lord a day is like a thousand years, and a thousand years are like a day.   (2 Peter 3:8)

7,000 Years in the Talmud:

The Jewish people consider the Talmud to be the most authoritative source of Judaism after the Bible.[1] It contains the early oral law and discussions of all facets of Jewish life. Though dating back earlier, this information was compiled between 70 A.D. and 500 A.D. by their teachers.

The view frequently expressed in the Talmud is that the world would last for seven thousand years, which they founded upon the Sabbath division of time. The Jews had fully developed the doctrine of the millennium long before the New Testament book of Revelation (c. 90 A.D.) dealt with it (Revelation 20:2ff). For example:

> Rabbi Kattina said: Six thousand years shall the world exist, and one [thousand, the seventh] it shall be desolate, as it is written, *And the Lord alone shall be exalted in that day* (Isaiah 2:11). Abaye said: It will be desolate two [thousand], as it is said, *After two days will he revive us: in the third day, he will raise us up, and we shall live in his sight* (Hosea 6:2).
>
> It has been taught in accordance with R. Kattina: Just as the seventh year is one year of release in seven, so is the world: one thousand years out of seven shall be fallow, as it is written. *And the Lord alone shall be exalted in that day*...and it is also said, *For a thousand years in thy sight are but as yesterday when it is past* (Psalm 90:4).[2]

---

1.   Bridger, p. 475.
2.   *Sanhedrin II,* 97a

The Tanna debe Eliyyahu teaches: The world is to exist six thousand years. In the first two thousand there was desolation (Editor's note: no Torah...From Adam until then [Abraham], two thousand years elapsed.); two thousand years the Torah flourished; and **the next two thousand years is the Messianic era** (Editor's note: Messiah will come within that period.), but through our many iniquities all these years have been lost. (Editor's note: **He should have come at the beginning of the last two thousand years;** the delay is due to our sins.)[3]

Our Rabbis taught: In the seven year cycle at the end of which the son of David will come...[4]

For they (those who calculate Messiah's advent) would say, since the predetermined time has arrived, and yet he has not come, he will never come. But [even so], wait for him, as it is written, *Though he tarry, wait for him* (Habakkuk 2:3)....Scripture saith, *And therefore will the Lord wait, that he may be gracious unto you, and therefore will he be exalted, that he may have mercy upon you.* But since *we* look forward to it, and *He* does likewise, what delays [his coming]?[5]

Rab said: All the pre-destined dates [for redemption] have passed, and the matter [now] depends only on repentance and good deeds.[6]

R. Eliezer said: If Israel repent, they will be redeemed; if not, they will not be redeemed....But the Holy One, blessed be He, will set up a king over them, whose decrees shall be as cruel as Haman's, whereby Israel shall engage in

---

3.   *Ibid.,* p. 657.
4.   *Ibid.,* p. 654.
5.   *Ibid.,* 97b, p. 659.
6.   *Ibid.,* p. 660.

repentance, and he will thus bring them back to the right path.[7]

This cruel king is the false messiah, described by the prophet Daniel (Daniel 9:27).

When the power of the holy people [the Jews] *has been finally broken, all these things will be completed.*
                                                    (Daniel 12:7)

Rabbi Hanan b. Tahlifa sent [word]...the Holy One, blessed be He, will renew His world only after 7,000 years.[8]

7,000 Years in Early Christian Writings:

For the first 300 years of this era, the early Christian Fathers and the Church held that at the end of 6,000 years, Christ would come and reign for 1,000 years. Among these men were: Barnabas (c. 100 A.D.), Justin Martyr and Irenaeus (c. 150 A.D.), Lactantius (c. 325 A.D.), and Methodius, Bishop of Tyre (c. 300 A.D.). This view of the millennium met with no opposition previous to Origen (185–254 A.D.).

Barnabas, the Apostle Paul's first partner, wrote in his epistle: As there had been 2,000 years from Adam to Abraham and 2,000 from Abraham to Christ; so there would be 2,000 years for the Christian era and then would come the Millennium.[9] (This epistle, written around 100 A.D., is not in the Bible.)**Will the time allotted for the nations to respond to God under grace equal the interval given to the Jewish nation to obey Him under the law?** (cf. John 1:17)

7.   *Ibid.,* p. 660.
8.   *Ibid.,* p. 658.
9.   Halley, p. 33.

Lactantius, tutor of the son of the Roman Emperor Constantine, categorically stated in his *Divine Institutes,* Chapter 14:

...let the philosophers...know that the six thousandth year is not yet completed; and when this number is completed, the consummation must take place.[10]

After the conversion of Constantine I, the Great (272–337 A.D.), the Roman Empire became nominally Christian. In addition, the third-century school of interpreters, headed by Origen, taught Scripture from a figurative rather than a literal viewpoint. Such factors led to the decline in the purity of the Church.

Gibbon, the historian, said:

The ancient and popular doctrine of the Millennium was carefully inculcated by a succession of Fathers from Justin Martyr and Irenaeus, who conversed with the immediate disciples of the Apostles, down to Lactantius, who was the teacher of the son of Constantine. It appears to have been the reigning sentiment of orthodox believers...
As long as this error [as he calls it] was permitted to subsist in the Church, it was productive of the most salutary effects on the faith and practice of Christians.[11]

The Church did not throw off its shackles until the reformers of the sixteenth century. Martin Luther severely condemned the system of making Scripture non-literal or "spiritualizing" it.[12] He came into direct conflict with the Church with his insistence on the authority and inerrancy of Holy Scripture.

The Apocrypha:

The Apocryphal books were a part of the Septuagint, the first translation of the Old Testament prepared by Jewish scholars

---

10.   Jeffrey, p. 173.
11.   *Milman's Gibbon's Rome,* Vol. 1, p. 262; quoted by Blackstone, p. 67.
12.   Blackstone, p. 36.

(250–150 B.C.) for non-Hebrew-speaking Jews. Although these books are not accepted in the Hebrew nor Protestant Bibles, they provide information on that era.

They indicate that God rules the world according to a predetermined time schedule (2 Esdras 4:35–37). The end awaits the death of a certain number of the righteous (1 Enoch 47:4).[13]

> *Israel has experienced a hardening in part until the full number of Gentiles has come in.*   (Romans 11:25)

Other Precedents

Two Consecutive Jewish Generations as a Nation

Though not generally realized, Moses spent not one, but two, periods of 40 days each on Mount Sinai with the Lord. He received the stone tablets with the Ten Commandments on two separate occasions before his people were ready to accept them.

Similarly, it required two consecutive generations, **as a nation,** before Israel was willing to enter the Promised Land. And, so it may be with their acceptance of their Messiah (p. 218ff).

The Second Son

Under the ancient law of primogeniture, at least a double portion of the father's property was given to the firstborn son. It also provided that the younger of two sons would serve the older, under normal circumstances. However, God frequently elects the second son, signifying that the Lord intervenes according to His perfect will.

Examples of God's choosing the second son ahead of the first were Abel instead of Cain (Genesis 4:4); Isaac over Ishmael (Genesis 17:19); Jacob over Esau (Genesis 25:25; Malachi 1:2);

---

13.   *The NIV Study Bible,* Note 6:11, p. 1,933.

Moses over Aaron (who was three years older); Ephraim over Manasseh (Genesis 48:19); and figuratively speaking, Jesus (the "last Adam") over Adam (1 Corinthians 15:45).

The Third Day

Scripture states that the Lord's complete restoration of the Jewish people will take place on the *"third day"* (Hosea 6:2). So important is this interval that it is repeatedly used on other major occasions (see p. 312). Four examples are:

1. Isaac was released from death on the third day (Genesis 22:4).
2. The Jews took a three-day journey to offer sacrifices to the Lord and escape from Egypt (Exodus 8:27).
3. God spoke the Ten Commandments to Moses and the Israelites on the third day (Exodus 19:16).
4. Joshua led the Israelites into the Promised Land on the third day (Joshua 1:11; 3:2).

After ["achar"—the hind part of] *two days, he will revive us; on the third day he will restore us that we may live in his presence. Let us acknowledge the Lord; let us press on to acknowledge him. As surely as the sun rises, he will appear.*   (Hosea 6:2f)

In spite of the many powerful miracles Jesus had already done, the Pharisees asked Him for a sign. The one He chose to give was that of the prophet, Jonah.

A wicked and adulterous generation asks for a miraculous sign! But none will be given it except the sign of the prophet Jonah. For as Jonah was three days and three nights in the belly of a huge fish, so the Son of Man will be three days and three nights in the heart of the earth.   (Matthew 12:39f; cf. Jonah 1:17)

In light of Hosea's prophecy, the three-day entombment of Jonah is **the single most important sign Jesus could have left with His people about their future and their resurrection as a nation.** Forty years after the death of Jesus, the Jewish nation was dispersed and became a non-functioning unit.

Since the nation is now revived at the end of *"two days,"* should we not expect their full restoration at the dawning of *"the third day?"* The third millennium since the birth of Jesus Christ is soon to begin.

Jesus was also using the Jonah example as a foreshadowing of the three days that He himself would be entombed in the earth before being raised from death at dawn of the third day. Surely, David could not have been referring to himself when he said:

My body will also rest secure, because you will not abandon me to the grave, nor will you let your Holy One see decay.   (Psalm 16:9, 10)

Note: In general, bodies start to decompose within four to eight hours after death. However, it is not always that rapid, as "some bodies may remain in a state of natural preservation for several days." Such circumstances as age and health of a body and the weather would affect the rate of deterioration.[14]

Jesus Christ was raised from the dead by dawn of the third day. It was a common Jewish idea that the soul stayed near the deceased for three days and corruption commenced on the fourth day. By then, the soul took its final leave beyond recall.[15]

(In the Old Testament reckoning of time, a partial day was still reckoned as a day.[16] Of course, the Jewish day starts at sundown.)

---

14.   *Funerals: Consumer's Last Rights,* p. 100.
15.   Edersheim, Vol. 2, p. 324; quoting: *Abhodah Zarah,* 20b; *Bereshith Rabba,* 100; *Vayyikra Rabba* 18.
16.   *The NIV Study Bible,* p. 1,460, Note 12.40; Unger, p. 1,099.

The "three-day journey" seems to be pointing to the two entombments: first of the Messiah and then of His nation, with each coming to life on the third "day." The Jewish nation did not reach the goal, acceptance of Messiah and His salvation, on their first three-"day" journey. It is as if they have had to repeat the two-"day" period a second time before they will accept the Messiah at the dawn of the third "day."

The Twenty-First Century As Focal Point

We are given three different timespans, all of which converge at the start of the 21st century. These are the seventh, the fifth, and the third "day":

On the Seventh "Day"—Freedom for Men

If the age of each father at the birth of his son in the lineage from Adam to Abraham is added together, the total is **2,008 years.** Abraham is thought to have lived around 2000 B.C. or about four millennia ago. Near the close of the 20th century, we are at the end of about 6,000 years since Adam. [It was in Noah's 600th year that God's judgment came upon mankind (Genesis 7:6, 11)]. Thus the year 4009 B.C. is arbitrarily chosen as the year of the creation of Adam, since there is no zero-year between 1 B.C. and 1 A.D.

The Lineage from Adam to Jacob

(Genesis 5:3–32; 9:28; 11:10–12:4; 21:5; 25:26).

Adam		if Adam was created in the year	4009 B.C.
Adam	age 130	at birth of Seth	3879 B.C.
Seth	age 105	at birth of Enosh	3774 B.C.
Enosh	age 90	at birth of Kenan	3684 B.C.
Kenan	age 70	at birth of Mahalalel	3614 B.C.
Mahalalel	age 65	at birth of Jared	3549 B.C.
Jared	age 162	at birth of Enoch	3387 B.C.
Enoch	age 65	at birth of Methuselah	3322 B.C.
Methuselah	age 187	at birth of Lamech	3135 B.C.

Lamech	age 182	at birth of Noah	2953 B.C.
Noah	age 502	at birth of Shem	2451 B.C.
Noah	age 600	at Flood	2353 B.C.
Shem	age 98	at Flood	
Shem	age 100	at birth of Arphaxad	2351 B.C.
Arphaxad**	age 35	at birth of Shelah	2316 B.C.
Shelah	age 30	at birth of Eber	2286 B.C.
Eber	age 34	at birth of Peleg	2252 B.C.

Peleg ("division"): In Peleg's lifetime, the earth was divided.

Peleg	age 30	at birth of Reu	2222 B.C.
Reu	age 32	at birth of Serug	2190 B.C.
Serug	age 30	at birth of Nahor	2160 B.C.
Nahor	age 29	at birth of Terah	2131 B.C.
Terah***	age 130	at birth of Abram (Abraham)	2001 B.C.
	2,008 years		
Abraham	age 100	at birth of Isaac	1901 B.C.
Isaac	age 60	at birth of Jacob	1841 B.C.

** There is mention of a Cainan, son of Arphaxad (Luke 3:36). However, he is not listed as a son of Arphaxad in Genesis 10:24 or 11:12f .

*** Terah was 130 at the birth of his son, Abram, because Abram was 75 when his father died at 205 years of age (Genesis 11:26, 32; 12:4; Acts 7:2–4).

Thus, the seventh millennia from Adam starts with the 21st century.

On the Fifth "Day"—God Does Not Derive Fruit from His "Fig Tree," Israel, until the Fifth Day (Leviticus 19:25).

Another law God gave Moses for the Israelites was upon entering Canaan and planting any kind of fruit tree, they could not eat its fruit until the fifth year (Leviticus 19:23f). Perhaps, the Lord Himself will not derive fruit from Israel, the *"fig tree"* He planted c. 2000 B.C. until the beginning of the seventh millennium, or five millennia later.

c. 2001 B.C.   Birth of Abraham, father of Hebrew nation. The fifth "day" after this date is the 21st century.

On The Third "Day"—Restoration for Nation of Israel

30 to 70 A.D.   Moral disintegration of nation really began in 30 A.D., 40 years before the destruction of the Second Temple (see p. 20f).

21st Century   Start of third "day" (Hosea 6:2) since the birth of Christ.

For other examples of the importance of the third "day" (see p. 312).

The 430-Year Intervals in History

Strikingly identical time periods have been repeated three times in Jewish history before they were offered their land, their Messiah and their nation. *Each period lasted 430 years.* The three cases are as follows:

CASE I.   Physical Bondage of Israelites—Before They Were Offered the Promised Land

Intervals:

30 years	Hebrews lived with Joseph in Egypt (not in slavery).
400 years	Hebrews in slavery in Egypt.
1st Generation— to be offered the land	The Wilderness Period: The Exodus generation (those OVER 20 years old) spent a total of 40 years in the wilderness, where they died off, because of their refusal to enter the Promised Land.
2nd Generation— to be offered the land	The 2nd Generation, those UNDER 20 years old at the rejection, learned obedience and later entered the Land led by Joshua.

Dates for Intervals of Case I:

430 years:

c. *Nisan* 15, 1711 B.C.	Jacob and his family entered Egypt.
c. *Nisan* 15, 1281 B.C.	The Exodus of the Hebrew nation.

1st Generation: c. 1281-1241 B.C.	The Wilderness Period: The first generation (AS A NATION). Moses died in the last month of the 40th year (on Hebrew calendar).
2nd Generation: c. *Nisan* 10, 1241 B.C.	The Second Generation entered the Promised Land in the 1st month of the 41st year (on Hebrew calendar).

CASE II.   Spiritual Defection by the People of Israel— Before They Were Offered the Messiah

Intervals:

400 years	The "silent years" with no Jewish prophets.
30 years	Jews lived with Messiah on earth before His ministry begins.
1st Generation— to be offered the Messiah	The Wilderness Period: Messiah's generation died off or was dispersed from Israel within the forty years after their rejection of their Messiah.

Dates for Intervals of Case II:

430 Years:

c. 400 B.C. to 30 A.D.	Approximately 400 "silent years" with no word from the Lord and no prophets. Malachi, the last Old Testament prophet, denounced the wickedness of the priests and the people. The period ended with the crucifixion of Jesus.
1st Generation: 30-70 A.D.	The Wilderness Period: This generation, as a nation, rejected their spiritual birthright by "cutting off" their Messiah. The Talmud describes 40 years of specific signs of national deterioration prior to dispersion in 70 A.D. (see pp. 20, 21)
2nd Generation: 1949 A.D.	No 2nd Generation AS A NATION until Jews won independence in 1949.

CASE III.   Captivity of Land of Israel—Before Jewish Nationhood and Messiah

Intervals:

400 years	The Holy Land under Turkish Moslem domination.
30 years	The Holy Land under British rule.
2nd Generation— Will it be offered Messiah?	The Restoration Period: The Second Generation (AS A NATION) since dispersion (no nation between 70–1948/1949 A.D.).

Dates for Intervals of Case III:

430 Years:

1517–1917	400 years—Ottoman Turks control *Erez* Israel.
1917–1947	30 years—Balfour Declaration— British administration of Palestine. Partitioned by United Nations in 1947.
1948	Israel declared nationhood.
1949	Israel wins War of Independence.
2nd Generation: 1930–2010 (lifetime)	Messiah may deliver Israel and be accepted by the Jewish nation during the lifetime of people 19 years old in 1949 (Matthew 24:30-35). A lifespan is 70–80 years (Psalm 90:10).
	This 2nd Generation should enter the spiritual Promised Land, God's kingdom established on earth, led by *Yeshua* (Jesus).

It is significant that God told Abraham that his descendants would be enslaved and mistreated for 400 years in Egypt, which nation is understood to symbolize the world system (Genesis 15:13). If the real Messiah comes at the end of this century, the Jews would have been in the world about 4,000 years, beginning with their father, Abraham. Thus we see finite periods for the Jews, whether it be in the wilderness (40 years), in Egypt (400 years), or in the world (4,000 years).

The last interval could have been cut in half if the Jewish leaders had received their Messiah when He first presented Himself. It was not the Promised Land that the Jewish leaders were spurning in 30 A.D. They were the first Jewish generation to be offered direct access into the very presence of God through Jesus. The proof of this accessibility was the supernatural tearing in two from *"top to bottom"* of the thick Temple curtain, which separated the Holy of Holies from all but the Jewish High Priest. This rending happened at the precise moment Jesus gave up His Spirit on the cross and died (Matthew 27:51).

The presence of the Lord dwelt in the Holy of Holies, which hitherto, the people could never enter. From that point on, God's presence could be entered by all who accept the sacrifice of Jesus and repent. The High Priest entered the Holy of Holies once a year with the blood of innocent animals to atone for his sins and those of his nation. This was in accord with God's command to Moses (Leviticus 16).

Similarly, Jesus Christ entered the Holy of Holies in heaven after His resurrection. Once and for all time, He offered the sacrifice of His own blood for the sin of the human race. He paid our penalty. His atoning death and His righteousness will cover our sinful nature and our sins, so that we need not be eternally separated from the Lord.

Once the sacrifice of God's Son had been made, the blood of bulls and goats was no longer effective. Jesus' generation was the last one God allowed to offer Temple sacrifices. That generation completed its allotted 40 years (30–70 A.D.) in a spiritual wilderness. The Temple was destroyed and the nation dispersed until the 20th century.

Israel has been gathered together as a nation for over 40 years since the cease-fire in 1949. There appears to be an additional waiting period, which will include the seven years of transition. These last years will be ones of deepest purification in Israel and in all the world before Messiah comes.

It is noteworthy that the Dead Sea Scrolls of the Old Testament were discovered the very year that the United Nations partitioned Palestine (1947). The Scrolls symbolize the restoration of God's Word to His nation.

So too, the unearthing of the flask of precious anointing oil at Qumran in May 1988 looks ahead to the coming of the Holy Spirit upon Israel. Anointing oil symbolizes the Spirit throughout the Old Testament. God placed His Spirit upon His servants to enable them to lead and serve His people. The Word alone is not enough as the Holy Spirit must also come before Israel's restoration will be complete (cf. Zechariah 12:10; 13:1). Both the shewbread (the Word) and the *Menorah* (oil and candlestick) were present in the Holy Place of the Temple.

Their rescue from Egypt began their religious year with Passover in the spring (Exodus 12:2). Deliverance for the Jewish nation will come in the fall if mankind's High Priest comes on *Yom Kippur,* the most holy day of the Jewish year.

A Cycle of Twenty Units before Fruition

There exists a pattern of a 20-year waiting period before fruition came to the patriarchs of the first three Hebrew generations. This interval was repeated again after the Israelites became a nation and entered the Promised Land under Joshua. Messiah has been waiting 20 centuries for His offspring, the fruition of His life, to become apparent.

Yet it was the Lord's will to crush him and cause him to suffer. And though the Lord makes his life a guilt offering, he [Messiah] *will see his offspring and prolong his days.*
(Isaiah 53:10)

Here are the examples:

1. Isaac: The first generation: Isaac was 40 years old when he married Rebekah. She did not bear him progeny until he was age 60 (Genesis 25:20, 26).

2. Jacob: The second generation: Jacob worked for Laban outside of Israel in Haran for 20 years before he was free to return home with his family to the Promised Land (Genesis 31:38-41; 35:27).

3. Joseph: The third generation: Joseph was beloved by his father, but his brothers were jealous of him. They placed him in a pit and sold him off to the Gentiles (see p. 90).

Joseph entered Egypt at 17, joined Pharoah's service at 30 as second-in-command (Genesis 41:43, 46), and administered the storage of grain during the next seven years of plenty until the age of 37. Therefore, Joseph was in Egypt for 20 years ahead of his brothers, during which time God used him to prepare the way for them to receive great abundance. His brothers made their first trip to get food at the start of the famine in the following year (Genesis 42:1).

4. The first Hebrew generation to enter Canaan: It took Joshua and the Israelites seven years to conquer Canaan and part of the next seven-year period to distribute the land among the 12 tribes. The Israelites could not celebrate the seventh year of rest for the land until they had cultivated it for the first six years of the cycle (Leviticus 25:1–7). Therefore, they were in the land for 20 years, before they kept the first Sabbatic year of rest in the 21st year, as commanded by the Lord.[17]

---

17.   Grunfeld, p. 87.

The Lord went ahead of His people when they entered the Promised Land under Joshua. By how much distance did the Ark of the Covenant, the symbol of His Holy Presence, precede them? The nation was told to keep a distance of *"2,000 cubits by measure"* behind the priests carrying the Ark (Joshua 3:4, KJV). Jesus Christ will have gone ahead of His people by 2,000 years or 20 centuries if He returns at the dawning of the 21st century. *"He will see his offspring"* (Isaiah 53:10).

Note: This measure of 2,000 cubits is related to ordinary Jewish life, as it was the basis of their Sabbath day's journey. The rabbis concluded that the distance between the ark and the people on the march under Joshua was the same as that between the Tabernacle and the people's tents encamped close to it in the wilderness. (They would have had to have been able to walk that distance to attend Tabernacle worship on a Sabbath.)

Therefore, the rabbis set 2,000 cubits as the limit one could walk without breaking the Law against working on the Sabbath (Exodus 16:27ff).[18] The Sabbath day's journey (*tehum shabbat*) was still practiced in the time of Jesus (Acts 1:12).

God's 120 Years of Building—His Warning to Man

Then, there is the significant 120-year period in which Noah built the ark (Genesis 6:3). By way of actual evidence, seals under the Flood deposit and written records on tablets that refer to the Flood have been found at different sites by archaeologists, Dr. Langdon at Kish, Dr. Schmidt at Fara, and Dr. Wooley at Ur. One ancient Babylonian king wrote that "he loved to read Writings of the age before the Flood." Assurbanipal, founder of Ninevah's library, alluded to "inscriptions of the time before the Flood."[19]

18.   Orr, p. 2,634.
19.   Halley, p. 44.

A large vessel the size of Noah's ark has been seen on Mount Ararat in Turkey. A group of 500 men sent by the Russian Czar in 1916 and other expeditions have contributed descriptions, pictures, measurements, and chunks of hand-tooled hardwood. Though this wood may not necessarily belong to the ark, there are no such hardwood trees within 100 miles of the mountain.[20]

In 1972, the Earth Resources Satellite photographed Mount Ararat from an altitude of 570 miles. The photos are made from signals transmitted by the satellite and are stored in the Earth Resources Satellite library in Sioux Falls, South Dakota. Objects as small as 100 feet by 100 feet have been identified.

On the larger of the two peaks of Mount Ararat, there is a deep chasm called the Ahora Gorge. There is a long, narrow, rectangular formation in the gorge. Careful study shows this to be a ledge of about 1,000 feet long on which there is a lighter formation of about 600 feet in length. When the signals are analyzed by computer, this lighter object appears uniquely different from other substances on the mountain.[21]

As mentioned, Noah's generation could gauge the approach of God's coming judgment by the actual progress in Noah's construction of the ark of safety. Similarly, God has been stirring up the Jews to rebuild Zion as their *"refuge"* (Isaiah 14:32b). Petah Tikvah and Rosh Pinnah were the first villages to be established in the Holy Land and were both started in 1878. The new *Yishuv* (community) started evolving from 1880. Their "ark" will be complete when we see:

1.   The extension of Israel to its Biblical boundaries.

20.   Anderson film.
21.   *Ibid.*

2. The return of Jews from all nations to Israel (Ezekiel 39:28).

3. Israel's complete spiritual restoration.

Then they will know that I am the Lord their God, for though I sent them into exile among the nations, I will gather them to their own land, not leaving any behind.

(Ezekiel 39:28)

The 120 and Man's Government

The first mention of a subject in the Bible is of significance, because that is the initiation of the original pattern. Notice the timeline of the life of Moses, the first leader of the Israelite nation. There were three phases, each of which lasted precisely 40 years (cf. Deuteronomy 31:2).

Under the first three kings of Israel, the Holy Land was united. Each king reigned for 40 years: Saul (Acts 13:21), David (2 Samuel 5:4), and Solomon (1 Kings 11:42) with a total of 120 years.

40 years of Saul: This unrighteous ruler could symbolize the two millennial rule of pagans from Adam to Abraham.

40 years of David: The beloved Jewish king may represent the 20 centuries of the Hebrews.

40 years of Solomon: This king expanded international trade. His involvement with many foreign wives and rulers of the Gentile nations, may signify *"the time of the Gentiles"* for two millennia.

There are other examples of 120 as a pattern within government. The Jews required 120 members to form a ruling body which still applies in Israel's *Knesset* today. This stems from the *minyan,* the quorum of ten adult male Jews, which is the legal minimum requirement for communal prayer or public services. Ten would be multiplied by the 12 tribes.

The Medo-Persian King Darius appointed 120 governors to rule in his kingdom (Daniel 6:1). This was the specific number of Jewish Christians who assembled to receive the Holy Spirit and to choose a replacement for the apostle Judas (Acts 1:15). The number of priests that sounded the trumpets at the dedication of Solomon's Temple were 120 (2 Chronicles 5:12). Only the priests could sound the trumpets (Numbers 10:8).

Daniel's 69th *Shemittah* (Seven-Year Cycle): 25-32 A.D.

A master revelation in the Bible is Daniel's seven-year periods (*shemittot*). **As the Feasts of Israel imply the meaning and days of past and future events, Daniel's prophecy deals with intervals in history.**

To recapitulate, God exiled the Hebrews to one nation and later to all the nations. God's warning of this possibility is found in the first books of the Bible.

Then the Lord will scatter you among all nations, from one end of the earth to the other.
(Deuteronomy 28:64, cf. 4:27; Leviticus 26:33, 38)

The Israelites left Egypt **the very day** that Jacob had entered many years before. However, after the Exodus, there was a delay of 40 years and only those under 20 years old were allowed to enter the Promised Land.

(1) The Jews were punished by a 70-year exile in Babylon, after which only a remnant wanted to return.

(2) While Daniel was petitioning the Lord about ending the 70-year Babylonian exile, the prophet was told that **an even longer period was coming—70 times seven.** Between the 69th and the 70th seven-year intervals, there has been a long interruption.

The specific length of Jewish exile is not haphazard. It is underscored by **God's concern for their land as well**.

I will scatter you among the nations...The land will enjoy its sabbath years all the time that it lies desolate and you

*are in the country of your enemies…The land will have the
rest it did not have during the sabbaths you lived in it.*

(Leviticus 26:33f)

*The land enjoyed its sabbath rests; all the time of its deso-
lation it rested, until the seventy years were completed in
fulfillment of the word of the Lord spoken by Jeremiah.*

(2 Chronicles 36:21)

Daniel was told that a decree would go out to restore
Jerusalem. The Persian King Artaxerxes I (step-son of Jewish
Queen Esther) issued the only such edict to rebuild **the city** in
Nisan 445 B.C., the 20th year of his reign (Nehemiah 2:1). In the
"hind part" (*achar*) of the 69th *shemittah* from the date, Messiah
would be killed [69 x 7 = 483 years] (Daniel 9:24-27).

The Bible uses a year of 360 days **in prophecy**, instead of a
solar year of 365.2422 days. Therefore, 483 prophetic years =
476.07 solar years:

445 B.C. - 476 years = 31 A.D. + 1 year (as no "0" year
between 1 B.C. to 1 A.D.) = 32 A.D.

Thus, the 69th *shemittah* would have extended from 25 A.D. to
32 A.D.

Indeed, Messiah was killed in the latter part of the 69th
shemittah. Jesus was born before Herod the Great died on April 1,
4 B.C. and during *"the first census"* of Quirinius (Luke 2:2)
between 6 to 4 B.C.

Jesus was probably born in the fall since the Bethlehem shepherds were still tending their sheep in fields at night at His birth
(Luke 2:8). They were not in the shelter of the nearby caves, which
would be necessary by December 25. (The December date was
chosen by Pope Liberius in 354 A.D. to coincide with the Roman
festival to the sun.)

The Wise Men came to *worship* Jesus and were warned in a
dream not to go back to Herod. King Herod was *"furious and*

gave orders to kill all the boys in Bethlehem and its vicinity who were two years old and under in accordance with the time he had learned from the Magi" (Matthew 2:16).

John the Baptist prepared the way **right before** Messiah by preaching repentance *"in the 15th of the reign of Tiberius Caesar"* (Luke 3:1). This would have been in the year 25-26 A.D. since Tiberius had authority in the provinces beginning in 11 A.D. This placed the birth of Jesus in the fall of 5 B.C. With only one year between 1 B.C. and 1 A.D., Jesus would have started His ministry at age 30 in the fall of 26 A.D. Crucifixion came three-and-a-half years later in the spring at Passover in 30 A.D. "The majority of scholars choose A.D. 30" which would place Passover (*Nisan* 14) on Friday, April 7.[22]

It was also in 30 A.D. that the Jewish *Sanhedrin* (court) could no longer meet on the Temple Mount and were soon exiled from Jerusalem altogether. Other disturbing signs started occurring in the Temple in the same year. They continued until its destruction in 70 A.D. (*Talmud: Shabbath* 15a; *Yoma* 39 a, b; 67a, 68b—see p. 20f).

The Long Interval until the 70th *Shemittah*

Not only does Daniel identify the *shemittah* in which Messiah would be killed. He also makes it possible to determine that the end of the 69th *shemittah* is in 32 A.D. **Forty 49-year cycles (1,960 solar years) have passed since 32 A.D.**

[As stated, 49 solar years is a complete period in which the sun and moon return nearly to their original positions relative to each other, with an error of only 32 hours—see p. 197].

Forty represents completion and full testing in the Bible. [Four of the many examples are: the Flood waters increased for 40 days.

22.   Meier, p. 402; quoting Blinzler, p. 431.

Twice Moses spent 40 days on Mount Sinai receiving the Law. Jesus was tempted 40 days in the wilderness. The gestation period for a baby is 40 weeks. Following the birth of a son, a Jewess had to wait 40 days before offering a sacrifice for her purification in the Temple (Leviticus 12:1-8; Luke 2:22). Forty may symbolize the duration of 40 centuries of full formation and testing of the Jewish nation as well.]

Maybe the Lord will take the Jews out of the spiritual wilderness following these 40 cycles of 49 years each, just as He did out of the physical wasteland of Sinai after 40 years.

However, before release and restoration, God will first: (1) awaken the world; (2) give humanity one last call to repent and come to Him; (3) remove His people; (4) take the restraint off wickedness so that it will reveal its true nature; and (5) punish evil. (Deceived or uncommitted people will have the maximum opportunity to make an informed choice.)

All this must happen before the world is ready to receive Messiah. Thus, the 70th *shemittah* will be an earth-shaking time of transition.

Chapter Twelve

GOD'S "APPOINTED FEASTS"

These are my appointed feasts.   (Leviticus: 23)

The Seven Feasts of Israel—God's Schedule

There is a correlation between the Seven Feasts of Israel and prophetic events. Several authors point out that the meaning behind the first four feasts has been brought to fruition by a major Bible event on the exact day of each of these feasts (Buksbazen; Fuchs; Glaser; Larkin; Ritchie; Levitt, *The Seven Feasts of Israel*).

It seems logical that the Lord will consummate the last three with the same degree of precision. By considering the clear significance of the last three Feasts, one can gain insight into the way these "appointed times" may be fulfilled in the future.

God's time frame is embedded in His handiwork like a seal. Events must conform to His timing which may be viewed in the:

   I. Annual Jewish religious calendar
  II. Human development in the womb

III. Major events in pre-Mosaic, Jewish, and Christian history

IV. Agricultural year of Israel (see p. 160f)

Only God could design and execute such an all-encompassing master plan.

I. Annual Jewish Religious Feasts

The Biblical order of Jehovah's Feasts is Passover, Unleavened Bread, Firstfruits, Pentecost, Trumpets, Day of Atonement and Tabernacles. They cluster around the three times at which Jewish men had an appointment to appear before the Lord in Jerusalem (Exodus 23:14ff). Originally, all Jewish men were called to be Jehovah's priests, not only the Levites (Exodus 19:6). The three occasions were: (1) the week of Unleavened Bread; (2) Pentecost; and (3) the seven-day Feast of Tabernacles or Ingathering.

According to the Bible, the Jewish religious calendar started in the spring with *Nisan* as the first month (Exodus 12:2; 23:15b). The first four feasts encompass 52 days, followed by a long, dry summer. The last three feasts in the fall cover 22 days during the seventh Biblical month, *Tishri* (Chart 2, p. 326f).

II. Human Gestation and the Feasts

We see that each person is under the time frame of the seven feasts while he is being formed in the womb.

The average pregnancy is 280 days, and it is calculated from the first day of the last menstrual cycle before conception. (Zola Levitt offers these correlations in *The Seven Feasts of Israel*, pp. 21–31):

1. Passover—is on "the 14th day of the first month"—*Nisan* 14 (Leviticus 23:5). The angel of death passed over the Jewish homes that had the blood of the lamb on them, thus granting life to those inside.

The appearance of the egg is on the 14th day of the first month of pregnancy. Of course, the egg brings new life.

2. Unleavened Bread - begins on the 15th day of the first month - *Nisan* 15 (Leviticus 23:6).

The fertilization of the egg must occur within 24 hours, therefore by the 15th day.

3. Firstfruits is on the Sunday that falls during the week of Unleavened Bread (*Nisan* 15–21). Firstfruits celebrates the spring planting (Leviticus 23:11). (See "Note" on next page.)

The fertilized egg takes anywhere from two to six days to travel down the Fallopian tube before it implants during the first week.

4. Pentecost - *Sivan* 6 - the 50th day after *Nisan* 16 (Leviticus 23:15ff).
   (1) On this day, Israelites were given the Law at Mount Sinai and were recognized as a nation henceforth.
   (2) The Jews who believed Jesus to be the Messiah received the Holy Spirit on Pentecost and became known as the Church.

The embryo becomes a recognizable human fetus 50 days after implantation.

5. The Feast of Trumpets is on the first day of seventh month, *Tishri* 1 (Leviticus 23:24). Though not fulfilled yet, this Feast speaks of our ability to hear.

The hearing of the child is fully developed by the first day of the seventh month. The baby can discriminate a sound now.

6. The Day of Atonement (*Tishri* 10) - The blood sacrifice was offered once a year in the Holy of Holies of the Temple to atone for the sins of Israel (Leviticus 23:27). "It is the blood that makes atonement for one's life" (Leviticus 17:11).

On the tenth day of the seventh month, the hemoglobin of the blood of the baby changes to prepare it to carry oxygen from the air after birth.

7. Feast of Tabernacles (*Tishri* 15) - is a reminder to the Jews of their continued dependence upon God's Spirit to guide them now, just as much as during the 40 years when they

lived in tabernacles (booths) in the wilderness and required His daily provision.

The completion of the lungs on the 15th of the seventh month starts the baby's safe period. If born now, the baby could exist outside the womb. After birth, the baby will not be able to survive without breath. (Wind, breath, and spirit are the same word, *"ruach,"* in Hebrew.)

Note: The Bible dictates that Firstfruits must fall on Sunday **and** on *Nisan* 16, but it is ignored by all. Why is this requirement so important?

Modern Judasim does not always connect Firstfruits with *Nisan* 16. Due to the luni-solar Jewish calendar, the numerical dates do not fall on the same day of the week each year. This presents a dilemna.

Firstfruits must fall on *"the day after the Sabbath"* (a Sunday), **but it is also 50 days before Pentecost (*Shavuot*)** (Leviticus 23:11, 15f). Since Pentecost is on *Sivan* 6, fifty days prior would place Firstfruits on *Nisan* 16.

As Sunday does not always coincide with the 16th, the rabbis chose to celebrate Firstfruits on the Sunday during the week of Unleavened Bread. Nevertheless, they begin to count the days until Pentecost from *Nisan* 16.

After the Church became separated from its Jewish roots and calendar, Easter (the day of Jesus' resurrection) was no longer set to fall on **either** *Nisan* 16 or Firstfruits.

Jesus was *"the firstfruits"* from the dead. His resurrection on Firstfruits, *Nisan* 16, was the new beginning for mankind on Sunday, the first day of the new week. And the Holy Spirit was sent 50 days after Jesus' resurrection to empower the Church. These divine events are the reason for these two Feasts and their precise timing.

Of course, Pentecost, *Shemini Azeret* (the day after Tabernacles) and *Hanukkah* also fall on or include eight days.

III. Pre-Mosaic, Jewish, and Christian Events and the First Four Feasts

Pre-Mosaic events: God recognized His first triad of Feasts on two separate occasions, **centuries before He gave Moses the seven Feasts at the birth of the Israelite nation!**

Occasion 1—The Timing of the Flood

In addition to the 120 years warning during the building of the ark, there was another signal of the coming judgment. It was the name of Noah's grandfather, "Methuselah." The latter's claim to fame is usually his longevity (969 years), the timing of his life. More important than this was **the timing of his death!** He lived until the year of the Flood, but died before it started. His name may be translated "In the full (mature) length of time, it will be sent." (This comes from *math, mathay, shalach,* and *shelach.*)

Noah was 600 years old before both his grandfather's demise and the start of the Flood (Genesis 7:6). Noah's birthday was on the first day of the first month, *Nisan* 1 (Genesis 8:13). (Methuselah must have died on or by *Nisan* 10, causing Noah to be in mourning for the usual 30 days.)

Had it not been for the death and the one-month postponement allowed for mourning (cf. Numbers 9:10ff), God would no doubt have called Noah and his family into the ark on the 10th of the first month (*Nisan* 10) rather than of the second month. We know that God closed the door to the ark on the 16th and began the Flood on the 17th (of the second month).

Thus, there is a connection between the dates of the Flood and the Feasts. For example, the setting apart of both the Passover lamb and Jesus as the Sacrifice also took place on *Nisan* 10.

Note: *Nisan* 10 has two opposite aspects:
(1) Noah and his family entered the ark of safety in the second month (after one month's delay): victory.
(2) The Israelites selected the Passover lamb to sacrifice for their sins: sacrifice.

(3) The Israelites entered the Promised Land under Joshua: victory.

(4) Jesus made a triumphal entry into Jerusalem and offered Himself to the Jewish nation as their King/Messiah, but was rejected: sacrifice.

Projected to occur on *Nisan* 10:

(5) God's two witnesses will be killed by the beast, the world dictator: sacrifice.

(6) The 144,000 men will enter heaven led by Jesus: victory.

(7) The beast will enter the Temple and will demand worship of his image there: sacrilege.

There emerges a vitally important precedent: God rescued His people and they entered a new environment on *Nisan* 16, or Firstfruits. We shall see if this will apply again in the future.

To summarize:

1. Noah *et al.* entered on the 10th and were safely shut inside the ark on the 16th. The Flood began on the 17th day of the second month (Genesis 7:11). There was probably a one-month postponement (cf. Numbers 9:10f) of the Flood due to Noah's mourning for his grandfather, Methuselah. The latter died in the year of the Flood.

2. Pharaoh and his army pursued the Israelites who were fleeing Egypt on *Nisan* 15 and 16. The Egyptians were destroyed at daybreak (Exodus 14:27f) on *Nisan* 17. If Pharaoh had not been killed by the third day, Moses would have been legally obligated to take the Hebrews back. [Moses' request, which Pharaoh finally granted, was to take a three-day journey to offer sacrifices to God (Exodus 3:18; 8:27; 12:31.] The Israelites escaped out of Egypt and through the Red Sea before dawn of the third day, *Nisan* 17th.

3. Joshua and the Israelites were no longer given manna from heaven on *Nisan* 16 as they had now passed over the Jordan and entered their new environment, the Promised Land (Joshua 5:12).

4. Jesus resurrected victorious over the power of death and entered the dimension of heaven by daybreak on *Nisan* 16.

Occasion 2—The Timing of Jacob's Entrance into Egypt and the Subsequent Departure of the Israelites

Jacob offered a sacrifice on *Nisan* 14 and went into Egypt on *Nisan* 15. It was *"430 years to the very day"* before the Israelites departed from Egypt under Moses on *Nisan* 15 (Exodus 12:41; cf. Genesis 46:1, 5; Exodus 12:17; Numbers 33:3).

Jewish and Christian Historic Events

Not only have the first four feasts been fulfilled for Israel but for the Church as well, by separate sets of historic events (see Chart 2, p. 325f).

IV. Israel's Crop Harvests (see p. 160f)

The Last Three Unfulfilled Feasts

The three fall Feasts of Jehovah were never celebrated by the Church, but have remained solely within Judaism over the long centuries. They will soon command world attention. No longer will they be *"a shadow of things to come"* (Colossians 2:16f, KJV). Their reality is found in Messiah. **It seems logical that they will inaugurate His arrival and the establishment of His kingdom on earth as the first four did originally.**

The Fifth Feast—THE AWAKENING

Rosh Hashanah - The Feast of Trumpets - *Tishri* 1
The Profound Call to Return to God (Leviticus 23:22–25)

Even though the major concept connected with the feast in modern Judaism is New Year's Day, the Biblical name for it is Trumpets. As implied, the sounding of the trumpet or ram's horn (*shofar*) is the matter of central importance. The long, stirring wail and staccato blasts on the *shofar* have varying meanings: an announcement of the Sabbath, a call to assemble, the summoning of troops, or a battle cry (Numbers 10:1ff). In addition, there is the special connotation of calling the dispersed Jews home to Israel.

And in that day a great trumpet will sound. Those who were perishing in Assyria and those who were exiled in Egypt will come and worship the Lord on the holy mountain in Jerusalem.   (Isaiah 27:13)

On this feast, the Mighty God may awaken Israel, the Church, and the entire world. He will gain the attention of all.

God speaks of sounding the trumpet on stupendous occasions. There was a very loud trumpet blast, *"which grew louder and louder"* when the Israelites received the Law at Mount Sinai. Fire, darkness, thunder, and lightning accompanied this blast (Exodus 19:16; 20:18; Hebrews 12:18). It was to be sounded at the start of the Jubilee year (Leviticus 25:9), at the accession of a new king (1 Kings 1:34, 39), and on the day of the Lord's arrival (Zephaniah 1:14, 16; Zechariah 9:14). All three will be the case on the day the Messiah appears.

When Jesus comes to catch up believers to meet Him in the air, *"the trumpet will sound"* (1 Corinthians 15:52). The seven angels who administer God's wrath on earth during the Great Tribulation will blow a trumpet before each judgment begins (Revelation 8 and 9). Messiah will also send forth His angels with a great *shofar* call to resurrect His righteous dead (Matthew 24:31).

The Jewish oral tradition associates this festival with three themes: **the anniversary of Creation, the day of Judgment, and the day to renew the bond between God and Israel.**[1] The first two are universal, while the last is national.

Jewish tradition also holds that Adam was created on *Tishri* 1 (*Sanhedrin,* 38b). The first word of the Bible is *"Bereshit"* (In the beginning) can be changed to *"Aleph b' Tishri"* (on the first of

---

1.   Winter, *The High Holy Days,* p. 9.

Tishri). It was assumed that all men would be held accountable and judged on the anniversary of their Creation, *Tishri* 1.[2]

The Jewish civil year begins with an annual reckoning, at which time the actions of the past year are evaluated by the Lord. On *Tishri* 1, the judgment is "written," but it does not become final until the Day of Atonement on the 10th. In the intervening Days of Awe, the Jews are to examine themselves, repent, and ask God for mercy.

The blast of the *shofar* reminds the Jews of God's faithfulness to Abraham, who was ready to sacrifice his son to God. Instead, the Lord provided a substitute sacrifice so that Isaac could go free. God supplied a ram caught in a thicket (Genesis 22). The thicket symbolizes the thorns and thistles which are evidence of God's curse upon the earth (Genesis 3:17f). Like Isaac, Israel will be delivered from certain death. We can go free for eternity if we accept the sacrifice that God has provided for us through the Lamb of God.

The Old Testament mentions three events occurring on *Tishri* 1. The first two are connected with rededication of the nation after returning from Babylonian exile. These are the rebuilding of the altar to God (Ezra 3:3–6) and the reading of the Law to the people, indicating renewal of the relationship between both parties (Nehemiah 8:2ff).

The third event concerns Gedaliah, the governor appointed by King Nebuchadnezzar over the Jewish remnant in Judah. The king of the Ammonites (Arabs) arranged for Ishmael of Judean royalty to murder the governor. Since Gedaliah would not heed a timely warning, he was killed (2 Kings 25:25; Jeremiah 41:1ff). (No date is stated in *Tishri;* therefore, it is understood to be the *Tishri* 1.)

As we have seen in the prophet Ezekiel (Ezekiel 38 and 39), some Arab nations and other countries will attempt to annihilate "Gedaliah" (Israel). If these nations execute their full-scale inva-

---

2.   *Vayikra Rabba* 29:1; Glaser and Glaser, *The Fall Feasts of Israel,* p. 45.

sion on the Day of Judgment, they will no doubt consider they have chosen a most appropriate day to bring destruction. (This would not be the first time Arab neighbors have attacked Israel on a holy day.) After these nations invade, they will encounter God's fury unabated. This Feast of Trumpets may well plunge man into the most climactic period of history.

> *Surely the Sovereign Lord does nothing without revealing his plan to his servants the prophets. The lion has roared— who will not fear? The Sovereign Lord has spoken—Who can but prophesy?* (Amos 3:7f)

God will sound an alert of the most grave and crucial magnitude. His full-scale deliverance of Israel will cause a worldwide awakening. Many will become interested in God's Word.

God will cause Israel to renew her affiliation with Him, Jehovah (Ezekiel 39:22). It will indeed be the Judgment Day for the invaders. The God of Jacob will have intervened in the affairs of men, piercing us to the core and bringing many to their moral senses. God will no longer seem cosmic, but acutely personal. The final spiritual renewal of the people of Israel and of the nations will have begun. They will see that the Bible is accurate in all details and is coming to pass speedily.

The Sixth Feast—MESSIAH AS HIGH PRIEST

Yom Kippur - The Day of Atonement - *Tishri* 10

The Return to Divine Favor in a Single Day (Leviticus 23:26–32; Zechariah 3:9; Romans 3:24–26; Hebrews 10:19–22).

The 10 days of repentance culminate on the holiest day of the year, *Yom Kippur. Kippur* (atone) comes from *kaphar,* which means to cover, pitch (as with tar), placate, or cancel. The *Rosh Hashanah* judgment is either changed or finalized on *Yom Kippur.* On this day God covers or forgives sins that are repented of and closes His books until the next year. It is a day of solemn fasting and self-examination.

These 10 days are the most important interval in man's spiritual year. The sages pointed out that the Hebrew letters of *"Rosh Hashanah* and *Yom Kippur"* are an acrostic for the verse: "I am my Beloved's and my Beloved is mine" (Song of Songs 7:10).[3]

Though the date is not specified in the Bible, traditionally it is thought that Moses ascended Mount Sinai the second time on *Elul* 1 and returned 40 days later on *Yom Kippur,* bearing the second set of stone tablets of the Law. Moses also brought down God's forgiveness for Israel's worship of the golden calf.[4] As with the Law, Messiah will be given the second time to the Jews. He will bring forgiveness for the nation with Him too (Zechariah 12:10; 13:1).

God taught reconciliation between Himself and His people via two powerful symbols, while the Temple was in existence (Leviticus 16). On *Yom Kippur,* two goats were chosen and lots were drawn, one *"for the Lord"* and one *"for azazel"* (scapegoat or goat of removal).

The first goat was sacrificed, and the High Priest sprinkled some of its blood on the mercy seat in the Holy of Holies, which he could only enter on *Yom Kippur.* Like that of Passover, this sacrifice of an innocent animal was vividly embedded in the Jewish psyche. They knew it was God's plan by which He would deliver them from their sins. Someone is always hurt by the sins that are committed in daily life.

After this sacrifice was accomplished, the High Priest placed his hands upon the second goat in front of the entire congregation. All their sins were symbolically transferred to its head, and it was led through the streets of Jerusalem. The people showed contempt for the sins it carried by hitting and spitting upon it. The scapegoat was then led into the wilderness and pushed over a cliff. The Sanhedrin also struck and spit upon Jesus before He was crucified (Matthew 26:67; Mark 14:65).

---

3.   Winter, *The High Holy Days,* p. 1.
4.   *Ibid.,* pp. 1, 60.

These two goats taught the dual work of Messiah: the goat *"for the Lord"* was sacrificed for our sinful nature and the goat *"for azazel"* for our sins. Sin causes alienation from God, each other, and self. It brings death. Jesus' atonement frees us from the power and guilt of our sinful nature. If we will receive it, He will forgive our sins.

> *I do not understand what I do...When I want to do good, evil is right there with me. For in my inner being, I delight in God's law; but I see another law at work in the members of my body, waging war against the law of my mind and making me a prisoner of the law of sin at work in my members. What a wretched man I am! Who will rescue me from this body of death? Thanks be to God—through Jesus Christ our Lord!*
> *So then, I myself in my mind am a slave to God's law, but in the sinful nature, a slave to the law of sin. Therefore, there is now no condemnation for those who are in Christ Jesus; because through Christ Jesus, the law of the Spirit of life set me free from the law of sin and death.*
> (Romans 7:15; 21–25; 8:1–2)

Even if God forgave our sins daily, we would still be under the power of our sinful nature if God did not release us from that as well.

> *You will...hurl our iniquities into the depths of the sea.*
> (Micah 7:19)

> *He* [Jesus] *was delivered over to death for our sins, and was raised to life for our justification.*   (Romans 4:25)

God will remove our sins from us as far as the east is from the west (Psalm 103:12). Jesus will cover us with His righteousness if we repent and turn to Him.

Why could not God have forgiven our sins and ended the matter there? He said from the start that partaking in sin would cause certain death (Genesis 2:17).

For the wages of sin is death.   (Romans 6:23)

Justice in His universe demands punishment of sin (Psalm 89:14). Nevertheless, the Lord's love and mercy caused Him to send a substitute to take our penalty. Thus, we are able to avoid eternal separation from Him in hell. **At the crucifixion of Jesus, God Almighty directed His wrath against man's sin upon His only Son, instead of on disobedient mankind.**

God made him who had no sin to be sin for us, so that in him we might become the righteousness of God.
                                        (2 Corinthians 5:21)

If we do not accept the garment of righteousness with which Messiah offers to cover our sinfulness, then we will encounter the Lord's judgment directly, without a mediator. Sinful man has an account that must be settled with a holy God. There are only two options available. Those who refuse the Lord's love, mercy and rescue will receive His justice. Finally, His cup of wrath will be poured out full force after His call to repent.

Knowing therefore, the terror of the Lord, we persuade men.   (2 Corinthians 5:11, KJV)

If Messiah returns on this most holy day of the year, the God from whom *"no secrets are hidden"* will seal His judgments written on *Rosh Hashanah.* On Passover, Jesus was the sacrifice. On *Yom Kippur,* He is our High Priest who presented the sacrifice of His own blood to His Father in heaven. His blood, applied to the doorposts of our heart, is God's provision to prevent our second death, eternal separation from God in the lake of fire (Revelation 20:14). This place of torment was prepared for the devil and his angels (Matthew 25:41).

Each year, the Jews waited for the High Priest, when he went into the Holy of Holies, to see if the sacrifice would be accepted. As no sacrifice has been offered on *Yom Kippur* since 69 A.D., how can the Jews be sure their sins are forgiven for any given year?

The life of a creature is in the blood, and I have given it to you to make atonement for yourselves on the altar. It is the blood that makes atonement for one's life.

(Leviticus 17:11)

The sacrifice on Passover was offered by the individual for his household. The sacrifice on the Day of Atonement was made by the High Priest for the forgiveness and return of all Israel to divine favor.

When Messiah appears this time from the Holy of Holies of heaven, there will be no doubt in anyone's mind that His blood sacrifice was accepted by His Father. Messiah's sacrifice must be accepted by an individual to be effectual.

Yom Kippur underscores the fact that the High Priest-Messiah has paid the price to deliver Israel and all of us from our sinful nature and has forgiven our sins. Judgment has been averted through the life of another. Jesus gained our acceptance and entrance into God's holy presence. Heaven is the ultimate Promised Land which God's children will inherit. Israel is the physical symbol of God's spiritual kingdom to come. Messiah will deliver Israel from her physical enemies as well.

The Seventh Feast—MESSIAH AS KING

Sukkot - The Feast of Tabernacles - *Tishri* 15–21
God Dwells with Men Again (Leviticus 23:33ff; John 7:2, 37).

It was not the duty of Jewish people to go up to the Temple for the fifth and sixth Feasts as it was for *Sukkot*. This is a thanksgiving for the harvest, hence the name, Feast of Ingathering.

During this week, the Jews live in *sukkot* (booths), rejoice before the Lord, and wave the *lulav* (palm branch—victory of the people) and *etrog* (citrus fruit—productivity of the land) (Leviticus 23:39ff).

A total of 70 bullocks were sacrificed over the seven days of the feast on behalf of the nations of the world. This anticipated the conversion of the Gentiles to the God of Israel and their gathering under His *shekinah* glory along with the Jewish people. Seventy nations are listed in Gensis 10.

The two traditional ceremonies of this feast at the time of Christ were the illumination of the Temple and the water drawing. The illumination was at the end of the first day. Four huge golden candlesticks (75 feet tall) were set up and lighted in the Temple Court of the Women. The Levitical musicians played many instruments, while the priests, Levites, leaders, and men of Israel danced all night. They praised God and held burning torches (*Sukkah* 5:3, 4). This was an attempt to depict the light or presence of God, without which all is pitch-black. Without the God of Israel, man is without hope in the world (Ephesians 2:12).

When the cock crowed at dawn, two priests started down from the Upper (Nicanor) Gate and walked eastward, through the Beautiful (eastern) Gate, sounding blasts on the *shofar* as they went. The two then turned towards the west and faced the Temple. The worshipers said a prayer to remind themselves of their ancestors who had wickedly bowed down to the sun and turned their backs on God's eternal light.[5]

Note: God's glory had filled the wilderness Tabernacle (Exodus 40:34f) and Solomon's Temple (1 Kings 8:11) from which His presence subsequently withdrew (Ezekiel 10:18f). Though Zerubbabel's Temple was dedicated, there was no indication that the glory descended upon it (Ezra 6:16ff). Instead:

---

5.   Edersheim, *The Temple: Its Ministry and Services,* p. 285.

...the Lord had filled them with joy...   (Ezra 6:22)

In Herod's rebuilt Second Temple, Jesus taught during this feast:

I am the light of the world. Whoever follows me will never walk in darkness, but will have the light of life.

(John 8:12)

His presence will finally return to the rededicated Third Temple (Ezekiel 43:4). After the millennium, there will be no more night, and the Lord God will provide the light (Revelation 22:5). The Holy City will shine forth with His glory, and its brilliance will be *"like that of a very precious jewel"* (Revelation 21:11).

On the last day of Tabernacles, the water-drawing ceremony took place. A priest descended to the pool of Siloam and filled a golden pitcher with water. After returning to the Temple, he poured it into a silver basin by the great altar and chanted the 12th chapter of Isaiah, the song of praise.

Although you were angry with me, your anger has turned away, and you have comforted me... With joy you will draw water from the wells of salvation. In that day you will say: Give thanks to the Lord, call on his name. Make known among the nations what he has done, and proclaim that his name is exalted.   (Isaiah 12:1ff)

With all Israel present, Jesus stood and invited them in a loud voice to drink of the living water He provides. By "standing," He is calling special attention to His message. He, as well as the other teachers, usually sat.

On the last and greatest day of the Feast (sukkot) *Jesus stood and said in a loud voice, "If anyone is thirsty, let him come to me and drink. Whoever believes in me, as the Scripture has said* [Isaiah 58:11], *streams of living water*

*will flow from within him." By this, he meant the Spirit,
whom those who believed in him were to receive. Up to that
time, the Spirit had not been given since Jesus had not yet
been glorified.*   (John 7:37ff)

Water overflowing and bringing life to barren areas is a
repeated theme. A river watered the garden and flowed from Eden
to bring life to other areas (Genesis 2:10). Water issued from the
side of Jesus at His death (John 19:34).

On that day [Messiah's arrival], *a fountain will be opened
to the house of David and the people of Jerusalem to
cleanse them from sin and impurity.*
(Zechariah 13:1; cf. Leviticus 16:30)

Life-giving water will come from the south side of the Temple
at Messiah's return. (Even today, underground water may be seen
running in Solomon's Quarries under part of the city of
Jerusalem.) It will empty into the Dead Sea and will cause that sea
to become fresh with all kinds of fish living there. Creatures will
be able to live wherever the river flows. All kinds of fruit trees will
grow on both banks of the river (Ezekiel 47:1–12; Joel 3:18).

In the New Jerusalem, there will also be a river of the water of
life which flows from the throne of God and of the Lamb. On each
side of the river will stand the fruit-bearing tree of life. Its leaves
are for the healing of the nations (Revelation 22:1f).

Sukkot looks backward as a memorial to the impermanent wilderness tabernacle or shelter (*sukkah*) in which the Israelites lived
after they left Egypt. These structures also remind us of our own
temporary physical bodies in which we live on earth. **This Feast
points toward the fact that Messiah will not only come to us
as High Priest (*Yom Kippur*), He will dwell with us as King in
the millennium and beyond.**

"Tabernacles" represents His inauguration as the rightful ruler
in His worldwide kingdom of both Jews and Gentiles. He is the
only King ever to be worthy of worship. His throne will be His

Temple in Jerusalem, where He will live among the Israelites forever (Ezekiel 43:7). Israel will be holy when His sanctuary is among them forever (Ezekiel 37:28).

Note: [As we have seen, the Syrian Antiochus Epiphanes took the Temple on Tabernacles. The evil Herod the Great, one of the last kings of Judea, chose *Yom Kippur,* 37 B.C., on which to capture Jerusalem. He had himself inaugurated immediately after on Tabernacles when all the people would be in the city for the Feast.[6]

Since Satan counterfeits God's plan in order to deceive, Tabernacles would be the appropriate day for the false king/ messiah's inauguration as well.]

The Prince of Peace will make a *"covenant of peace"* with Israel (Ezekiel 37:26ff). Peace can only radiate out to the world at large after it resides in Jerusalem. Israel will truly be able to rejoice after they receive God's redemption from the sin nature and forgiveness of their sins through their Messiah. The Gentiles will celebrate this Feast as well:

> *Then the survivors from all the nations that have attacked Jerusalem will go up year after year to worship the King, the Lord Almighty, and to celebrate the Feast of Tabernacles. If any of the people of the earth do not go up to Jerusalem to worship the King, the Lord Almighty, they will have no rain...This will be the punishment of Egypt and the punishment of all the nations that do not go up to celebrate the Feast of Tabernacles.*
> (Zechariah 14:16ff; cf. 1 Kings 8:35)

> *In that day, the Root of Jesse will stand as a banner for the peoples. The nations will rally to him and his place of rest will be glorious.*   (Isaiah 11:10)

---

6.   Josephus, p. 336.

Passover and Tabernacles are the only two Feasts mentioned in Jewish millennial worship (Ezekiel 45:21–25; Zechariah 14:16). They represent the beginning and the end of God's redemption.

At the transfiguration of Jesus, shortly before the crucifixion, Peter wanted to prolong the visit of Moses and Elijah with Jesus in His glorified state. Peter zealously offered to build three tabernacles, ignoring the suffering that Jesus had said would soon follow. However impulsive Peter's suggestion was, he had experienced a foretaste of the glorified Christ among men and desired to remain there. It was a supremely satisfying moment.

He [Jesus] *took Peter, John, and James with him and went up onto a mountain to pray. As he was praying, the appearance of his face changed, and his clothes became as bright as a flash of lightning. Two men, Moses and Elijah appeared in glorious splendor, talking with Jesus…they spoke about his departure, which he was about to bring to fulfillment at Jerusalem…As the men were leaving Jesus, Peter said to him, "Master, it is good for us to be here. Let us put up three shelters—one for you, one for Moses and one for Elijah."*

(Luke 9:28ff; Matthew 17:1ff; Mark 9:2f)

When Jesus returns, the seventh redemptive name of the Lord will be fulfilled in Jerusalem. *Jehovah-Shammah, "THE LORD IS THERE"* (Ezekiel 48:35).

In summary, these remarkable Feasts take us into the presence of our Creator. The LORD commanded the men of Israel to apprear before Him at the three annual harvests: Unleavened Bread, Pentecost and Tabernacles (Exodus 23: 14ff).

Those who accept the blood of *the New covenant* are received into the presence of the God of Israel also (Jeremiah 31: 34 repeated in Hebrews 8: 8-12). As noted, the harvests point to the three sets of people that God will remove from earth and bring to His throne in heaven (p. 161f).

Motivated by love, God calls us to Himself. He desires life on earth to lead us to spiritual reality...the temporal to reflect the eternal. The Feasts speak of the coming of the Law, the Holy Spirit and both advents of Messiah. The Feasts outline God's ONLY way to redeem mankind.

Jesus is calling us personally. There is no sin so great that He will not forgive us, but we must come and ask His forgiveness. Only a lack of understanding, sin or pride can hold us back. Respond while there is still time. Do not remain outside of His presence and love!

Chapter Thirteen

REVIEW OF DATES

He changes times and seasons.
He sets up kings and deposes them.   (Daniel 2:21)

Section One: Approximate Chronology of the Last 6,000 Years

Identifying dates helps us to see people and events of the past more clearly. The Bible is used exclusively to arrive at the intervals from Adam to the distribution of the Promised Land to the Hebrew nation under Joshua. **In other words, the Bible supplies the exact information necessary to form an unbroken chain of events from Adam to Israel's possession of their land.** Thereafter, history is the major source of the dates (see p. 12f). "C" (circa) is used to indicate an approximate date.

The first month of the Biblical calendar year starts with *Nisan* in the spring (Exodus 12:2). However, Moses also retained their civil year, which began in the fall with *Tishri*.[1]

If Adam (not the world) was created in 4009 B.C., then Abraham would have been born in 2001 B.C. since there are

---

1.   Josephus, p. 28.

2,008 years between these two men (see p. 215f). This meshes with the approximate time that archaeologist Albright and other sources have concluded that Abraham lived (see p. 12f). Thus, we begin with the reasonable, but arbitrary starting date of 4009 B.C. There is no zero year between 1 B.C. and 1 A.D.

God's plans run like a thread through history. The restoration of Israel and the Church from the 1880s onward are highlighted (pp. 303-306).

(From Adam to Jacob see Genesis 5:3–32; 9:28f; 11:10–12:4; 21:5; 25:26).

c. 4009 B.C.	Adam was created; lived to 930 years of age.
3879 B.C.	Seth was born; lived to 912 years of age.
3774 B.C.	Enosh was born; lived to 905 years of age.
3684 B.C.	Kenan was born; lived to 910 years of age.
3614 B.C.	Mahalalel was born; lived to 895 years of age.
3549 B.C.	Jared was born; lived to 962 years of age.
c. 3500 B.C.	The rise of civilization in Mesopotamia of the Tigris-Euphrates river valley.
3387 B.C.	Enoch was born; lived to 365 years of age.
3322 B.C.	Methusalah was born. He died in the year of the Flood; lived to 969 years of age.
c. 3200 B.C.	The rise of civilization in Egypt.
3135 B.C.	Lamech was born; lived to 777 years of age.
2953 B.C.	Noah was born on the first day of the first month (Gen. 8:13); lived to 950 years of age.
c. 2800–2400 B.C.	Supremacy of cities of the Sumerians in the lower Euphrates area.
c. 2500 B.C.	Rise of civilization in the Indus Valley (Pakistan).

2451 B.C.	Shem was born, lived to 600 years of age.
c. 2400 B.C.	The Semitic Akkadians rule area north of Sumer under Sargon I (the Great) and others.
1st month, Day 1, 2353 B.C.	Noah's 600th birthday (Gen. 7:6; 8:13).
1st month, 2353 B.C.	Methuselah died before the Flood. Noah would have mourned for his grandfather 30 days, as customary (Deut. 21:13).
2nd month, Day 10, 2353 B.C.	Noah and his family of seven entered the ark as God had commanded. Pairs of all creatures came to Noah (Gen. 7:1–11).
2nd month, Day 16, 2353 B.C.	THE FLOOD: Then, God closed the door to the ark at the end of the 7th day that Noah was on board (Gen. 7:4, 10, 16). This cut off escape from God's wrath for anyone else.
2nd month, Day 17, 2353 B.C.	The judgment by Flood began and the rain continued for 40 days (Gen. 7:11f).
1st month, Day 1, 2352 B.C.	Noah was 601 years old (Gen. 8:13). A new start.
2351 B.C.	Arphaxad was born; lived to 438 years of age.
2316 B.C.	Shelah was born; lived to 433 years of age.
2286 B.C.	Eber was born; lived to 464 years of age.
Post-Flood B.C.	Men built Tower of Babel in Shinar (Babylon/Iraq), probably in Peleg's lifetime.
2252 B.C.	Peleg was born; lived to 239 years of age.
2222 B.C.	Reu was born; lived to 239 years of age.
2190 B.C.	Serug was born; lived to 230 years of age.
2160 B.C.	Nahor was born; lived to 148 years of age.

2131 B.C.	Terah was born; lived to 205 years of age.
2001 B.C.	Abram was born 2,008 years after creation of Adam. (Derived by adding ages of each father in Biblical genealogy); lived to 175 years of age.
1926 B.C	Abram leaves Haran for Canaan at age 75 (Gen. 12:4).
1915 B.C.	Birth of Ishmael (Abram–age 86) (Gen. 17:24).
1901 B.C.	Birth of Isaac (Abraham–age 100) (Gen. 21:5).
c. 1900 B.C.	First Babylonian dynasties (north of Sumer).
1861 B.C.	Isaac (40 years old) married Rebekah (Gen. 25:20).
1841 B.C.	Birth of Jacob and Esau (Isaac–age 60) (Gen. 25:26).
1826 B.C.	Abraham dies at age 175 (Gen. 25:7).
1750 B.C.	Joseph was born (his father, Jacob–age 91) (Jacob was 130 and Joseph was 39 years old the year that Jacob entered Egypt.)
1733 B.C.	Joseph entered Egypt at age 17 (Gen. 37:2).
1721 B.C.	Isaac dies at age 180 (Gen. 35:28); Jacob is then 120 years old.
1720 B.C.	Joseph rose to power in Egypt under Pharaoh at 30 years old (Gen. 41:46).
c. 1720/1710–1550 B.C.	Hyksos ruled Egypt (Semitic invaders from Asia with horse and chariot).
1713 B.C.	End of seven years of abundance under Joseph (Gen. 41:47, 53f).
1712 B.C.	First year of famine–Joseph–age 38. Ten of his brothers went to Egypt (Gen. 42:1ff).

1711 B.C.	Second year of famine (Gen. 45:6). Joseph's brothers second trip to Egypt (Gen. 43:15). Joseph sent for his father (Gen. 45:18).
Nisan 14, 1711 B.C. (Day)	Jacob offered sacrifice to the God of Isaac at Beersheba (Gen. 46:1). This foreshadowed the first Passover, after which God would enable Moses and the Hebrew nation to leave Egypt centuries later.
Nisan 15 (Night)	God reaffirmed His covenant with Jacob in a vision (Gen. 46:2ff).
Nisan 15, 1711 B.C. (Day)	JACOB AND *"ALL"* HIS FAMILY ENTERED EGYPT on *Nisan* 15 because Israelites left that country 430 years later, *"to the very day"* (Ex. 12:41, 51; cf. Gen. 46:5–27). Jacob was 130 years old upon entry (Gen. 47:28).
1694 B.C.	Jacob died in Egypt at age 147 (Gen. 47:28).
1640 B.C.	Joseph died in Egypt at 110 years (Gen. 50:26).
1364 B.C.	Birth of Aaron, Moses' brother. (Both Aaron and Moses died in the same year: Aaron at 123 and Moses at 120 years of age—Num. 33:38f; Deut. 34:7.)
1361 B.C.	Birth of Moses. Moses was born when Jews had spent 350 years in Egypt.
1361–1321 B.C.	Moses was a Prince in Egypt for 40 years (Acts 7:23). He then fled from Egypt.
1321–1281 B.C.	He was a shepherd in Midian for 40 years (Acts 7:30). Moses was 80 at the Israelite Exodus from Egypt (Ex. 7:7) after they had spent 430 years there (1711 B.C. - 430 years = Exodus at 1281 B.C.).
c. 1309–1290 B.C.	Seti I was Pharaoh of Egypt.
c. 1290–1216 B.C.	Rameses II (Ex. 1:11, 12:37; Num. 33:3, 5), Merneptah, and others.

1281–1241 B.C.	Moses was leader of Israel for 40 years (Acts 7:36).
Nisan 14, 1281 B.C.	First Passover was celebrated.
Nisan 15, 1281 B.C. (March–April).	THE EXODUS: 430 years after the very day Jacob and his family entered Egypt, the Hebrew nation set out from Ramses. This included 603,550 fighting men over age 20 (not counting Levites, women, children, and Gentiles) (Num. 33:3; Ex. 12:17; Lev. 23:6). They took the bones of Joseph and escaped through the parting of the Red Sea.
Nisan 17, 1281 B.C.	Egyptian Pharaoh and troops perished in Red Sea on the third day.
Sivan 1, 1281 B.C. (May–June)	Israelites arrived and camped at the foot of Mt. Sinai (Ex. 19:1f).
Sivan 2, 1281 B.C.	Moses ascended Mt. Sinai to hear God (Ex. 19:3).
Sivan 3, 1281 B.C.	Moses returned and summoned the elders (Ex. 19:7).
Sivan 4, 1281 B.C.	Moses reascended Mt. Sinai with their answer. He descended (Ex. 19:8b).
Sivan 4 and 5, 1281 B.C.	Moses consecrated the people, and told them to be ready on the third day (Ex. 19:14f).
Sivan 6, 1281 B.C.	God came down to Moses and Israelites on the third day (Ex. 19:16ff).
Sivan 6, 1281 B.C. *Shavuot* or Pentecost	God spoke the TEN COMMANDMENTS to them at Mt. Sinai (Ex. 20:1ff). Birth of the Hebrew nation upon receiving the Law. After 40 days on the mountain with God, Moses returned with the Ten Commandments on two tablets. He broke these, as Israelites worshiped Golden Calf. Three thousand souls died because of disobedience (Ex. 24:3, 18; 32:19ff).
Later that year	Moses later went back upon the mountain for another 40 days and returned

	with a second set of tablets and God's forgiveness. Jewish tradition says his second return was on *Yom Kippur* (Winter, *The High Holy Days*, p. 60).
Nisan 1, 1280 B.C.	Wilderness Tabernacle set up under Moses' direction (Ex. 40:17).
Av 9, 1280 B.C.	Israelites refused to enter Promised Land after leaving Egypt. (Date is derived from passage of time in Num. 1:1–14:1).
***Av* 9, 1280 B.C.**	**(1) God decreed that this generation would never enter His land.**
Av 1, 1241 B.C.	Death of Aaron on Mt. Hor at age 123 (Num. 20:27f; 33:38f). Israel mourns for 30 days (Num. 20:29).
Adar 1241 B.C.	Moses died on Mt. Nebo at 120 years of age in last month of 40th year (Deut. 34:7). (Possibly on *Adar* 1). The Lord buried him in a valley opposite Beth Peor in Moab (Deut. 34:6). Israel mourned for 30 days (Deut. 34:8).
Nisan 7, 1241 B.C.	The Israelites camped on east bank of Jordan River. God told Joshua to have the people prepare to enter the Promised Land in 3 days (Josh. 1:11). Joshua sent out two spies who were gone for three days (Josh. 2).
Nisan 10, 1241 B.C.	ENTERED PROMISED LAND: Spies returned to Joshua, who assumed full command. ISRAELITES CROSSED JORDAN with ark leading the way by 2,000 cubits (Josh. 4:19; 3:4). Israelites were circumcised at Gilgal (Josh. 5:8).
Nisan 14, 1241 B.C.	They celebrated Passover at Gilgal (Josh. 5:10).
Nisan 15, 1241 B.C.	Israel ate produce of the land for first time.
Nisan 16, 1241 B.C.	The manna from heaven stopped, as they were now living off their new land (Josh. 5:12).

Nisan 22, 1241 B.C.	Israelites took Jericho on seventh day.
1241–1234 B.C.	First seven years for Hebrews to conquer the land. Caleb was 40 when sent by Moses to explore Canaan (Josh. 14:7) just prior to their refusal to enter Promised Land on *Av* 9, 1280 B.C. Thirty-eight years and seven months later, they finally entered land. Since Caleb was about 85 years old when the land distribution began (Josh. 14:10), it took about 7 years to conquer the land under Joshua.
1234–1227 B.C.	About seven years to distribute the land.
1220 B.C.	After the Israelites had cultivated the land for an entire six-year period, the first sabbatical year was celebrated in the 21st year after they entered the Holy Land (Grunfeld, p. 88).
From Joshua to the Monarchy	THE JUDGES—God used 12 consecutive Judges to rule Israel. There were recurring cycles of falling away from God, oppression by other nations, crying out to God, and God raising up a deliverer (Judg. 3:7–16:31).
The Monarchy	UNITED KINGDOM under Saul, David and Solomon. (*The NIV Study Bible* Frontispiece states that their three reigns are historically verifiable dates).
1050 B.C.	Saul anointed as king, reigned 40 years (Acts 13:21).
1040 B.C.	Birth of David.
1010 B.C.	Death of Saul—David (age 30) reigned over Judah for over seven years from Hebron (2 Sam. 5:5).
1003 B.C.	Start of David's rule over all 12 Tribes and capture of Jerusalem at age 37 (2 Sam. 5:5).
970 B.C.	End of David's 40-year reign (2 Sam. 5:4; 1 Kin. 2:10, 11).
970 B.C.	Start of Solomon's reign (1 Kin. 11:42).

Iyyar (Ziv) 2 967/966 B.C.	First Temple was started *"in the fourth year of Solomon's reign"* in *"the 480th year"* after the Exodus (1 Kin. 6:1; 2 Chr. 3:2). It is thought that the number, "480," is a representative one, referring to the 12 generations of Judges and High Priests that extended from Aaron to Zadok's son in Solomon's day (1 Chr. 6:50–53; 6:3–8). These 12 were multiplied by 40, the conventional number of years for a generation (12 x 40 = 480). It was of tremendous importance to legitimize the lineage of Zadok, as he was the only authorized High Priest of the Temple from Solomon's time on (1 Kin. 2:27, 35; 1 Chr. 29:22). The 315 years between the Exodus in 1281 B.C. and 966 B.C. were more likely the number of actual years after the Exodus until the Temple was started.
c. *Heshvan* 959 B.C.	Completion of the Temple 7-1/2 years later (1 Kin. 6:38). Zadok was High Priest (1 Chr. 29:22).
c. *Tishri* 8–22. 958 B.C.	Dedication of the First Temple (1 Kin. 8:2ff.) 120 priests sounded trumpets (2 Chr. 5:12).
930 B.C.	End of Solomon's reign. DIVIDED KINGDOM
930 B.C.	Division of Holy Land into Israel in the north and Judah in the south.
883 B.C.	Assyrian Empire began to expand.
753 B.C.	Settlement of Rome and start of Roman Kingdom under Romulus (101 Rulers from Romulus to end of Empire in the West in 476 A.D.).
729–625 B.C.	Assyria controlled Babylon.
721 B.C.	FALL OF NORTHERN KINGDOM (ten tribes of Israel taken captive to Assyria) (2 Kin. 17:23). Some people of the ten

	tribes later returned to Israel under Cyrus (2 Chr. 36:23).
626–539 B.C.	BABYLONIAN EMPIRE.
606 B.C.	The overthrow of Zedekiah, the last Hebrew king. First captives taken from Judah to Babylon.
Av **10, 586 B.C.**	**(2) Burning of Temple. Jews deported to Babylon (Jer. 52:12f).**
539–330 B.C.	MEDO-PERSIAN EMPIRE. Darius, the Mede, and Cyrus, the Persian, conquered Babylon.
536 B.C.	RETURN TO ZION: Cyrus set the Jews free from Babylonian captivity. Zerubbabel led 42,360 Jews (Neh. 7:66) back to Zion after 70 years in Babylon (606–536 B.C.) (Ezra 2:2; Neh. 7:7). People from the 10 tribes returned also.
Tishri 536 B.C.	Jews built an altar and offered sacrifices (Ezra 3:1).
Iyyar 535 B.C.	Zerubbabel (governor), priests, and Levites began work on Second Temple in the same month Solomon started First Temple (Ezra 3:8; 1 Kin. 6:1).
520 B.C.	Zerubbabel and Jeshua were able to renew the work on Temple because of decree by Darius (Ezra 5 & 6).
Adar 3, 516 B.C.	Second Temple completed (Ezra 6:15) and dedicated before Passover (Ezra 6:16–19).
c. 500 B.C.	The Roman state (which would expel Jews from their land 5 centuries later) was a solid political entity with a republican form of government by that time. They grew increasingly stronger. By contrast, the Turkish Empire, which gained control of the Holy Land in 1517, began to lose power over the ensuing centuries (see p. 271).
485–465 B.C.	King Xerxes I (Ahasuerus) of Persia.

478 B.C.	Esther, a Jew, became Queen of Persia.
473 B.C.	Esther saved the Jews from massacre.
Adar 13, 473 B.C.	Jews victorious over their enemies, killing 75,000 of them (Esth. 9:16).
Adar 14, 473 B.C.	*Purim* (lots): The Jews rest and celebrate their victory (Esth. 9:17).
465–425 B.C.	Artaxerxes I (Son of Xerxes I and stepson of Esther) looked upon the Jews with favor.
	Jews in Judah allowed to practice their religion and rule themselves via High Priests.
Nisan 445 B.C.	Artaxerxes I issued decree to restore and rebuild Jerusalem in the first month of 20th year of his reign. He authorized Nehemiah to do so (Neh. 2:1f). The job took 49 years (Dan. 9:25).
Tishri 1, 445 B.C.	Ezra reads Book of the Law on *Rosh Hoshanah* (Neh. 8:2).
c. 400 B.C.	About 400 "silent years" with no prophetic voice from God speaking to the Jews after Malachi.
336–330 B.C.	Darius III (Codomanus).
334–331 B.C.	Alexander the Great conquered Persia, Egypt, Gaza, Judah, Tyre, and east to India.
331 B.C.	Fall of Persia at Battle of Arbela to Alexander—The Empire passed from Asia to Europe (Dan. 8:5–8, 21f).
330–164 B.C.	THE HELLENISTIC PERIOD in Judah. Alexander allowed Jews to observe their religion, exempted them from taxes during their sabbatical years, and granted them some privileges of Greek subjects (*The NIV Study Bible,* p. 1,430).
June 13, 323 B.C.	Death of Alexander the Great. His generals divided his domain into four: (Dan. 11:4) Ptolemy I in Egypt and

	North Africa; Seleucus I in Syria and Mesopotamia; Lysimachus in Thrace and Asia Minor; and Cassander in Macedon.
320 B.C.	Ptolemy I of Egypt—Conquered Jerusalem. The Ptolemies were tolerant of Judaism.
265 B.C.	Roman state controlled Italian peninsula.
250–150 B.C.	Septuagint (LXX)—First Greek translation of Old Testament by Jewish scholars in Egypt for Greek-speaking Jews.
219–217 B.C.	The Seleucid Antiochus III (of Syria) conquered most of Judah. The Syrian rulers were determined to Hellenize the Jews.
217 B.C.	Ptolemy IV defeated Antiochus III at Battle of Rafah and recovered Judah.
198 B.C.	Antiochus III defeated Egypt and gained Judah at Battle of Panias (Banias).
175–163 B.C.	Antiochus IV Epiphanes, King of Syria.
169 B.C.	He plundered Temple treasury and outlawed the practice of Judaism.
Tishri 15, 167 B.C.	Antiochus IV stopped the Temple sacrifices on the first day of *Sukkot*.
Kislev 25, 167 B.C.	Antiochus IV set up an altar to Zeus; sacrificed swine.
Kislev 25, 164 B.C.	Judah Maccabee ("the hammer") of the Hasmonean family and his men crushed the Syrians, captured the Temple, and rededicated it to God after 2,300 sacrifices (1,150 days) had been stopped (Dan. 8:14).
164–63 B.C.	THE JEWISH HASMONEAN (MACCABEAN) PERIOD in Judah.
163 B.C.	Antiochus IV died of illness in Tabae, Asia Minor.
142 B.C.	Hasmonean High Priest, Simeon, secured Jewish independence from

	Demetrius II of Syria (I Maccabees 13:42).
142–134 B.C.	Simeon ruled as High Priest.
63 B.C.	ROMAN PERIOD IN JUDAH: General Pompey captured Jerusalem and Temple and entered Holy of Holies (Josephus, p. 292). Judea was subject to Rome.
October 5, 37 B.C.	Herod the Great took Jerusalem on *Yom Kippur,* overthrowing Hasmonean family.
37– 4 B.C.	Herod ruled as king, subject to Rome.
27 B.C.– 476 A.D.	ROMAN EMPIRE IN WEST.
27–14 B.C.	Augustus (Octavianus)—first Roman Emperor. The Roman state grew from kingdom to republic to empire.
20/19 B.C.	Herod began rebuilding Second Temple in 18th year of his reign (Josephus, p. 334). Sanctuary of white marble with plates of gold was completed in 18 months. Courts and colonnades were finished eight years later, but project continued (*Ibid.,* p. 336).
8 B.C.	Dedication of Herod's rebuilt Second Temple on anniversary of his inauguration on *Sukkot* (Tabernacles—Josephus p. 336).
6–4 B.C.	Quirinius ordered census in Judea (Luke 2:1f).
6 B.C. c. *Kislev* 25 (November/December) *Hanukkah*—The Feast of Lights Rededication of Temple	Because of God's symbolic and exact ordering of sacred events to occur on the Feasts, Jesus may have been conceived in the Virgin Mary by the Holy Spirit on *Hanukkah,* which celebrates God's miracle of light in the Temple. At the conception of Jesus, the Light of the world was sent from heaven to earth. (Man's body is intended to be the Temple in which God's Spirit desires to

	dwell—1 Cor. 6:19.) Human gestation averages 280 days.
Nisan in 5 B.C.	Birth of John the Baptist, who was six months older than his cousin, Jesus.
5 B.C. c. *Tishri* 10 September/October	BIRTH OF JESUS CHRIST in Bethlehem where His family had to go for the census. Such a stupendous event as this birth must have been on *Tishri* 10—*Yom Kippur,* which would have been 285 days after conception. This birth fulfilled the *"sign"* God gave that a virgin would bear a Son and call Him *"Immanuel,"* (God with us) (Is. 7:14). The shepherds were watching over their flocks *"in the fields"* by night at His birth (Luke 2:8). This suggests that the weather was still warm enough that the flocks did not have to be kept in the winter shelter of the nearby caves. Pope Liberius of Rome (354 A.D.) ordered the people to celebrate Jesus' birth on Dec. 25, which was already the pagan Roman feast to the sun (p. 228).
April 1, 4 B.C.	Herod died in Jericho within 2 years or less of Jesus' birth (Matt 2:18).
Nisan in 26 A.D.	The brief ministry of John the Baptist (age 30) of calling people to repentance before Messiah's coming.
Tishri in 26 A.D.	Jesus was baptized, tempted and began His ministry at age 30 (Luke 3:21ff; 4:1-21; Is. 61:1f).
Nisan 10, 30 A.D. (Monday)	3½ years later, Jesus made His Triumphal Entry into Jerusalem on a donkey's colt (Zech. 9:9; Matt. 21:1ff; Mark 11:1ff; Luke 19:28ff; John 12:12ff). He offered Himself as the King/Messiah and was rejected by Jewish religious authorities. Jesus wept over the city, saying: *"If you had only known on this day what would bring you peace"* (Luke 19:42).

Jesus arrived from the village of Ephraim (John 11:54) *"six days before Passover"* (John 12:1). Since the Jews counted both the first and the last day, this would place His arrival in Bethany on Sunday, *Nisan* 9. He could not have arrived on Saturday, as Mosaic law restricted travel on the Sabbath. *"The next day"* (John 12:12), Monday, *Nisan* 10, would have been the day of the Triumphal Entry with Passover on Friday, *Nisan* 14.

Friday, *Nisan* 14, 30 A.D.
Passover
April 7

THE CRUCIFIXION OF JESUS CHRIST: A decree would be issued to rebuild Jerusalem (Dan. 9:24ff). Artaxerxes issued the only such decree in 445 B.C. (Neh. 2:1). In the "hind" part (*achar*) of 69 *shemittot* (seven-year periods) later, Messiah would be killed.

483 Biblical prophetic years (360 days each) equals 476.07 solar years (365.2422 days each). Since there is only 1 year from 1 B.C. to 1 A.D., the end of the 69th *shemittah* was 32 A.D. [445 B.C. - 476 years = 31 + 1 = 32 A.D.]

Messiah was crucified in 30 A.D. He hung on the cross from 9 a.m. to 3 p.m. and was taken down and place in a nearby tomb before sundown, the start of the Sabbath.

30 A.D. (Sunday, *Nisan* 16)

Jesus rose from the dead before dawn on *"the third day"* on Sunday, the Feast of Firstfruits, *Nisan* 16. Christ is the firstfruits from the dead (1 Cor. 15:20f). He appeared to the disciples for 40 days on earth.

30 A.D. (*Iyyar* 26)

Ascension of Jesus Christ to heaven on the 40th day after His resurrection.

30 A.D. (Sunday, *Sivan* 6)

Coming of the Holy Spirit: Birth of the Jewish Church at Jerusalem on Pentecost (*Shavuot*)—50 days after Jesus' resurrection (*Nisan* 16). The fire of the Holy Spirit fell upon the believers (Acts 1:15).

30–324 A.D.	Persecution of Christians by Rome.
32 A.D.	The last year of Daniel's 69th *shemittah* (7 years). 38 years later, the Jews were *"vomited"* from the land (Lev. 18:25).
37 A.D.	Birth of Joseph ben Matthias (Jewish historian-Flavius Josephus).
64 A.D.	Entire project of Herod's Temple Mount was completed two years before Jewish Revolt.
May 66–September 70 A.D.	The Jewish Revolt.
October 67 A.D.	Vespasian and his son, Titus, led Roman victory over Jews in Galilee.
April–September 70 A.D.	Siege of Jerusalem by Titus. Jews who believed the words of Jesus fled to Pella before 4 Roman legions (about 80,000 men) attacked the city. Simon bar Giora defended the city on north. John of Gischala protected the Temple area and Tower of Antonia. Romans crucified 500 Jews daily outside the city (Keller, p. 408f).
Av 9, 70 A.D.	**(3) The Temple was set afire by soldiers,** contrary to Titus' orders: Titus entered the "Holy Place" of the Temple and ordered his six commanders to save the Temple. The unrestrainable soldiers hoped for plunder, seeing all the gold on the building, and threw fire upon the Temple itself. This fulfills *"The people of the ruler who will come will destroy the city and the sanctuary"* (Dan. 9:26).
September 70 A.D.	Dispersion of Jews. Jerusalem under Tenth Fretensian Legion ("Legion XF").
70 A.D.	Sanhedrin established at Jabneh (Yavne or Jamnia).
70–324 A.D.	Jerusalem under Roman rule.

79–81 A.D.	Titus was Roman Emperor.
79 A.D.	Eruption of Mt. Vesuvius, near Rome, destroyed Pompeii and Herculaneum.
79 A.D.	Fire in Rome destroyed Pantheon, temple to Roman gods.
81 A.D.	Arch of Titus—Commemorated his victory over Jerusalem and depicted the captured Jews, Temple furnishings and the Menorah. The Arch still stands in Rome today.
90 A.D.	Rabbinic Council of Jabneh. Condemnation of heretics (*"minim"*), Jewish Christians.
c. 90 A.D.	The Revelation, the last book of the New Testament was written by John.
Av 9, 130 A.D.	**(4) Plowing of Jerusalem**—Emperor Hadrian ordered Governor Tineius Rufus to plow Jerusalem along the line of the projected walls of new city, "Aelia Capitolina" (*Jerusalem,* p. 38). This "plowing" fulfilled Micah 3:12; Jer. 26:18. To erase "Judea" from memory, Hadrian changed its name to "Palestine."
132–135 A.D.	Second Jewish Revolt—under Simeon Bar Kokhba. Jerusalem occupied for $3\frac{1}{2}$ years.
Av 9, 135 A.D.	**(5) Romans Crush the Second Revolt**—Last Jewish fortress at Betar fell. Bar Kokhba and his men were killed and Rabbi Akiva was executed.
c. 200–500 A.D.	The Jewish oral laws were put into writing and compiled into the Palestinian and the Babylonian Talmuds.
324–337 A.D.	Emperor Constantine Constantine granted the Christians freedom of religion. It became the official religion of the Roman Empire. Christianity became worldly as emphasis was no longer upon personal

	commitment to Jesus Christ by a persecuted minority. Jerusalem regained its name.
364 A.D.	Roman Empire was divided into the West (Rome) and the East (Constantinople).
476 A.D.	Fall of Roman Empire in West under Odoacar.
c. 500 A.D.	The final editing of the Babylonian Talmud.
525–565 A.D.	Justinian's Reign.
570?–632 A.D.	Mohammed, the founder of the Islamic religion.
July 22, 622 A.D.	Mohammed's flight (*hegira*) from Mecca to Medina. Start of Moslem Calendar.
638 A.D.	Jerusalem captured by Moslems.
638–1099 A.D.	**EARLY ARAB PERIOD** In Judea.
688–691 A.D.	Dome of Rock was built on Temple Mount.
706 A.D.	Al Aksa Mosque was built in stone.
732 A.D.	Moslems threatened Western Europe until defeated by Charles Martel at the Battle of Tours, outside Paris.
742–814 A.D.	Charlemagne—King of the Franks.
December 25, 800 A.D.	Charlemagne crowned "Holy Roman Emperor" by the Pope. First Germanic ruler to assume this title. Both men believed that if **the Roman Empire could be restored and united, there would be peace (Pax Romana)**. He extended civilization, maintained law and order, raised the standard of living, and unified people. His vast realm included most of the western part of the Roman Empire. "The empire he revived lasted in one form or another for one thousand years (800–1806)." His capital

was never at Rome, but at Aachen near the Rhine.

800–814 A.D.	Charlemagne's reign as Emperor.
962 A.D.	Otto of Germany crowned Holy Roman Emperor of Germany and Italy by the Pope.
962–1806 A.D.	"HOLY ROMAN EMPIRE," or The First *Reich* (empire or state), was under the German kings. Its yellow flag with a black eagle was flown until 1806. The eagle was the symbol of Roman power.

1000 A.D. (NOTE: All remaining dates are A.D.)

"Widespread fear of the End of the World and the Last Judgment at the end of first millennium...Spiritual center of Judaism moved from Mesopotamia to Spain" (Grun, p. 124f).

1054	Schism in Church between Russian Orthodox (East) and Roman Catholic (West) one millennium after Christ. (About midway through their 2,000 years, Israel divided into north and south, after the reign of Solomon).
1099–1187	CRUSADER PERIOD in Jerusalem.
1187	Saladin, Sultan of Egypt, captured Jerusalem from the Crusaders. Regained by Crusaders in 1229.
1244–1291	Khorezmians, Tartars, and Mongols overran Jerusalem.
Av 9 (July 18), 1290	**(6) King Edward I banished all Jews from England**. They had to leave by All Saints Day, October 31 (Croner, ed., p. 4).
1291–1517	MAMELUKE PERIOD: Sultans from Egypt provided Islamic rule over Jerusalem.
1347–1350	Black Death killed one quarter of European population.

1388	First complete English translation of the Bible (initiated by John Wycliffe).
c. 1440	Johannes Gutenberg invented printing with movable type. The first means of mass communication made the Bible available to the common man.
1453	Roman (Byzantine) Empire in the East fell to the Ottoman Empire.
January 2, 1492	Granada, the last Moslem fortress in Spain fell to the Spanish crown.
January 1492	Royal decision to expel the Spanish Jews and send Christopher Columbus on his expedition (according to first words of his journal).
March 31, 1492	Royal edict for expulsion of Spanish Jews was signed.
April 17, 1492	Ferdinand and Isabella signed contract with Columbus.
Av 9 (August 2), 1492	**(7) Expulsion of all Jews from Spain by midnight.** This was a seventh major Jewish disaster on *Av* 9.
August 2, 1492	Columbus's sailors boarded ship before midnight. It was illegal for a Jew to remain in Spain after the deadline (Weisenthal, p. 3).
August 3, 1492	Columbus set sail at dawn.
October 12 (*Tishri* 21), 1492	Columbus discovered New World on *Hoshana Rabbah*, the seventh day of *Succot*, the seventh Feast of the Lord. This is "the day when man's blessings for the coming year are finally decreed in heaven," according to Jewish tradition (Bridger, p. 211).
1496–97	Expulsion of Jews from Portugal.
1490s	Sultan opened Ottoman Empire to Jewish refugees from Spain and Portugal.
1500s	33 major explorers and discoveries.

1512–1520	Turkish Sultan Selim I reigned.
August 24, 1516	War between Ottoman Turks and Mameluke forces.
1517	Selim I defeated Mamelukes of Egypt and gained Egypt, Arabia, Palestine, and Syria.
1517–1917	OTTOMAN EMPIRE.
	Ottoman Turks ruled the Holy Land in which small minorities of Jews and Christians lived. Their empire grew progressively weaker, but was kept alive by Europe to counteract Russian extension of influence to the Mediterranean. (On the other hand, Rome grew in strength for five centuries before expelling the Jews—see p. 260).
October 31, 1517	Protestant Reformation of Church began in Germany when Martin Luther published his *Ninety-Five Theses,* which effectively divided the Church. He fought to restore the supreme authority of Scripture, reform Church practices, and bring back the truth that salvation is by God's grace and not by human works. Salvation must be accepted personally as a gift through the life, death and resurrection of Jesus Christ.
1520–1566	Suleiman I, the Magnificent (*al-Qanuni* —"the Law-giver"), son of Selim I, ruled the Ottoman Empire.
1537–1541	Suleiman restored Jerusalem's walls, gates, and fountains. The Jews rejected Suleiman's offer to rebuild the Temple. The Eastern (Golden) Gate, the only one that leads directly into the Temple area, was rebuilt and blocked off. The Bible said that this gate must remain shut. *"No one may enter through it...the Lord, the God of Israel, has entered through it"* (Ezek. 44:2).

1588	Defeat of Spanish Armada of 132 vessels by England's 32 ships opened world to English trade and colonization as Spain's leadership was destroyed.
Av 9, 1626	Birth of Shabbetai Zevi, a false messiah.
1654	Jews arrived in New Amsterdam, New York, and started a congregation.
December 4, 1655	English declared that there was no statute to exclude Jews from England.
1658	Jews started congregation at Newport, Rhode Island.
1665	In Smyrna, Shabbetai Zevi proclaimed himself Messiah. Messianic fervor spread throughout Jewish world.
Sivan 15 (June 18), 1666	Zevi set this date for the restoration of Israel.
September 5, 1666	Zevi converted to Islam.
1676	Death of Zevi.
1695	Jews settled in Charleston, South Carolina.
1720s	The Great Awakening—Religious revivals in American colonies. Leaders: J. Edwards, T. Frelinghuysen, G. Tennent, G. Whitefield.
July 4, 1776	United States Declaration of Independence.
1789–1799	French Revolution.
1799–1815	Napoleon Bonaparte ruled France.
August 1799	Rosetta Stone (c. 916 B.C.) found in Egypt by officer of Napoleon's engineering corps. Its trilingual inscription provided the key to decipher Egyptian demotic and hieroglyphic scripts by using its Hellenistic Greek.
1799 onward	Major findings in Biblical archaeology have been uncovered in the last two centuries.

1799	Napoleon invaded Palestine with the intention to establish a Jewish state there.
Beginning of 1800s	Interest by European powers in Middle East. Establishment of Consulates in Jerusalem and increased Christian activities there.
1806	End of Holy Roman Empire in Germany due to Napoleon's conquests.
1840	Jews gained right to a Chief Rabbi of Palestine with seat in Jerusalem. Sultan included the Jews in a type of religious bill of rights. Permission was given Jews to hold public worship. Synagogues were protected.
1841	Michael Solomon Alexander—First Anglican Bishop sent to Jerusalem. Alexander was also the first Hebrew-Christian bishop of Jerusalem since 135 A.D.
1849	Establishment of Christ Church, an Evangelical Protestant church, in Jerusalem on site of Herod's palace, the first large structure built in Jerusalem in 500 years. The presence of this church body challenged the religious status quo, causing a dramatic increase in Christian activities and foreign visitors. Turks were forced to propel Jerusalem into the 19th century.
Mid 1800s	European nations gained economic and political influence over much of Ottoman Empire.
1856	American Revival by the Holy Spirit.
1859–1860	The Welsh Revival in Christianity.
1859–1860	The Ulster Revival, Ireland.
1859	Charles Darwin's theory of evolution in his book, *The Origin of Species.*

1867	Last restriction of Jewish residence in Jerusalem was removed. Many Jews moved there.
November 17, 1869	Suez Canal opened.
1871–1918	The Second *Reich*—German Empire.
1877	Russia declared war on Turkey.
1878	Russia defeated Turkey; took Balkans in Treaty of San Stephano.
1878	Berlin Congress—European powers forced Russia to give back her gains, but Turkish Empire continued to lose territory.
1878	Establishment of *Petah Tikvah* in Judea and *Rosh Pinnah* in Galilee by religious Jews. These were the first Jewish villages in Palestine in our times.
1879	Eliezer Ben-Yehuda advocated a national rebirth in Palestine.
1880	RETURN TO ZION: The New *Yishuv* began in *Erez* (land of) Israel. This was the secular, nationalist community whose goal was to build an economy based on Jewish labor and agriculture. Prior to 1880, the Old *Yishuv* of mostly Orthodox Jews were opposed to all modern trends and depended on contributions from abroad (*halukkah*) to exist. Ottoman rule had opposed Jewish participation in economic life. About 12,000 Jews lived in Jerusalem then.
1881	Ben-Yehuda moved to *Erez* Israel and began to revive the Hebrew language.
1881–82	*Pogroms* in southern Russia hit about 100 Jewish communities. Massacres and arson became endemic.
1882	First *Aliyah* (ascent)—Jewish immigration to Holy Land on a large scale.
1893	Term "Zionism" coined.

January 1895	The Dreyfus Affair—A French court martial accused the innocent Jewish Captain Dreyfus of high treason and Parisian mob rioted against him.
1895	Anti-Semitic riots and election of a mayor on an anti-Semitic platform in Vienna.
August 29, 1897	First World Zionist Congress in Basel, Switzerland, led by Dr. Theodor Herzl, the founder of Zionism.
1897	Armistice between Old and New *Yishuv* in Israel.
1900	World Zionist Congress met.
January 1, 1901	Modern Pentecostalism began with the outpouring of the Holy Spirit on Agnes Ozman in Bethel Bible School in Topeka, Kansas.
1902	World Zionist Congress met. Collapse of British offer of land in Sinai for the Jews.
1902, 1903, 1905, 1906	New wave of Russian *pogroms* against Jews.
1903	World Zionist Congress met. No agreement on British offer of Uganda as a place of refuge for Jews.
November 1903–1905	Welsh Revival led by Evan Roberts.
1904	World Zionist Congress met. Abandoned Uganda plan.
April 14, 1906–1909	Holy Spirit Revival led by William J. Seymour at Azusa Street in Los Angeles, California, started a worldwide Pentecostal movement.
August 1, 1914 (*Av 9*)	**Germany declared war on Russia (Av 9).**
1914–1918	WORLD WAR I.
March 1917	Czar Nicholas II of Russia overthrown. (Czar and Kaiser mean "Caesar" in Russian and German.)
October 31, 1917	British offensive took Beersheba, Gaza, and Jaffa from Turks.

November 2, 1917	Balfour Declaration favoring "a National Home for the Jewish people" in Palestine.
November 7, 1917	Start of Communism in Russia with the Bolshevik Revolution.
November 9, 1918	Kaiser Wilhelm II fled. Germany became a republic.
December 10, 1917 *Hanukkah, Kislev* 25	English General Allenby took Jerusalem from Turks without firing a shot, ending 400 years of Turkish rule in Palestine.
1917–1947	BRITISH PERIOD in Palestine.
1920	League of Nations established.
1920	England received the British Mandate of Palestine from League of Nations.
April 24, 1920	Balfour Declaration approved by the Allies' Conference at San Remo.
1921	Winston Churchill, British Secretary of the Colonies, signed 77.6% of Palestine over to Arabs, creating Transjordan (see p. 39). This was the first partition of Palestine.
July 1922	The League of Nations confirmed Transjordan's boundaries. President Woodrow Wilson, a Christian Bible student, protested this arbitrary partition, as he was concerned about Biblical boundaries.
July 24, 1922	League of Nations incorporated the Balfour Declaration into British Mandate of Palestine.
1927	Recognition of future state of Israel by a Protestant denomination in their creed: "This millennial reign will bring the salvation of national Israel" (General Council of Assemblies of God, Constitution Article V-Item 14 on "The Millennial Reign of Christ").

1928	British recognized Transjordan as independent state.
1933	*Humanist Manifesto I* signed.
January 30, 1933	Adolf Hitler made chancellor; consolidated his power within 6 months.
1934–1945	The Third *Reich*—German government under Hitler.
1935	Vast oil fields discovered in Saudi Arabia. It has larger oil reserves than any area of similar size in the world.
1936–1939	Major Arab uprisings in Palestine.
July 7, 1937	British Peel Commission: three-way partition plan and restriction on European Jews escaping to Palestine and on Jewish land purchases.
August 1937	Nazi reorganization of four concentration camps in Germany.
1938	About 30,000 Jews taken to German concentration camps.
1938	Pan-Arab Conference in Cairo adopted policy that all Arab states and communities would prevent development of Zionist state.
March 1938	Hitler annexed Austria.
July 1938	President Franklin D. Roosevelt organized a conference of 32 nations at Evian-les-Bains, France, to rescue Jews in the Third *Reich*. Most countries refused to help, which Hitler interpreted as approval of his "Final Solution" (killing all Jews).
November 9, 1938	Crystal Night (*Kristallnacht*)-Nazis looted and burned 119 Jewish synagogues and 7,500 shops in Germany, causing economic ruin for the Jews.
May 17, 1939	British MacDonald White Paper abandoned Peel Partition Plan and Balfour Declaration policy. The White

	Paper severely restricted Jewish immigration and land purchase in Palestine and left Jews in Europe to their fate.
September 1, 1939	German invasion of Poland.
1939–1945	WORLD WAR II.
1939–1945	THE HOLOCAUST: Six million Jews murdered by Nazis.
1940–1945	Palestinian Jews joined Allies to fight Nazis. Amin al-Husseini, the Islamic Mufti of Jerusalem, collaborated with the Nazis as proven at the 1946 Nuremberg trials. British refused immigration to Jewish survivors from Europe.
January 20, 1942	15 Nazis officials met at Wannsee, near Berlin, to map out the identification, transportation, and murder of every Jew in Europe.
May 8, 1945	V-E DAY—VICTORY IN EUROPE.
June 16, 1945	First test of the atomic bomb—White Sands, New Mexico.
September 2, 1945	V-J DAY—VICTORY OVER JAPAN. End of World War II.
1945	Many Jews immigrated to Palestine after the war.
October 24, 1945	Establishment of the United Nations, to which most nations belong.
1945	Arab League formed.
1946	Transjordan granted complete independence by Britain.
Spring 1947	Bedouins discovered Dead Sea Scrolls in Qumran caves.
April 1947	British government turned Palestine problem over to U.N.
May 1947	Special session of U.N. General Assembly convened to deal with Palestine. They appointed U.N. Special Committee on Palestine (UNSCOP) to study issue.

July 1947	British refused to allow the *"Exodus 1947"* to dock at Haifa with its survivors of Nazi death camps. This became a world-renowned symbol of Jewish need for a homeland.
Saturday, November 29, 1947	PALESTINE PARTITION PLAN gained a majority vote in United Nations. Israel was granted 16.1% of original 1920 British Mandate of Palestine, or the equivalent of one tenth of 1% of the total land of the 21 Arab nations. Arabs did not accept a Jewish state, and planned to take all of Palestine by force.
1948	National Council of Churches organized.
Friday, May 14, 1948	PROCLAMATION OF INDEPENDENCE OF ISRAEL. Government established.
12:01 a.m., May 15, 1948	British withdrew the last of their forces and government from Jerusalem.
Saturday, May 15, 1948	Armies of Egypt, Transjordan, Syria, Lebanon, Saudi Arabia, and Iraq attacked the new state. Eight months of warfare ensued. Israel's Provisional Government remained in Tel Aviv.
1948–1977	Labor Party in full control of government.
1948–1951	Mass immigration of Jews to Israel.
January 7, 1949	WAR OF INDEPENDENCE ended by cease-fire: Jerusalem was divided between Israel on the west and Jordan on the east. Arab League declared "a permanent state of war" against Israel.
1949–1967	Jordan denied Israeli access to Temple Mount in East Jerusalem.
May 14, 1949	Israel admitted to United Nations.
October 1, 1949	Communist government in China.
1949	Billy Graham's First Crusade.

1949	North Atlantic Treaty Organization (NATO) was formed to prevent Russia from taking over Western Europe. The Council of Europe was organized.
October 1949	Communists rule East Germany.
January 23, 1950	West Jerusalem was proclaimed the capital of Israel and seat of the Knesset.
April 1950	Transjordan changed its name to "Jordan" after annexing the West Bank. Only Britain and Pakistan recognized the annexation *de jure*.
1951	Six nations formulated European Coal and Steel Community (ECSC) (Precursor of the European Union—E.U.).
October 1956	WAR: Israel, supported by Britain and France, launched preemptive attack on Arab neighbors. Cease-fire came on November 5.
1957	Treaty of Rome. European Community's Parliament set up. Members to be voted to office by direct suffrage in the future. European Economic Community (EEC) and European Atomic Energy Community (Euratom) established.
1958	World Bible Conference in Jerusalem sponsored by Israeli government. Increasing emphasis on Jewish cultural and spiritual heritage.
1960s	Viet Nam demonstrations. "Hippie" generation. U.S. campuses abandoned many traditional restrictions on students.
November 14, 1960	Creation of Organization of Petroleum Exporting Countries (OPEC). After World War II, the world's need for oil became an issue in international politics. Important oil discoveries were made in Iran in 1908; Iraq in 1927; Saudi Arabia in 1935. The Middle East has about three-fifths of the world's oil resources.

1967	Spain repealed 1492-Edict of Expulsion of the Jews. Jews could now obtain legal recognition as a religious body in Spain.
Monday, June 5, 1967 (*Iyyar* 26)	SIX-DAY WAR began. Israel bombed airfield of Egypt, Syria, Jordan and Iraq. Jordan seized U.N. headquarters in Jerusalem and attacked Israel. (Jesus ascended on *Iyyar* 26, 30 A.D.)
Wednesday, June 7, 1967	JERUSALEM UNITED: Israel took Temple Mount and entire city.
Saturday, June 10, 1967	Cease-fire—Israel gained East Jerusalem with Temple Mount, West Bank, Gaza, Sinai, and Golan Heights.
1967	Israel united all of Jerusalem as their capital. Their claim is still unrecognized by the United Nations.
1967	The Soviet Union and Eastern European satellites, except Romania, severed diplomatic relations with Israel.
1967	Billy Graham first preached in the Communist countries of Eastern Europe.
1967 onward	Soviet propaganda was the main source of anti-Semitic material.
1967 onward	Archaeology now possible on Temple Mount and all Jerusalem.
1967	ECSC, EEC, Euratom merged to form European Union (E.U.).
1968	E.U. abolished all tariffs between members. Common tax on imported goods.
1968	Formation of the Club of Rome, an international body that seeks solutions to earth's problems. 100 leaders meet regularly.
1972	Euthanasia legalized in Holland.
1973	*Humanist Manifesto II.*
January 22, 1973	Supreme Court legalized abortion in United States in *Roe v. Wade.*

October 6 (*Tishri* 10), 1973	*YOM KIPPUR* WAR: Egyptians and Syrians attacked on two fronts.
November 11, 1973	Cease-fire signed on Armistice Day.
November 1973	Most African nations broke relations with Israel due to Arab oil concerns.
November 10, 1975	37th anniversary of "Crystal Night" (November 9, 1938)—United Nations passed a resolution condemning Zionism as a form of racism.
November 19, 1977	By visiting Jerusalem, Anwar Sadat acknowledged the Jewish state. His subsequent Peace Treaty with Israel prevented Egypt from joining other Arab nations to attack Jews. Without Egypt, the Arab neighbors did not invade Israel.
December 1977	Syria broke ties with Egypt.
1977–90	Coalition governments in Israel between liberal Labor Party and conservative Likud.
September 17, 1978	Camp David Peace Accords were signed by Begin and Sadat and witnessed by Carter.
March 26, 1979	Israel signed a Peace Treaty with Egypt and returned Sinai to Egypt. The boundary line was east of El Arish.
1979	Ayatollah Khomeini came to power in Iran. A fervent believer in anti-Semitic classic, *Protocols of the Elders of Zion.* He called America "the Great Satan."
June 7 and 10, 1979	First election of "The Assembly", the parliament of the E.U.
July 16, 1979	Saddam Hussein assumed undisputed power in Iraq after a coup.
July 20, 1980	First Global Conference of the Future.
July 30, 1980	After an Israeli law which formally recognized Jerusalem as the capital of Israel, foreign embassies left that city.

	Those of El Salvador and Costa Rica are the only ones there today.
September 1980	Iraq invaded Iran.
June 5, 1981	First published case report of AIDS by Centers for Disease Control in Los Angeles.
June 14 and 17, 1984	Second election of "The Assembly" of the E.U. This happens every fifth year.
March 11, 1985	Mikhail Gorbachev became General Secretary of the U.S.S.R. and instituted *perestroika* (restructuring) and *glasnost* (openness) reforms soon thereafter.
1986	British scientists discover a hole in the Antarctic ozone layer.
April 25, 1986	Chernobyl (Ukraine) nuclear power plant exploded and released 50 tons of radioactive material (10 times more than at Hiroshima). Chernobyl means "wormwood" (bitter or grievous) in their dialect. Is this a sample of the destruction called "wormwood" (Rev. 8:11)?
December 9, 1987	Palestinian *intifada* (uprising) began.
1987	70 years after Bolshevik Revolution, Russian Communist system is in deep trouble.
1988	Communist governments collapse in Eastern Europe.
1988	Israel defines "who is a Jew" for the purposes of the Law of Return to that land (also in 1984 and 1990).
May 1988	A flask of 1900-year-old persimmon oil of a kind used to anoint Judah's kings, was found in a cave near the Dead Sea.
August 1988	Iran-Iraq War ended with cease-fire.
December 1988	Palestinian Liberation Organization (P.L.O.) recognized Israel and renounced terrorism. U.S. opened dialogue with P.L.O.

1989	U.S. and Egypt attempted to bring Israel and Palestinians to peace table.
January 1989	George Bush became U.S. President. His policy was not as supportive of Israel as previous presidents.
July 1989	Supreme Court in *Webster v. Reproductive Health Services* permitted state legislatures to consider additional restrictions on abortion. All subsequent anti-abortion laws passed have been enjoined until they go through the court system.
End of 1980s	The improvement of U.S.-U.S.S.R. relations made global co-operation easier.
November 9, 1989	Berlin Wall came down exactly 51 years after "Crystal Night" (Nazi destruction of Jewish property in Germany).
December 1989	Egypt and Syria restored diplomatic relations after 12 years, marking the end of Egypt's ostracism in Arab world.
1989-1990	Collapse of Soviet regimes in Eastern Europe.
March 15, 1990	Collapse of Labor-Likud coalition government due to a 60-60 vote deadlock in the *Knesset*.
April 1990	Saddam Hussein threatened to burn half of Israel.
May 30-*Shavuot,* 1990	Israeli forces blocked attack by Palestinian gunboats on Tel Aviv beach.
June 1990	U.S. suspended dialogue with the P.L.O.
June 11, 1990	Conservative Likud government took office in Israel.
August 1990	Saddam Hussein annexed Kuwait and the Allied forces mobilized for war in Saudi Arabia.
September 1990	Soviet legislature adopted a law that ended Bolshevik policy of atheist education and state control of religious institutions.

October 2, 1990	Unification of West and East Germany.
October 1990	Israel distributed gas masks to citizens.
October 8-*Sukkot,* 1990	Palestinians attacked Jewish worshippers at "Western Wall," Jerusalem. Jewish police fire on Palestinians.
November 22, 1990	Margaret Thatcher resigned. This removed her restraint on rapid unification of E.U.
December 14, 1990	Leaders met in Rome to approve a blueprint for political and economic union of E.U.
February 1991	Iraq launched 39 Scud missiles against Israel and several against Saudi Arabia.
February 27, 28, 1991 (*Adar* 13 and 14)	Allies defeated Saddam Hussein's army in 100 hours by midnight of the 27th and celebrated victory the next day. On these two days, the Feast of *Purim,* Jews still celebrate their defeat of Haman and their enemies in 473 B.C. in Persia (Esth. 9:17). "Many Orthodox Jews believed that the war against Iraq was the beginning of the coming of Messiah" (*The Washington Post,* March 2, 1991, p. B-6).
March 12, 1991	British Prime Minister John Major put aside his predecessors' hostility to European unity and sought key role for Britain in creating E.U. policy.
April 1, 1991	Israel's new entry restrictions cut in half the number of Palestinians working in Israel. Their standard of living has plummeted due to Gulf War and *intifada.*

June 5, 1991	Episcopalian Diocese of Washington, D.C. ordained a homosexual woman to the priesthood (See June 5, 1981).
December 1991	Collapse of Soviet Union.
1996	**2,000 years since Jesus Christ.**
1996	Israelis celebrate 3,000 years in Jerusalem
1996	Decision regarding future of Jerusalem.
1996	Presidential elections–U.S., Russia, Israel.
1996	Efforts toward greater unity in E.U.

Section Two: Coming Events—Proposed

Future days are suggested because coming Biblical events seem to fulfill the last three Feasts of Israel (see chapter 12).

A. The Invasion of Israel

Rosh Hashanah Judgment Day (*Tishri* 1)—Year 1	The invasion will be brief, since God will disarm the invaders (Ezek. 39:3). The whole attack may be over in six days, as was the Six-Day War. The invaders will be destroyed in Israel.
Tishri 6—Year 1	At the end of the invasion, half of the Christians (Matt. 25:1–9) will go forth immediately to call the world to repent, accept the righteousness that Jesus Christ offers, and expect to be *"caught up"* by Jesus Christ to escape God's coming wrath.
Tishri 6—Year 1	Israel also will go forth immediately to bury the dead and cleanse the land for seven months (Ezek. 39:12–14).

B. The Seven-Year Transition to Messiah's Rule

The First Three-and-One-Half Years

Tishri 10—Year 1	*Yom Kippur;* God's two witnesses will appear and do powerful miracles in Israel for 1,260 days.
	An exceptional leader *"will confirm a covenant with many"* (in Israel) for one seven-year period. This will be the start of his seven-year reign and the transition to Messiah's rule on earth. Many Jews will go to Israel believing him to be their Messiah.
Tishri 15-21—Year 1	Inauguration of Israel's king.
Iyyar (April/May)—Year 1	The Temple may be started right after the seven months of cleansing the land and after Passover. (*Iyyar* was also the month in which the work on both prior Temples was begun).... A man thought to be Messiah must be present to authorize the construction of the Temple. There must be peace with the Moslems for this to happen.
Sivan 20 or *Tammuz* 20—Year 1	Israel brings forth her progeny, the 144,000 (Rev. 12:1–5), 280 days (average human gestation) after leader confirms a covenant. This encompasses *Tishri* 10 to *Sivan* or *Tammuz* 20, depending on whether there is an added month that year.
Sivan 20 or *Tammuz* 20—Year 1	The leader of Israel will become ruler of the E.U.
Tishri—at start of Year 3	The Temple may be completed after 18 months of construction.
Tishri 8–21—Year 3 Feast of Tabernacles	Dedication of the Temple may take two weeks if done in keeping with that of Solomon's Temple (1 Kin. 8:65f; 2 Chr. 7:8f) and at the start of the Israeli leader's 3rd year in office. (see p. 122.)

Tishri 22—Year 3

Shemini Atzeret—Final Assembly on the eighth day of the Feast of Tabernacles (*Sukkot*) and the end of the dedication. The Temple may then be used for 18 months for worship before the sacrificial system is halted in the middle of the leader's 4th year in office.

About Midpoint—Year 4

The false messiah of Israel ("Caesar" of the E.U.) will receive a fatal wound from a sword but yet will live. The whole world will be astonished and will follow him after he arises as the beast (Rev. 13:3, 12, 14).

The Second Three-and-One-Half Years

Nisan 10— Year 4
The Midpoint

The exact midpoint of the seven years of transition will be a fateful day. The 144,000 Jewish servants of our God are *"caught up"* and enter heaven, led by Messiah. They are called *"firstfruits of God and the Lamb"* (Rev. 14:4). (On the same day, the Israelites entered the Promised Land under Joshua.) The families of these men will be protected by God for the remaining 1,260 days in the desert (Rev. 12:6, 14).

Nisan 10—Year 4

God's two witnesses will be killed by *"the beast"* (Rev. 11:7) after completing their assigned 1,260 days.

Nisan 10— Year 4

The Messianic pretender of Israel ("Caesar" of the E.U.) will stop the Temple sacrifices, declare himself to be God, and demand worship of his image in the Temple. The Jews will realize this man is the prophesied false messiah and flee (Dan. 9:27; 2 Thess. 2:4; Rev. 13:14f). He will become dictator for 42 months (1,260 days) of the world, which is divided up into ten regions. Each area will have a king, who gives

Nisan 10—Year 4

his authority to the dictator (Rev. 13:1,5; 17:12f). He arises from the sea of humanity.

Nisan 10—Year 4

The false prophet will emerge and exercise the beast's authority, making the people of earth worship the beast and his image. The false prophet will perform great miraculous signs and deceive those who reject the real Messiah (Rev. 13:11ff).

Nisan 10—Year 4

"The woman" (the families of the 144,000) is flown to the place prepared for her by God in the desert, where she will be taken care of for the 1,260 days of wrath (Rev. 12:6, 14). Those in Judea flee to the mountains (Matt. 24:16ff; cf. Rev. 12:17).

Nisan 10—Year 4

THE GREAT TRIBULATION:

The wrath of Almighty God will start on earth, and extend for three-and-a-half years.

Nisan 14—Passover—Year 4

A breath from God will bring the two witnesses to life in Jerusalem. They will be *"called up"* to heaven immediately. People worldwide will see them ascend (via television). Within the same hour, an earthquake in Jerusalem kills 7,000 people and one-tenth of the city will collapse (Rev. 11:11f).

From the Midpoint to the end of the 7 years

The false prophet will force people to receive the mark of the beast on the forehead or right hand in order to buy or sell. Of those who are not beheaded by the beast, half of unrepentant mankind are killed by sword, famine, plague, wild beasts, and troops (Rev. 6:8; 9:15).

The Harlot Church will back Anti-Christ, but be destroyed by him subsequently. The world's economic/commercial system will crash. There will be unimaginable ecological destruction. Some will even hide in caves.

The 7th year	The last year that the nations trample upon Jerusalem (Rev. 11:2).
Before the end of the 7th year	The marriage and wedding supper of Messiah and His Bride (Rev. 19:7ff; Matt. 22:2–14; 25:10; Eph. 5:31f. This has its roots in Is. 54:5–7; Hos. 2:19f).
Tishri 1–*Rosh Hashanah*— Year 8	The beast, the ten kings, and their armies from all nations may begin to assemble at the Plain of Jezreel at Armageddon (*Har Mageddon*—Mount of Megiddo— Rev. 16:16) on the same day a few nations invaded Israel seven years before. They will attack Jerusalem.
Tishri 10–*Yom Kippur*— Year 8	Israel's Deliverer will be *"revealed from heaven in blazing fire"* (2 Thess. 1:7). He will be seen by all eyes as He descends (Rev. 1:7). The Mount of Olives, just east of the Temple, will split from east to west when His feet touch down upon it. (Zech. 14:4)
	Jesus Christ brings His angelic hosts and all His saints with Him. He fights the armies gathered to make war against Him. The Anti-Christ and false prophet will be cast into lake of fire. Satan will be bound and thrown into the Abyss for 1,000 years. The kings of the earth and their armies will be slain (Zech. 14:2f, 12; Rev. 19:11f). CHRIST AS HIGH PRIEST.
	The First Resurrection concludes with: (1) The Old Testament people written in the book of life (Dan. 12:1, 2, 13). (2) The post-Rapture Christians who had been beheaded by the Anti-Christ (Matt. 24:31; Mark 13:27; Rev. 20:4ff).
Tishri 10–*Heshvan* 10— Year 8	All levels of Israeli society will mourn and grieve bitterly as for an only child

when they look upon their Redeemer with His pierced hands and feet (Zech. 12:10; Is. 53:5; Ps. 22:16). This will include the clans of David (political leadership), Nathan (the prophets), Levites (the priests), Shimei, and all the rest (Zech. 12:12ff). Shimei represents the ones who have cursed the Lord's anointed (2 Sam. 16:5). The traditional mourning period lasts 30 days.

JUDGMENT OF THE SURVIVORS ON EARTH:

King Messiah will judge the nations for their treatment of the least of His brethren, *"whoever does the will of my Father in heaven"* (Matt. 12:50).

Tishri 10–*Tishri* 1
Entire 8th year

THE JUBILEE YEAR OF RESTORATION—(*Yobel*) beginning on *Yom Kippur* has probably not been celebrated in Israel since the days of Jeremiah (before Jewish exile into Babylon). At the end of the time decreed for Daniel's people and their city, everlasting righteousness will be brought in and the land of Israel will be returned to the Jewish tribes.

Tishri 15–21 *Sukkot*—
Year 8

INAUGURATION OF THE KING IN HIS KINGDOM to dwell (*shakan*) with His people permanently.
The Feast of Tabernacles looked backward to the tabernacles or shelters (*sukkot*) in which the Israelites dwelt in the wilderness after they left Egypt.

Heshvan 10—Year 8

Israel's mourning period will conclude Daniel's 1,290 days (1,260 of wrath and 30 days of mourning—Dan. 12:11).

Kislev 25—Year 8

REDEDICATION OF THE MILLENNIAL TEMPLE 45 days after the mourning period is over appears to fall on the first day of *Hanukkah,* ("dedication")! It was the day the Second Temple was rededicated after the Maccabees seized it from Antiochus Epiphanes, the Syrian tyrant. Note: This follows Daniel's schedule: (1,290 + 45 = 1,335 days—Dan. 12:12). (see p. 198.)

C. The Millennium and Beyond

7th Millennium

One thousand years of peace under Messiah who will rule with an iron scepter (Ps. 2:9; Rev. 2:27; 19:15). The saints (Jews and Gentiles) will reign with Jesus (2 Tim. 2:12; Rev. 3:21) and be given authority over the nations (Rev. 2:26). They will govern the 12 tribes of Israel (Matt. 19:28), administer cities (Luke 19:17ff), and ultimately judge the world and (fallen) angels (1 Cor. 6:2f).

End of 7th Millennium

Satan will be released briefly to test those born on earth during the millennium. A huge number will band together and rebel against God's authority. They will march across the earth and surround Jerusalem. Fire will come down from heaven and devour them. Then, Satan will be thrown into the lake of fire to join the beast and the false prophet. They will be tormented day and night forever (Rev. 20:7ff).

After Man's Final Rebellion

The Resurrection of the wicked dead.
The Great White Throne Judgment: (Rev. 20:11-15)
(1) People who will not accept Messiah's covering of righteousness and forgiveness will stand before God's Judgment, clothed in their own self-will and deeds.
(2) Fallen angels who have been waiting in darkness and chains (2 Pet. 2:4; Jude 6).

Post Judgment

At the start of the eighth millennium: *"The heavens will disappear with a roar; the elements will be destroyed by fire, and the earth and everything in it will be laid bare (burned up, KJV)"* (2 Pet. 3:10; Matt. 24:35). *"Earth and sky fled from His presence"* (Rev. 20:11). There will be a new heaven, a new earth, and a new Jerusalem. There will be no more death, mourning, crying, or pain for the old order of things will have passed away (Rev. 21:1–5). *"NO LONGER WILL THERE BE ANY CURSE"* (Rev. 22:3). God says, *"I AM MAKING EVERYTHING NEW!"* (Rev. 21:5)

Section Three: Projected Timeline

Tishri 1	Tishri 6	Tishri 10
Rosh Hashanah Feasts of Trumpets		*Yom Kippur* Day of Atonement
1ST YEAR	**1ST YEAR**	**1ST YEAR**
The invasion of Israel by Russia and specified countries will end, perhaps by the sixth day as in the Six-Day War.	God's Deliverance Israelis bury invaders for seven months. Christians go forth, calling the world to repent and accept Jesus as Savior and Lord before God's coming wrath.	Leader confirms the covenant with Israel. God's two witnesses appear. Many Jews believe the leader to be Messiah and go to Israel. Hostility of neighbors is no longer a problem in Israel.

Tishri 15-21	Iyyar	Tammuz 20
Tabernacles		
1ST YEAR	**1ST YEAR**	**1ST YEAR**
Inauguration of Israel's king.	Israel starts to rebuild Temple by authority of (false) messiah in the same month the First and Second Temples were begun.	280-day gestation period after leader signs covenant. 144,000 Jewish servants of God come forth. Israel's ruler becomes leader of E.U. with ten nations, but supported by only seven heads of state. (An added month that year would make date one month earlier.)

Tishri 8-22	Nisan 10	Nisan 10
Yom Kippur and Tabernacles		
START OF 3RD YEAR	**MIDDLE OF 4TH YEAR**	**MIDDLE OF 4TH YEAR**
Dedication of the Temple. Second anniversary of ruler's reign in Israel.	144,000 Jews, *"caught up"* to heaven. Families of 144,000 are flown to a place prepared for them in the desert by God. Those in Judea flee to the mountains. God's wrath begins. It extends for 1,260 days or 42 months (of 30 days each).	The two witnesses are killed by the ruler. Ruler (the beast) stops Temple sacrifice and offering. Appearance of the false prophet. The beast and false prophet command worship of the *"abomination"* (image of ruler) in the Temple. Beast becomes ruler of world divided into 10 areas, each with a king, for 1,260 days.

Nisan 14	Tishri 1	Tishri 10
Passover	Rosh Hashanah	Yom Kippur
4TH YEAR	START OF 8TH YEAR	START OF 8TH YEAR
God's two witnesses brought to life and "called up" to heaven. A terrible earthquake in Jerusalem.	Armies from all nations gather at Armageddon to go up and attack Jerusalem. They are led by the beast and the 10 kings.	Messiah Jesus arrives with His angels and saints. He delivers the Jews and Jerusalem. Satan is bound and hurled into the Abyss for 1,000 years. Beast and false prophet are thrown into lake of fire. Ten kings and their armies are killed. Old Testament and post-Rapture saints are resurrected. Year of Jubilee begins. All Israel mourns for their Messiah for 30 days. The 1,000 years of peace under the Messiah starts at the Year of Jubilee.

Kislev 25		
Hanukkah		
8TH YEAR	END OF 1,000 YEARS	BEGINNING OF THE EIGHTH MILLENNIUM:
Rededication of the Temple to God 75 days after arrival of the Messiah. This day is Hanukkah.	Satan released from his prison and goes out to deceive the nations. He gathers them together for battle against the camp of God's people in Jerusalem. This is the final rebellion against God. Satan is cast into the lake of fire. His followers are killed by fire from heaven. The wicked dead are resurrected. The Great White Throne Judgment of: those born during the 1,000 years, the wicked dead and fallen angels.	The New Heaven The New Earth The New Jerusalem

Section Four: The Jews and Jerusalem in 2,000 Years

1 B.C.	(No zero year)
70 A.D.	The destruction of Jerusalem and the Jewish nation.
1897 A.D.	The First World Zionist Congress.
1967 A.D.	Israel gained and united Jerusalem.

(1,897 Years)

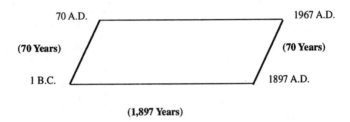

(1,897 Years)

Section Five: God's 120 Years of Building and Warning

Precedent: Noah's generation was given a grace period in which to repent during the 120 years between God's warning of the Flood and its arrival. During this time, Noah, *"a preacher of righteousness,"* built the ark as God had commanded.

> *Then the LORD said, 'My Spirit will not contend with man forever, for he is mortal. His days will be a hundred and twenty years.'*   (Genesis 6:3; cf. 1 Peter 3:20)

The Present: the Jewish community which started evolving in Israel in the 1880s was called the new *Yishuv.* Israel is their ark of *"refuge"* (Isaiah 14:32b). Their "ark" will be complete with (see p. 225f):

1. The extension of Israel to its Biblical boundaries.
2. The return of Jews from all nations to Israel (Ezekiel 39:28).
3. Israel's complete spiritual restoration.

The 120 years may be the timespan allotted for all mankind to prepare to meet the Messiah.

Early Settlement of *Erez* Israel: 1880–1897

1878	Russia defeated Turkey—this foreshadowed the loss of Turkish control over the Holy Land with the breakup of the Turkish Empire in 1917.
1878	The establishment of the first two villages in *Erez*-Israel: Petah Tikvah in Judea and Rosh Pinnah in Galilee by religious Jews.
1880	Agriculture began in earnest with the secular "new *yishuv*" (settlement).
1881	Eliezer Ben Yehuda moved to Israel and began to revive the Hebrew language.
1881–1882	Pogroms (devastation of Jews) in Southern Russia caused large scale Jewish immigration to *Erez* Israel in the First Aliyah (ascent).
1895	Dr. Theodor Herzl covered the Dreyfus Court Martial for his newspaper.

50 Years of Pre-Statehood: 1897–1947 for *Erez* Israel

1897	Dr. Herzl—the father of Zionism convened the First World Zionist Congress.
1902–1906	More Russian pogroms against Jews.
1917	The Balfour Declaration. England favored "A National Home for the Jewish people" in Palestine.
1917	General Allenby captured Jerusalem from Turkey on *Hanukkah*.
1927	Recognition was given to national Israel in the Creed of a major Pentecostal Protestant denomination.

1937	The British Peel Commission restricted Jewish immigration to and land purchases in Palestine. The Nazi concentration camps were reorganized.
1939–1945	The Nazi Holocaust of 6 million Jews.
1947	God's Holy Word: the Dead Sea Scrolls discovered in caves.
1947	The United Nations voted to partition Palestine, and create Israel.

Israel Wins Nationhood–Present

1948	The Proclamation of Independence of Israel.
1948	Six Arab neighbors attack Israel the day after her Proclamation of Independence.
1949	Cease-fire ends Israeli War of Independence. Israel stands as a nation.
1956	Israel's preemptive "Sinai Campaign."
1967	The Six-Day War: Israel gained all Jerusalem, especially the Temple Mount, for first time since 135 A.D.
	Israel also held Sinai, the Gaza Strip, the West Bank, and the Golan Heights.
1973	*Yom Kippur* War.
1977	Egyptian President Anwar Sadat recognized Israel's right to exist and visited Jerusalem.
1978	The Camp David Accords—The Israeli-Egyptian peace treaty.
1981	Israel destroyed an Iraqi atomic reactor.
1987	Palestinian *Intifada*—an internal Arab uprising in Israel began.
1988	A flask of ancient anointing oil (which represents the Holy Spirit in the Bible) was discovered in the anniversary month of Israel's Proclamation of Independence.

1991   Saddam Hussein attacked Israel with 39
                                        Scud missiles.

COMING:
                                        The invasion of Israel led by Russia.

                                        The seven years of transition from man's
                                        to Messiah's rule on earth.

                                        The gathering of armies at Armageddon
                                        to attack Jerusalem by Anti Christ.

                                        The arrival of Jewish Messiah on the
                                        Mount of Olives to deliver Israel.

                                        The Jewish Messiah will bring the Jubi-
                                        lee Year of restoration and liberty. The
                                        1,000 years of peace under Messiah will
                                        start at the Jubilee Year.

Section Six: Parallels Between Israel and the Church

I. Over a 2,000-Year Period

Approximately midway in the Jewish era (930 B.C.) and halfway through the Christian epoch (1054 A.D.), each split radically. The kingdom of Israel divided into the north and south, and the Church separated into east and west.

II. The Last 500 Years

A. The World—1492

This was a watershed year due to the transcendent effect of three events:

(1) The Spanish defeat of the Moors in Granada ended centuries of civil war in Spain and ejected Islam from Europe.

(2) The expulsion from Spain of the largest, most affluent community of Jews in the world caused the destruction of a Golden Age of Jewry.

(3) With the discovery of the New World by Christopher ("Christ-bearer") Columbus on *Tishri* 21 (the seventh day of *Sukkot*) God-released rich virgin land in the west. It has provided

a haven for Jews, religious freedom for Christians, and a new start for people of all nations.

[Note: Perhaps, God's intention to provide a future opportunity in the west was intimated by a specific vision and guidance He gave Paul. His apostle to the Gentiles was directed to head west to Macedonia (Greece) (Acts 16:6–10).]

The intersection of the three events in one year suggests divine timing. They were not occurring in some obscure corner of the world, but at the hub of the preeminent world power. (The Spanish Empire reached its height during the next 100 years. Under the Hapsburgs, Spain ruled the vast domain of the Holy Roman Empire and great portions of the New World.)

The three events seem to foreshadow the Lord's future intervention in the same three areas. Is this year a punctuation mark from the past that points to a great move of God in the near future? God has promised that after Israel became a nation, the world will see Him strike the death blow to the forces that attack Israel (Ezekiel 38 and 39).

He will also shake the earth and the heavens before Messiah comes (Haggai 2:7; Hebrews 12:26f). This will free His people (Jews and Gentiles) from the materialistic society which captures their minds and subjugates their energies, leaving nothing for God.

Thirdly, people of all nations will discover and inhabit the true New World, the kingdom of God, which Messiah will establish on earth.

B. The Holy Land—1517

Palestine came under the Ottoman Turks, whose empire declined and was largely held together by European powers. The latter did not want a Russian foothold in the area of the Mediterranean Sea. The Turkish Empire finally lost control of Palestine to the British in 1917.

C. The Church—1517

It was Martin Luther's finding a Bible that was the impetus behind the Protestant Reformation. (Finding the Book of the Law also brought King Josiah's great reformation [2 Kings 22:8ff; Halley, p. 236].)

On October 31, 1517, Martin Luther's *95 Theses* fueled an explosion in the Church. This led to reformation of its doctrines, practices and worldly power. He restored the Biblical principle that we are saved through faith in God's grace and not by our works. God's salvation is a gift to be accepted (Ephesians 2:8f). It causes good works to issue from a life; however, our works can never purchase our salvation. The authority of Scripture was emphasized by Luther.

Since then, other reformers have gradually rediscovered foundational truths. John Wesley stressed the holy, disciplined, and separated life of a Christian. The sovereignty of God was balanced by the responsibility of men. The coming of Christ, the Rapture of the Church, and Messiah's millennial reign were proclaimed by W.E. Blackstone and others.

A.B. Simpson anticipated the outpouring of the *"latter rain"* of the Holy Spirit (Joel 2:23, 29, KJV) in the 20th century. He said that openness to the Holy Spirit was our only defense against formalism. With the Baptism of the Holy Spirit and the gifts of the Spirit (including divine healing), the Church has been regaining truth and power it had lost since the days of the early Christians. Many born-again Christians have become aware of their Jewish roots, which produces a special bond with God's ancient people and their land.

Thus, the restoration of the authority and inerrancy of God's Word began in 1517, but the baptism of the Holy Spirit was not sent again to the Church until this century (1901). Man has experienced the restoration of God's Word for about **four centuries** and **one century** of waiting for the final renewal that the Holy Spirit will bring. It will be *"life from the dead."* We await:

...the glory that will be revealed in us. **The creation waits in eager expectation for the sons of God to be revealed...We wait** *for our adoption as sons, the redemption of our bodies.*   (Romans 8:18, 23)

This same four to one proportion exists in the 50-day period between the resurrection of Jesus from the dead and the coming of the Holy Spirit which give birth to the Church. Jesus, who is called "The Word" (John 1:1, 14), appeared to His apostles over a period of **40 days** between His resurrection and His ascension. He commanded them to wait for the promised Holy Spirit, who then came **ten days** later on the 50th day, Pentecost (*Shavuot*).

God has anointed the sons of God and set His seal of ownership on them. He has put His Spirit in their hearts as a deposit, guaranteeing their coming inheritance (2 Corinthians 1:21f; Ephesians 1:14).

Israel is also being prepared for her promised restoration and the coming of her Messiah in glory to Jerusalem.

On that day I will set out to destroy all the nations that attack Jerusalem. And I will pour out on the house of David and the inhabitants of Jerusalem a spirit of grace and supplication.   (Zechariah 12:9f; cf. 13:1; Ezekiel 39:29)

For if their (Israel's) *rejection is the reconciliation of the world, what will their acceptance be but life from the dead?*   (Romans 11:15)

III. Parallel Restoration in Israel and the Church began 1878/1880

Israel

The Church

1878—Petah Tikvah and Rosh Pinnah were the first villages established in Israel.
1880—The land began to be reclaimed for agriculture by waves of new Jewish settlers, the "new *yishuv*," escaping the Russian pogroms from 1881 onward.
1881—Revival of the Hebrew language began.

1878—*"Jesus Is Coming"* by W.E. Blackstone awakened the Church to the coming of Jesus Christ at the start, not the end, of His millennium of peace. Blackstone also proclaimed the future *"catching up"* (Rapture) of the Church to heaven.

1897—Zionism gained world recognition with the First World Zionist Congress at Basel, Switzerland. It was convened by Dr. Theodor Herzl.

1901—Modern Pentecostalism began with the outpouring of the Holy Spirit upon Agnes Ozman with the evidence of speaking in tongues at Bethel Bible School in Topeka, Kansas, on January 1.

1900 onward—Meetings of the World Zionist Congress. The continued reclaiming of the swamps and barren land for agriculture in *Erez* Israel through Jewish labor and hardship.

1903–1905—The Welsh Revival—Evan Roberts

1906–1909—The outpouring of the Holy Spirit at Azusa Street in Los Angeles, California was led by William J. Seymour. Pentecostalism became a worldwide movement.

1917—Balfour Declaration

1927—Recognition of Israel in a Pentecostal creed.

Israel	The Church
	1945—Christian Far East Broadcasting Company begins.
1947—The discovery of Dead Sea Scrolls. U.N. Partition Plan of Palestine.	1947—The First Pentecostal World Conference, Zurich, Switzerland. Oral Roberts' healing ministry begins.
1948—Israel's Proclamation of Independence. 1948–1951—Mass immigration of Jews.	1948—T.L. Osborn's healing ministry begins. Pentecostal Fellowship of North America founded. Kathryn Kuhlman, headquartered in Pittsburgh, held large healing services.
1949—Cease-fire between Jews and Arabs on January 7.	1949—Billy Graham's first crusade.
1950s—Progress in assimilation of Jewish immigrants with Hebrew language, jobs, and housing.	1950—Graham's Evangelistic Association and media ministry formed.
Low unemployment; agricultural self-sufficiency; new construction; nearly 100% of children in school; university students increase.	David du Plessis, the international Pentecostal spokesman, reported that God was pouring out His Holy Spirit in many lands.
Arabs and Druses shared in progress: 600% increase in agricultural productivity, free primary education, national insurance, welfare and health services, roads, water,	

Israel	The Church
electricity, sanitary facilities, and irrigation. They also participate in free elections and representation in the *Knesset,* the governing body. Relations with emerging nations began with technical aid to Africa and South America. The nations opened embassies in Jerusalem and supported Israel in the U.N. (Prince, p. 144f).	
1960s—Export of citrus crops; water made available to farm Negev Desert; increase in manufacture of consumer goods.	1960s—Charismatic (Pentecostal) Renewal in major Protestant churches: Baptist, Episcopalian, Lutheran, Mennonite, Methodist, Presbyterian and others.
	1962 to 1965—The Second Vatican Council sought: reconciliation between the Roman Catholic church and Protestant churches; acceptance of the charismatic gifts; and emphasis on the role of the laity and its call to holiness.
June 1967—Unification of Jerusalem, the heart of Israel, under Jewish control. This was 1900 years after the Jewish Revolt against the Romans.	February 1967—Roman Catholic Charismatic Renewal begins at Duquesne University, Pittsburgh, the same city in which Kathryn Kuhlman's healing

Israel

Most crucial was the gaining of East Jerusalem with the Temple Mount.

1980s to present—Soviet and Ethiopian Jews immigrate to Israel.

The Church

ministry was located. This renewal would have been unlikely without the decisions made at Vatican II.

True reunification of Christianity (Catholics and Protestants), under the power of the Holy Spirit in the Charismatic Renewal. This involved Britain, Eastern and Western Europe, Russia, Scandinavia, Australia, Africa, Asia, North, South, and Central America, and other areas.

1980s—Classical Pentecostals are the largest and fastest growing of Protestant churches in world (Burgess and McGee, p. 221). Revival of Christianity in the ex-Soviet Republics and the Third World nations.

Section Seven: The Fast of *Tishah be-Av* (*Av* 9)

Historic Disasters and Exiles of the Jewish People
"I will punish you for your sins seven times over"
(Leviticus 26:18, 21, 24, 28).

The rebellion:

Av 9, 1280 B.C.	The Israelites refused to enter the Promised Land after the Exodus from Egypt (Num. 1:1–14:1; *Taanith* 29a).

The disasters:

(1) *Av* 9, 1280 B.C.	God denied Israelites entry into the Promised Land. All those over 20 years old of that generation died off in the wilderness (Num. 14:30).
(2) *Av* 10, 586 B.C.*	The Burning of Solomon's Temple by Nebuzaraden, Commander of Nebuchadnezzer's army, who arrived on *Av* 7 (2 Kin. 25:8; cf. Jer. 52:12f).
(3) *Av* 9, 70 A.D.	The Second Temple was set afire by Roman soldiers under Titus (Tannith 29a; Josephus, p. 580ff).
(4) *Av* 9, 130 A.D.	The Roman Emperor Hadrian had Jerusalem plowed (Micah 3:12). He constructed a heathen temple on the Temple Mount and rebuilt Jerusalem as the pagan city, Aelius Capitolina, which the Jews were forbidden to enter, except to mourn on *Av* 9.
(5) *Av* 9, 135 A.D.	The Jewish Revolt was crushed. Fortress at Betar fell; Bar Kokhba, the leader, was killed; and Rabbi Akiva was executed.
(6) *Av* 9, 1290 A.D.	King Edward I's edict banished all Jews from England on July 18.
(7) *Av* 9, 1492 A.D.	The expulsion of all Jews from Spain by midnight of August 2.

* Note: On the seventh [of *Av*] the heathen entered the Temple...Toward dusk of the ninth day, they set fire to it, and it continued to burn the whole day.[1]

What is the probability of these disasters all happening on one day over so long a period of history?

We see that God has dealt charitably with Israel in setting the day of exile for later generations, on the very day of the original sin. The weeping of many generations of children, on that day, would rectify what the first fathers had spoiled.[2]

Upon seeing the Jews of Paris weeping on *Tishah be-Av* (*Av* 9), Napoleon said in amazement:

I vow that this people is destined for a successful future in its own land; for where can we find a single other people which kept alive similar mourning and hope for thousands of years?[3]

It was also on *Av* 9, August 1, 1914, that Germany started World War I by invading Russia. Following the two world wars, many Jews gained and returned to their homeland.

On the eve of *Av* 9, 1970, the Temple Mount archaeological team found evidence of Titus and his troops. It was a column with a royal inscription by the Tenth Roman Legion to Titus himself. This army had been storming the Temple area 1,900 years earlier, on that very day![4]

1. *Taanith* 29a, *Encyclopaedia Judaica*, Vol. 15, p. 945.
2. Kitov, Vol. 3, p. 242.
3. *Ibid.*, p. 242.
4. Ben-Dov, p. 189.

Chapter Fourteen

SUMMARY

When the Lord shall build up Zion, he shall appear in his
glory. (Psalm 102:16, KJV)

Arise, shine, for your light has come, and the glory of the
Lord rises upon you (Zion). See, darkness covers the earth
and thick darkness is over the peoples, but the Lord rises
upon you and his glory appears over you. Nations will
come to your light, and kings to the brightness of your
dawn. (Isaiah 60:1–3)

This is a summary of major Biblical and historical factors in
this book. Two topics have been repeated verbatim due to their
importance. **The conclusion is that the Jewish Messiah will
come to earth in this decade or the next.** This event must be
preceded by a seven-year transition, in which a leader will achieve
world power for the last half of the interval.

Only Israelites under 20 years of age at Israel's refusal to enter
the Promised Land could go into it years later under Joshua. **If
God employs this precedent, the transition to Messiah will**

happen during the lifespan of those under 20 years of age in 1949. This was the year that Israel won her War of Independence.

"This generation" that sees the fig tree (Israel) sprout leaves is mentioned in three of the four gospels of the New Testament in connection with seeing the coming of the Messiah. We are awaiting the prophet Daniel's last seven-year interval (*shemittah*).

Since there is ONLY ONE SEVEN-YEAR PERIOD remaining for Israel's spiritual restoration (Daniel 9:24-27), *the seven years of burning the invasion wreckage* (Ezekiel 39:9) must be the very same interval as *the final seven years that begin at the moment a brilliant leader "shall confirm the covenant" with Israel* (Daniel 9:27).

For there to be wreckage to burn, the invasion will have to take place immediately before the king (Daniel 11:36) confirms the covenant and begins to rule in Israel. (Burning is the only safe way to dispose of some war materiél today.)

The Armageddon military operation will take place at the end of the seven years, immediately prior to Messiah's arrival in glory on the Mount of Olives in Jerusalem.

The Factors

1. Noah's 600 Years and Mankind's 6,000 Years

The 6,000th year since Adam is at hand, since the Bible indicates there were a total of **2,008 years** between Adam and Abraham. There are about 4,000 years from Abraham to the present. There is a specific reason why God tells us twice that Noah had completed his 600th year before the Lord executed judgment on earth (Genesis 7:6, 11). The 6,000th year will bring closure to the children of Adam's sixth "day" on earth.

2. Six Days of Labor and One Day of Rest

Throughout God's Word, seven always brings completion of a cycle: six days of labor and one day of rest. This concept is so basic that it is embodied in the Fourth Commandment. Man has labored for six millennia. Will he find restoration in the seventh? God required His people to release a Hebrew slave in the seventh year (Exodus 21:2, Deuteronomy 15:12). Will the Lord grant His creation liberation from its bondage to decay and freedom for His children in the seventh millennium? The Bible declares there will be a millennium of peace on earth under Messiah (Revelation 20: 2-6).

3. Messiah and the First Day of the Year of Jubilee

However, the next millennium cannot bring peace *until* God deals with evil and Messiah establishes harmony on earth. After the seven years of transition, He will arrive in glory at the start of the eighth year and inaugurate the Jubilee (50th) year of restoration (Leviticus 25:10ff).

The Jubilee Year is the only year that starts on the *tenth* day of the month (*Yom Kippur*—the sixth Feast of Israel). It is possible that Messiah will come on Yom Kippur for several reasons (see p. 244). Ezekiel was shown a vision of someone who had feet (therefore a man) returning in glory (therefore God) to the Temple *"in the beginning of the year ["rosh hashanah"], on the tenth of the month"* (Ezekiel 40:1, 43:2–7).

4. The Seven Feasts of Israel—God's Signature on Life

The seven of the Feasts of Israel given to Moses (Leviticus 23) are embedded in the gestation of a baby; in pre-Mosaic, Jewish, and Christian history; and in Israel's agricultural year. The second triad of the Feasts appears to provide the meaning and timing for Messiah's return, as the first three did for His original presentation to the Jewish nation (see pp. 237-250).

5. The Third Day

The dawning of the seventh millennium begins on the third "day" (millennium), (cf. Psalm 90:4; 2 Peter 3:8) since the dispersion of the Jewish nation. This is of overwhelming significance since the Jewish people are told they will be restored on *"the third day"* (Hosea 6:2). Throughout the Old Testament, outstanding events took place on *"the third day,"* demonstrating its crucial importance to the Jewish people (see p. 213ff). For example:

I.   The release of Isaac from sacrifice (Genesis 22:4).
II. The Israelite journey to leave Egypt (Exodus 8:27).
III. The giving of the Law by God at Mount Sinai (Exodus 19:16).
IV. The entry of Joshua and the Israelites into the Promised Land (Joshua 1:11, 3:2).
V.   The release of Jonah from the large fish (Jonah 1:17).
VI. The one sign for the future which Jesus chose to leave for His people (Matthew 12:39f).
VII.The resurrection of Jesus from the dead (Matthew 27:63f; Luke 24:7).

6. The 120 Years of Building: Ark, Israel and Church

Noah's world was given 120 years to repent. Jews have been rebuilding the Holy Land visibly for nearly 120 years. The gifts and healing power of the Holy Spirit have also been under restoration within the Church during this same period. (This only applies to those Christians who are willing to receive them.)

7. 6,000-Year Concept in *Talmud* and Early Christian Writers

Some ancient Rabbis wrote in the Talmud, the most authoritative source of Judaism after the Old Testament, that this world will exist in its present state for 6,000 years. Then, the Lord will be exalted for 1,000 years.[1] Until about 300 A.D., early Christian fathers held the same conviction (see p. 208ff).

8. *"All the Trees"* Come to Independence

The coming to life of *"all the trees"* (nations—Luke 21:29) is a sign today. Of about 170 nations, 98 of them have been formed since 1945. This is due to the breakup of the Turkish, British, and French Empires in this century.

9. The "Fig Tree" Israel Blooms

The generation that sees the leaves coming out on the fig tree (the formation of Israel) is mentioned in connection with the Son of Man coming in great power and glory (Matthew 24:32ff; Mark 13:26ff; Luke 21:27ff; cf. Psalm 102:16, KJV). This prophecy identifies *actual Jewish possession of their nation (1949), not their control of Jerusalem (1967),* as the bench mark to which we must refer. (For example, the Israelites were in Israel for over two centuries before King David established Jerusalem as the capital (2 Samuel 5:4f).

10. Israel's "Second" Generation

It was the "second" generation of Israelites (those under 20 years of age—Numbers 14:29-31; 1:45) who entered the Promised Land under Joshua. We are still in the lifetime (70–80 years) of those under 20 years old in 1949. Their lifespan will extend to 2,000 or 2,010.

They are the "second" Jewish generation **as an entire nation**, after the "first" generation rejected Jesus Christ in 30 A.D. Will today's "second" generation accept the spiritual inheritance that God offers and enter His kingdom under the leadership of Jesus? Joshua and Jesus are translations of the same Hebrew name, *"Yeshua"* or salvation.

---

1.   *Sanhedrin* II, 97 a, b, pp. 657ff.

11. The Second Offer of the Law, the Land and the Messiah

Moses had to ascend Mount Sinai twice to receive the Law before Israel was in a condition to receive it. God offered two different generations the Promised Land before they entered. Messiah will be presented twice before He is accepted by Israel.

12. Pentecost (*Shavuot*) and the Jubilee—the 50th

The nation of Israel was born on Pentecost—50 days after leaving Egypt—when God descended on Mount Sinai and spoke the Law to them (Exodus 20:1ff). The Church was also established on Pentecost with the descent of the Holy Spirit on Jewish believers on the 50th day after Jesus' resurrection and the acceptance of His blood sacrifice by His Father in heaven (Acts 2:1ff).

When will the ultimate 50, the Jubilee, *"the year of the Lord's favor,"* for Israel and the world take place? Liberty will be proclaimed throughout the land on that day! (Lev. 25:10).

13. The 38th Century, the 38 Years, and the 38 Months

Will Israel soon come into her spiritual "promised land" by the 38th century after Jacob and his entire family entered Egypt on *Nisan* 15 c. 1711 B.C.? God left the Hebrew nation in the wilderness for over 38 years after they refused to enter the Promised Land. Thirdly, the prototype for the Anti-Christ, the Syrian King Antiochus Epiphanes, held the Temple for over 38 months before the Maccabees recaptured it [2,300 sacrifices (2/day) = 1,150 days ÷ 30 days/month = 38.3 months (Daniel 8:14)]. The Jews remained in Judah 38 more years after Daniel's 69th *shemittah* ended in 32 A.D.

14. Daniel's 69th Shemittah (Seven-Year Cycle): 25-32 A.D.

A master revelation in the Bible is Daniel's seven-year periods (*shemittot*). As the Feasts of Israel imply the meaning and days of past and future **events**, Daniel's prophecy deals with **intervals** in history.

The Bible stated that a decree would go out to restore Jerusalem. The Persian King Artaxerxes I (stepson of Jewish Queen Esther) issued the only such edict to rebuild **the city** in *Nisan* 445 B.C., the 20th year of his reign (Nehemiah 2:1). In the *"hind* part" (*achar*) of the 69th *shemittah* from that date, Messiah would be killed [69 x 7 = 483 years] (Daniel 9:24-27).

The Bible uses a year of 360 days **in prophecy**, instead of a solar year of 365.2422 days. Therefore, 483 prophetic years = 476.07 solar years: 445 B.C. - 476 years = 31 A.D. + 1 year (as no "0" year between 1 B.C. to 1 A.D.) = 32 A.D. Thus, the 69th *shemittah* would have extended from 25 A.D. to 32 A.D.

Indeed, Messiah was killed in the latter part of the 69th *shemittah*. Jesus was born before Herod the Great died on April 1, 4 B.C. and during *"the first census"* of Quirinius (Luke 2:2) between 6 to 4 B.C.

Jesus was probably born in the fall since the Bethlehem shepherds were still tending their sheep in the fields at night at His birth (Luke 2:8). They were not in the shelter of the nearby caves which would be necessary by December 25. (The December date was chosen by Pope Liberius in 354 A.D. to coincide with the Roman festival to the sun.)

The Wise Men came to *worship* Jesus and were warned in a dream not to go back to Herod. King Herod was *"furious and gave orders to kill all the boys in Bethlehem and its vicinity who were two years old and under in accordance with the time he had learned from the Magi"* (Matthew 2:16).

Jesus must have been born in 5 B.C., 30 years before John baptized in 25-26 A.D. (see p. 229). Since there was only one year between 1 B.C. and 1 A.D., Jesus' ministry would have started in 26 A.D., ending with His death on Passover in 30 A.D. at $33\frac{1}{2}$

years of age. "The majority of scholars choose A.D. 30" which would place Passover (*Nisan* 14) on Friday, April 7.[2]

It was also in 30 A.D. that the Jewish *Sanhedrin* (court) could no longer meet on the Temple Mount and were soon exiled from Jerusalem altogether. Disturbing signs started occurring in the Temple that very same year. The signs continued until the Temple's destruction in 70 A.D. (*Talmud: Shabbath* 15a; *Yoma* 39 a, b; 67a, 68b - see p. 20f).

15. The Long Interval until the 70th *Shemittah*

Not only does Daniel identify the *shemittah* in which Messiah would be killed, he also makes it possible to determine that the end of the 69th *shemittah* is in 32 A.D. **Therefore, forty complete 49-year cycles (1,960 solar years) have past since 32 A.D.**

[As stated, 49 solar years is a complete period in which ther sun and moon return nearly to their original positions relative to each other, with an error of only 32 hours - see p. 197].

Forty represents completion and full testing in the Bible. [Three of the many examples are the Flood waters increased for 40 days, twice Moses spent 40 days on Mount Sinai receiving the Law, and Jesus was tempted 40 days in the wilderness.]

Maybe the Lord will take the Jews out of the spiritual wilderness following these 40 cycles, just as He did out of the physical wasteland of Sinai. He brought them out in the very first month after the 40 original years were completed.

However before restoration, God will first: (1) awaken the world; (2) give humanity one last call to Himself; (3) remove His people; (4) remove the restraint off wickedness so that it will reveal its true nature (deceived or uncommitted people will be given the maximum opportunity to make an informed choice); and (5) punish evil.

---

2.   Meier, p. 402; quoting Blinzler, p. 431.

All this must happen before the world is ready to receive Messiah. It will all take place in that earthshaking 70th *shemittah* (seven-year period) before restoration.

The Timing

The proposed schedule of events within the seven-year transition to Messiah is based on the meaning of the Feasts of Israel (see chapter 12).

1. *Rosh Hashanah*—The Invasion

The attention of the world may be riveted on Israel on the Feast of Trumpets—*Rosh Hashanah*. Russia will lead five specified areas in an invasion of Israel perhaps on this day, the Jewish Day of Judgment. Instead of the troops laying waste to Israel, God Almighty's hot anger and fiery wrath will demolish the invaders, as He did the Pharaoh and the Egyptian army at the Exodus of the Israelites. The Lord's direct intervention in the affairs of Israel will be like a trumpet blast that will awaken the world to the presence and power of the God of the universe.

2. *Yom Kippur*—The Confirmation of the Covenant

The false messiah will *"confirm a covenant"* for an interval of seven years. This may happen on *Yom Kippur.* This agreement will establish this man's leadership and secure Israel's modern boundaries in accord with the land covenant which God originally made with Abraham for his descendants.

3. The Two Witnesses—First Day of the Seven Years

"The two witnesses" will come the day Israel confirms the covenant. The two men speak for God exactly 1,260 days, or during the first half of the seven years before they are killed.

4. The Rapture—Date Unknown

John the Baptist prepared the way for Messiah at His first appearance on earth for a little more than seven months (see p. 135). Like John, Christians may only be allotted a brief time after the invasion is over to call the world to repent and accept the real Messiah. The true Church will then be *"caught up"* to heaven. They are called *"a kind of firstfruits of all he created"* (James 1:18).

5. The Erection of the Temple

During the ruler's first seven months in office, Israel will be burying the dead invaders to cleanse the land. Then the false messiah will authorize the construction of the Temple to begin, perhaps in *Iyyar* (April/May). This was also the month in which both prior Temples were started. [The Temple may be completed in 18 months (as was Herod's Temple reconstruction), and used for worship for the next year and a half.] Then, the ruler *"will put an end to* [the Temple] *sacrifice and offering"* at the midpoint of the seven years (Daniel 9:27).

6. The 144,000 Jews—280 Days after the Covenant

About 280 days (the length of human gestation—cf. Revelation 12:1–5) after the confirmation of the covenant (Daniel 9:27, KJV), the 144,000 Jewish *"servants of our God"* will come forth to win Israel and the world to the Jewish Messiah, Jesus Christ (Revelation 7:3ff).

7. The E.U.—280 Days after the Covenant

On that same day, the king of Israel will become ruler of the European Union (E.U.). By then, the E.U. will consist of 10 nations; but only seven of those 10 heads of state will support him. The other three will fall from power.

8. God and the Midpoint of the Seven Years

At the seven-year midpoint, the 144,000 Jewish male progeny will be *"caught up"* and will enter the Promised Land of heaven. They will be led by Jesus, perhaps on *Nisan* 10. They are called *"the firstfruits unto God and to the Lamb"* (Revelation 14:4). As soon as they are caught up, the Messianic community that brought them forth is flown to a place in the desert under God's protection for 1,260 days.

[*Nisan* 10 was also the day that Noah *et al.* might have entered the ark of safety to avoid God's wrath had it not been for the one month postponement due to mourning for his grandfather (see p. 236). Joshua led the Israelites into the Promised Land on *Nisan* 10, and Jesus Christ made His triumphal entry into Jerusalem and the Temple area on *Nisan* 10 as well.]

God's wrath will then begin on earth at the midpoint.

9. The Beast and the Midpoint of the Seven Years

On the same day that the 144,000 Jews are removed by God, the ruler will kill the two witnesses. The king will be unrestrained and will therefore reveal his bestial nature fully. This is three and a half years after he becomes king of Israel. On that day he will stop the Temple sacrifice and offering, enter the Temple, demand that his image be worshipped as God in the Temple, and become dictator of a world divided into ten regions, each with a king. This time, all ten of these kings will champion the tyrant (Daniel 9:27; Matthew 24:15; Revelation 13:15).

10. Messiah's Arrival as High Priest—*Yom Kippur*

The Messiah/Deliverer of Israel may come to earth on the most holy day of the Jewish year. As Israel's High Priest, He will bring God's forgiveness to that nation. It will be a lasting atonement, not just one to cover the prior year.

Upon arrival, He will destroy Israel's enemies and resurrect the Old Testament and post-Rapture saints. His Bride (believers) and angelic hosts arrive with Him.

11. The King and His Kingdom—Tabernacles—*Sukkot*

On the Feast of Tabernacles, both Jew and Gentile will inaugurate Messiah, the King, as the rightful ruler of His kingdom on earth.

12. The Rededication of the Temple—*Hanukkah*

The millennial Temple may be rededicated on *Hanukkah* (*Kislev* 25), 75 days after Messiah's arrival (Daniel 12:11, 12).

Finale

No matter how hopeless your situation, or that of the world, righteousness and justice will prevail on earth at last. Man's inhumanity to man will cease. Daniel was told that *"70 sevens"* are decreed for his nation to put an end to sin and bring in righteousness (Daniel 9:24). Jesus told Peter to forgive *"70 times seven"* (Matthew 18:22, KJV). Notice that this is a finite number. At God's deadline, He will intervene and bring His consummation. The Jewish nation will be fully restored on the third "day." (Hosea 6:2)

Not to choose God is to lose Him. There is no neutral position. If we desire to relate to Him, we must seek, love, and obey Him, not disregard and reject Him and His commandments. We will each appear before Jesus one day. He will be either our Savior or our Judge. We make this choice now, not then.

Gather together, gather together, O shameful nation, before the appointed time arrives...before the fierce anger of the Lord comes upon you...Seek righteousness, seek humility...   (Zephaniah 2:1–3)

Write down the revelation and make it plain on tablets so that a herald may run with it. For the revelation awaits an appointed time; it speaks of the end and will not prove false. Though it linger, wait for it; it will certainly come and will not delay.   (Habakkuk 2:3)

When the time comes for me to punish, I will punish them...

(Exodus 32:34)

Then, suddenly, the Lord you are seeking will come to his
temple.   (Malachi 3:1b; cf. Haggai 2:7)

I foretold the former things long ago, my mouth announced
them and I made them known; then, suddenly I acted, and
they came to pass.   (Isaiah 48:3)

For he [the Lord] *will come like a pent-up flood that the*
breath of the Lord drives along. "The Redeemer will come
to Zion, to those in Jacob who repent of their sins,"
declares the Lord.   (Isaiah 59:19f)

I am the Lord; in its time I will do this swiftly.
                                        (Isaiah 60:22)

**We all have an eternal destiny. The crucial question is
not when will the prophecies happen, but where will I spend
eternity?** Do you want to go to heaven? Repent, accept the blood
of Jesus Christ to make atonement for your sinful nature, and
receive God's forgiveness of your sins. Messiah's dying for us
paid the penalty for our sins. This is God's provision by which we
may enter His holy presence in heaven.

The communication and fellowship which man broke with
God in the Garden of Eden will be fully restored:

A voice of one calling: "In the desert prepare the way for
the Lord; make straight in the wilderness a highway for
our God...And the glory of the Lord will be revealed, and
all mankind together will see it."
                              (Isaiah 40:3, 5; cf. Luke 3:4, 6)

On that day his feet will stand on the Mount of Olives, east
of Jerusalem.   (Zechariah 14:4)

The Jewish Messiah is coming.
Praise be to the Lord God, the Holy One of Israel.
Praise be to His glorious name forever.
Baruch Ha Shem Adonai.
Amen.

Chart One

THE BIBLICAL, JEWISH AND MODERN CALENDARS

	Month of Biblical Calendar	Month of Jewish Calendar	Hebrew Name	Month of Modern Calendar
Biblical year starts	1	7	*Nisan (Abib)*	March 15-April 15
	2	8	*Iyyar (Ziv)*	April-May
	3	9	*Sivan*	May-June
	4	10	*Tammuz*	June-July
	5	11	*Av*	July-August
	6	12	*Elul*	August-September
Jewish year starts	7	1	*Tishri (Ethanim)*	September-October
	8	2	*Heshvan (Bul)*	October-November
	9	3	*Kislev*	November-December
	10	4	*Tevet*	December-January
	11	5	*Shevat*	January-February
	12	6	*Adar I*	February-March
			Adar II (Veadar)	(This extra month is added every two to three years to make the lunar and solar calendars correspond.)

Chart Two

THE SEVEN ANNUAL FEASTS OF ISRAEL AND OTHER FESTIVALS

Leviticus 23

Feast	Biblical Calendar	Secular Calendar	Old Testament: Event in Israel	New Testament: Event in the Church
	Nisan 10	March/ April	Passover lamb was examined for imperfections until sacrificed on *Nisan* 14 (Ex. 12:3ff).	At His triumphal entry into Jerusalem, Jesus offered Himself as the King-Messiah of the Jews (Matt. 21:1ff).
1. Pass-over *(Pesach)*	*Nisan* 14		Symbol: Blood God's deliverance of the Jews from death. A lamb was sacrificed, its blood was put over the door, and the angel of death passed over the Jewish household in Egypt. The lamb was the substitute which received the death penalty instead of the Jews (Ex. 12:1-14).	Crucifixion of Jesus, the Lamb of God, who died to take away the sin of the world. He gives us the gift of everlasting life if we accept His sacrifice and righteousness (1 Cor. 5:7b).
2. Un-leavened Bread *(Hag Ha Matzah)*	*Nisan* 15-21 (one week)		Symbol: *Matzah* A week of eating bread made without yeast *(Matzah)*, to remember how God brought the	A godly life: Since yeast represents evil, eating unleavened bread represents the effort to live a life without sin,

Feast	Biblical Calendar	Secular Calendar	Old Testament: Event in Israel	New Testament: Event in the Church
			Israelites out of Egypt in haste (Ex. 12:15-20).	because Christ has set us free from our sinful nature and forgiven our sins (1 Cor. 5:7-8).
3. First-fruits*	*Nisan* 16 The day after the Sabbath		Presenting a sheaf of the first harvest.	Jesus' resurrection: He is *"the firstfruits"* from the dead (1 Cor. 15:20, 35).
4. Pentecost or Weeks* *(Shavout)*	Sivan 6	May/ June	Symbols: Two loaves containing leaven were waved before the Lord (Lev. 23:17). This represents Israel and the Church, in which the leaven of sin still exists.	
			Birth of the Jewish nation at the giving of the Law on Mt. Sinai. About 3,000 Jews** died for worshiping the golden calf (Ex. 32:28).	Birth of the Church by descent of the Holy Spirit on Jews in Jerusalem (Acts 2:1f). About 3.000 Jews were saved** that day (Acts 2:41).
5. Trumpets *(Rosh Hashanah* Jewish New Year's Day)	*Tishri* 1	September /October	Symbol: *Shofar* (ram's horn) Day of Assembly commemorated by trumpet blasts. Ten days of awe and repentance begin. Opening of Book of Life for God's judgment of people's sins of past year. **No fulfillment by an historical Christian event.**	Proposed: Invasion by Russia and 5 areas: Awakening of Israel, the Church and the world to presence, power, and will of God. Proposed: (7 years later) Armageddon invasion of Jerusalem begins.
6. Day of Atonement *(Yom Kippur)*	*Tishri* 10		Sacrifice offered for repentance, cleansing, and restoration of Israel; closing of the Book of Life until the next year. **No fulfillment by an historical Christian event.**	Proposed: Coming of Messiah. Defeat of false messiah and his forces. Resurrection of dead. Israel mourns for the One they pierced (Zech. 12:10ff). He is High Priest.
7. Tabernacles Booths *(Sukkot)* Ingathering	*Tishri* 15-21 (one week)	September /October	Symbols: Lulav and Etrog (palm branch and citron). Celebration of harvest. It is an eternal reminder of the booths, *sukkot*, in which Jewish ancestors	Proposed: Inauguration of Messiah as King in His Kingdom on earth. All nations will go to Jerusalem yearly at Tabernacles to worship

Feast	Biblical Calendar	Secular Calendar	Old Testament: Event in Israel	New Testament: Event in the Church
			lived during their desert wandering. **No fulfillment by an historical Christian event.**	the King of Kings! God dwells with men on earth. "THE LORD IS THERE" (Ezek. 48:35).
Hoshana Raba	*Tishri* 21		Last day of Week of Tabernacles.	
*Shemini Azeret**	*Tishri* 22		Final Sacred Assembly (On the eighth day).	
*Hanukkah** (Dedication or Festival of Lights)	*Kislev* 25	November/ December	God's miracle of light in Temple and rededication of the Temple. The oil lasts for 8 days.	
Purim	*Adar* 14, 15	February/ March	Saving of Jewish people by Queen Esther.	
Jubilee Year *(Yovel)*			The 50th year of restoration of people and land (Lev. 25:8ff; 27:17ff; Num. 36:4; Rom. 8:19-21).	

*The Eighth Day:

Firstfruits came on *"the day after the Sabbath"* (Lev. 23:11, 15) as did Pentecost (Lev. 23:16) and the final day of assembly of Tabernacles (Lev. 23:36). Hanukkah lasts eight days. As the first day of a new cycle, the eighth day offers a fresh start.

No new beginning is possible without the resurrection of Jesus Christ and His Father's acceptance of Jesus' blood sacrifice for us. Both these events took place on the eighth day of the week. The new heaven, the new earth, and the new Jerusalem will appear after the end of the seventh millennium, therefore, on the eighth "day" (Revelation 21:1).

It is also the day on which Jewish male babies are circumcised.

Note: Vitamin K, the blood-clotting element, is not produced in the normal amount until the fifth to seventh day of a baby's life. Prothrombin, the other clotting agent, is only 30 percent of normal until the eighth day, when it skyrockets to 110 percent. Thus, "the first safe day to perform circumcision would be the eighth day" in accord with God's instructions to Abraham (Genesis 17:12) (Dr. McMillen, p. 20f).

** The 3,000 is repeated:

There was a huge laver (basin) in the outer court of the Temple in which the priests had to purify themselves. (This symbolizes the need for purity in those who serve God.) The basin, including all its circulation pipes, received water for 3,000 baths (2 Chr. 4:5). (The actual basin itself held enough for 2,000 baths—1 Kin. 7:26). In addition:

3,000	Israelites died for worshipping golden calf at the birth of Jewish nation (Ex. 32:38).
3,000	Jews repented and were baptized at the birth of the Church (Acts 2:41).

It has been said that God is a good bookkeeper.

Chart Three

MULTIPLE FULFILLMENTS OF THE FEASTS OF ISRAEL

Feast	Biblical Calendar	Secular Calendar	Past and Proposed Fulfillments
	Nisan 10	March/April	1. Actually, Noah and family entered the refuge of the ark in second month on day 10. The Flood must have been delayed by one month due to the grandfather's death) (see Num. 9:10f) and 30 days of mourning.
			2. Identification and selection of the unblemished Passover lamb for observation until sacrifice on the 14th.
			3. Israelites enter Promised Land of Israel, led by Joshua.
			4. Triumphal entry of the sinless Jesus into Jerusalem as the King-Messiah of Israel (Mark 11:7f).
			5. Jesus identified as the One that should die instead of the whole nation (John 11:50-52) (see 2).
			PROJECTED:
			6. The two witnesses will be killed and observed by the world until the 14th (see 2).
			7. 144,000 servants of God will enter promised land of heaven, led by Jesus (see 1, 3).

Feast	Biblical Calendar	Secular Calendar	Past and Proposed Fulfillments
			8. False messiah enters the Temple and demands worship as God from all people (see 4 of Nisan 10).
Passover	*Nisan* 14	March/April	1. Jacob offered sacrifices to the God of Isaac before he and his entire clan entered Egypt.
			2. Angel of death passed over Jewish homes with the blood of the lamb on the doorposts before the Exodus.
			3. Jesus hung on the cross for 6 hours. His body was removed before sundown, the start of the Sabbath.
Unleavened Bread	*Nisan* 15	March/April	1. Entrance of Jacob and his entire family into Egypt (Gen. 46:6; Ex. 12:41).
			2. The Exodus: Departure of Moses and his entire nation from Egypt after removing bones of Joseph from his tomb in Egypt.
Firstfruits	*Nisan* 16	March/April	1. The door of ark is shut with Noah, his family, and the animals safe inside, before the Flood begins. (One month postponement - see 1 of *Nisan* 17).
			2. Continuing flight of Israelites under Moses. They camp at Pi Hahiroth where Pharaoh and his army approached them. Israelites escape through the Red Sea at night and enter Sinai.
			3. The manna from heaven is stopped because Israelites have entered the new environment of the Promised Land under Joshua 40 years later.
			4. The resurrection of Jesus Christ from His tomb. He is the *"firstfruits"* from the dead. He entered heaven on that day.
	Nisan 17	March/April	1. The Flood Judgment: Actually, the Flood began in the second month on day 17 (one month delay of Flood probably due to mourning for grandfather - cf. Num. 9:10f).

Feasts	Biblical Calendar	Secular Calendar	Past and Proposed Fulfillments
			2. The destruction of Pharaoh and his army at daybreak. The Bible does not state the date, but it must have been by *"the third day"* or Moses would have had to have returned to Egypt in keeping with his request to Pharaoh (Ex. 8:27; 12:31; 14:27). **THUS WE SEE A PRECEDENT OF RESCUE ON *NISAN* 16 AND ENTRY INTO A NEW ENVIRONMENT.**
Shavuot Pentecost	*Sivan* 6	May/June	1. God spoke the Law at Mt. Sinai at the birth of the Jewish nation. 3,000 souls died due to disobedience.
			2. God sent the Holy Spirit upon Jews who formed the Church. 3,000 souls were saved.
Yom Kippur Day of Atonement	*Tishri* 10	September/ October	1. Herod took Jerusalem (37 B.C.)
			2. Probably, the birthday of Jesus Christ.
			PROJECTED:
			3. False messiah confirms covenant.
			4. Jewish Messiah arrives and delivers the Jews and Jerusalem on first day of Year of Jubliee. He is Israel's HIGH PRIEST.
Sukkot	*Tishri* 15-21	September/ October	1. Dedication of Solomon's Temple.
			2. Capture of Temple by Syrian, King Antiochus Epiphanes.
			3. Inauguration of Herod the Great as King (Josephus, p. 336).
			4. Dedication of Herod's rebuilt Temple (8 B.C.).
			PROJECTED:
			5. Inauguration of false messiah as King of Israel.
			6. Inauguration of the "KING OF KINGS" in His Kingdom on earth.

Feast	Biblical Calendar	Secular Calendar	Past and Proposed Fulfillments
Hanukkah (Dedication) Festival of Lights	*Kislev* 25	November/ December	1. God's miracle of light in Temple and its rededication in 164 B.C. by the Maccabees. The saving of the Jewish religion.
			2. British General Allenby took Jerusalem without firing a shot.
			PROJECTED:
			3. Rededication of Third Temple.
Purim	*Adar* 14, 15	February/ March	1. Saving of Jewish people from Persian destruction in 473 B.C. by Queen Esther.
	Adar 14, 15		2. Saving of Israel from Iraqi destruction, concluding on February 27, 28, 1991.

Chart Four

A COMPARISON OF A HUMAN BEING AND THE TEMPLE

The temple is a pictorial representation of the way an individual enters into God's Holy Presence.

I. OUR PHYSICAL BODY

"The Outer Court." This contains the large bronze Altar of Sacrifice, where the entire animal was offered.

Once we enter the gates of the Outer Court, our first act before we can progress any further is to accept Jesus' bodily sacrifice for our sins.

II. OUR SOUL

"The Holy Place." It is the first room of the Temple and contains three pieces of furniture.

A. Our Intellect

The Table of Shewbread on the right side of the Holy Place represents God's sustaining Word.

Men must eat God's Word in order to live. (*"Man does not live on bread alone, but on every word that comes from the mouth of God"*—Deuteronomy 8:3; Matthew 4:4). The Word speaks to the mind.

B. Our Emotions

The Golden Seven-Branched Candlestick (*Menorah*) on the left side of the Holy Place represents the Holy Spirit. The Holy Spirit sheds light on the Word, brings life and vitality to our emotions, and helps us know God.

C. Our Will

The Altar of Incense was midway between the Table of Shewbread and the Menorah.

If our daily choices are to be balanced and acceptable to God, they must be influenced by both God's Word and His Holy Spirit. One without the other becomes dry legalism or excessive emotionalism.

III. OUR SPIRIT

"The Holy of Holies" is the second and final room. Here man may enter God's holy presence and experience His glory directly. Contained therein are:

A. The Ark of the Covenant

The golden chest with:

1. The two tablets of the Ten Commandments—the basic stipulations by which man must live in order to find peace with God, others, and himself. They were received by Moses at Mount Sinai.

2. Manna in a golden jar—represents God's daily provision for His people.

3. Aaron's rod that budded—symbolizes the life-giving power of God's High Priest, the Savior of mankind.

B. The Mercy Seat

The lid of the Ark of the Covenant.

Here the blood of the animal was sprinkled once a year. The blood symbolized the death of the sinless Lamb, Jesus Christ, who paid the penalty for the sin of mankind.

C. The Two Cherubim

The angels guarded the glory of God.

D. The *Shekinah* Glory

The magnificent, outshining light of God's Presence which dwelt over the Mercy Seat. It results from His Holiness and Power. To the Jews it looked like a consuming fire (Exodus 24:17). It was this same emanating radiance that Adam and Eve lost when they disobeyed God. This loss made them feel naked. (Man is the only one in creation who needs an added protective covering.) God's Presence will dwell with man again (Revelation 21:3).

"THE LORD IS THERE."
(Ezekiel 48:35)

SELECTED BIBLIOGRAPHY

Although over a hundred other books have been researched, the following have been quoted. All Bibles are identified by asterisks (**).

Anderson, Ken. Film: *Noah's Ark and the Genesis Flood*. Ken Anderson Films in association with Seven Star Productions (Contributors: Jack D. Dabner, Dr. Clifford Burdick, Harry Elders, Dr. John C. Whitcomb).

Background Notes–Israel. Washington, D.C.: U.S. Department of State, Bureau of Public Affairs, June 1987.

**Barker, Kenneth, ed. *The New International Version Study Bible*. Grand Rapids, Michigan: The Zondervan Corporation, 1985.

Bein-Dov, Meir. *In the Shadow of the Temple*. New York: Harper and Row, 1985.

The Bethany Parallel Commentary on the New Testament. Minneapolis, Minnesota: Bethany House Publishers, 1983.

The Bethany Parallel Commentary on the Old Testament. Minneapolis, Minnesota: Bethany House Publishers, 1985.

Blackstone, William E. *Jesus Is Coming.* New York: Fleming H. Revell Company, 1878.

Blaiklock, Edward M., R.K. Harrison, and David R. Douglas *The New International Dictionary of Biblical Archaeology.* Grand Rapids, Michigan: Zondervan Publishing House, 1983.

Breasted, James H., *Ancient Times.* New York: Ginn and Company, 1944.

Bridger, David, ed. *The New Jewish Encyclopedia.* New York: Behrman House, Inc., 1976.

Brown, Lester, et al. *State of the World* 1989. New York: W.W. Norton & Company, Inc., 1989.

Buksbazen, Victor. *The Gospel in the Feasts of Israel.* Fort Washington, Pennsylvania: Christian Literature Crusade, Inc., 1984.

Bureau of the Census: *Historical Statistics of the United States.* Part One, U.S. Department of Commerce, 1975.

Bureau of the Census: *Statistical Abstract of the United States - 1990.* The National Data Book - 110 Edition - U.S. Department of Commerce, 1990.

Burgess, Stanley M., Gary B. McGee, and Patrick H. Alexander, ed. *Dictionary of Pentecostal and Charismatic Movements.* Grand Rapids, Michigan: Zondervan Publishing House, 1988.

Charlesworth, James H. *The Old Testament Pseudepigrapha,* Vol. 1 and 2. Garden City, New York: Doubleday & Company, Inc., 1985.

Cohen, Abraham. *Everyman's Talmud.* New York: Schocken Books, 1975.

Cohen, Gary G., and Salem Kirban. *Revelation Visualized.* Huntingdon Valley, Pennsylvania: Salem Kirban Inc., 1981.

Colson, Charles. *Kingdoms in Conflict.* New York: Grand Rapids, Michigan: Zondervan Publishing House, 1989.

Cornell, Tim, and John Matthews. *Atlas of the Roman World.* New York: Facts on File Publications, 1986.

Croner, Gerald, ed. *England.* Jerusalem: Keter Publishing House Ltd., 1978.

Cumbey, Constance E. *The Hidden Dangers of the Rainbow.* Shreveport, Louisiana, Huntington House, Inc., 1983.

Daniel, Clifton, ed. *Chronicle of the Twentieth Century.* Mount Kisco, New York: Chronicle Publications, Inc., 1987.

Davis, Leonard J. and Moshe Decter, ed. *Myths and Facts 1982.* Washington, D.C.: Near East Research, Inc., 1982.

Davis, Leonard J. *Myths and Facts - 1989.* Washington, D.C.: Near East Research, Inc. 1989.

Dixon, Murray. *The Rebirth and Restoration of Israel.* Chicester, England: Sovereign World, 1988.

Donin, Hayim Halevy, ed. *Sukkot.* Jerusalem: Keter Publishing House Ltd., 1974.

Edersheim, Alfred. *The Life and Times of Jesus the Messiah.* Grand Rapids, Michigan: William B. Eerdmans Publishing Company, 1981.

Edersheim, Alfred. *The Temple: Its Ministry and Services.* Grand Rapids: Eerdmans, 1972.

Elson, Robert T. *Prelude to War.* Alexandria, Virginia: World War II Series, Time-Life Books Inc., 1979.

Encyclopaedia Britannica. Chicago: Encyclopaedia Brittanica, Inc., 1990.

Encyclopaedia Judaica. Jerusalem: Keter Publishing House Ltd., 1972.

Epstein, Rabbi Dr. I., translator. *Babylonian Talmud.* London: Soncino Press, 1952.

Estell, Kenneth, ed. *Encyclopedia of Associations - International Organizations,* 1990. New York: Gale Research, Inc., 1990.

The Europa Year Book 1987 - A World Survey, Vol. 1. London: Europa Publishing Ltd., 1987.

The Europa World Year Book 1990, Vol. I, II, 31st edition. London: Europa Publishing Ltd., 1990.

The Europa World Year Book 1991, Vol. I, 32nd edition. London: Europa Publishing Ltd., 1991.

Frank, Harry Thomas. *Atlas of the Bible Lands.* Maplewood, New Jersey: Hammond Inc., 1984.

Freeman, James M. *Manners and Customs of the Bible.* Plainfield, New Jersey: Logos International, 1972.

Fuchs, Daniel. *Israel's Holy Days.* Neptune, New Jersey; Liozeaux Brothers, Inc., 1985.

Funerals: Consumers' Last Rights, New York: W.W. Norton and Company, Inc., 1977.

Gardner, David E. *The Trumpet Sounds for Britain,* Vol. 2. Cheshire, England: Christian Foundation Publications, 1983.

Gaverluk, Dr. Emil and Dr. Patrick Fisher. *Fiber Optics: The Eye of the Antichrist,* Oklahoma City, Oklahoma: The Southwest Radio Church, 1979.

Glaser, Mitch and Zhava. *The Fall Feasts of Israel.* Chicago: Moody Press, 1987.

Goetz, William R. *Apocalypse Next.* Alberta, Canada: Horizon House Publishers, 1980.

Goodspeed, Edgar J. *The Apocrypha.* Chicago: The University of Chicago Press, 1946.

**Green, Jay P., Sr. *The Interlinear Hebrew-Greek-English Bible,* Vol. I–IV. Peabody, Massachusetts: Hendrickson Publishers, 1985.

Grun, Bernard. *The Timetables of History.* New York: Simon & Schuster, Inc., 1982.

Grunfeld, Dr. Dayan I. *Shemittah and Yobel.* New York: The Soncino Press, 1972.

Gur, Lt. General Mordechai. *The Battle for Jerusalem.* Israel: Hakorchim Press, 1986.

Halley, Henry H. *Halley's Bible Handbook.* Grand Rapids, Michigan: Zondervan Publishing House, 1978.

Hoffman, Mark S, ed. *The World Almanac and Book of Facts 1989.* New York: Pharos Books, 1988.

**The Holy Bible,* King James Version. New York: The World Publishing Company, 1924.

The Interpreter's Dictionary of the Bible, Vol. 4. New York: Abingdon Press, 1962.

Islamic Affairs Analyst, Intelligence International Ltd., Gloucester, UK, 11-94, 2-95.

Jeffrey, Grant R. *Armageddon: Appointment With Destiny.* Toronto, Ontario: Frontier Research Publications, 1988.

Jerusalem. Jerusalem: Keter Publishing House Ltd., 1973.

Johnson, Paul. *A History of the Jews.* New York: Harper & Row Publishers, 1988.

Josephus, Flavius. *Complete Works of Flavius Josephus.* Grand Rapids, Michigan: Kregel Publications, 1981.

Kah, Gary H. *En Route to Global Occupation.* Lafayette, Louisiana: Huntington House Publishers, 1992.

Kaufman, Asher S. "Where the Ancient Temple of Jerusalem Stood," *Biblical Archaeology Review,* Vol. IX, No. 2, Washington, D.C.: Biblical Archaeological Society, March/April 1983.

Kaplan, Aryeh. *The Real Messiah?* New York: National Conference of Synagogue Youth, 1985.

Keller, Werner. *The Bible as History.* New York: Bantam Books, 1988.

Kitov, Eliyahu. *The Book of Our Heritage,* Vol. 1–3. New York: Feldheim Publishers Ltd., 1978.

Lambert, Lance. *Battle for Israel.* East Sussex, England: Kingsway Publications Ltd., 1975.

Landman, Issac, ed. *The Universal Jewish Encyclopedia,* Vol. 5, New York: Universal Jewish Encyclopedia Co., Inc., 1948.

Larkin, Clarence. *Dispensational Truth.* Glenside, Pennsylvania: Rev. Clarence Larkin Est., 1918.

Levitt, Zola. *A Christian Love Story.* Dallas, Texas: Zola Levitt Ministries, Inc., 1978.

Levitt, Zola. *The Seven Feasts of Israel.* Dallas, Texas: Zola Levitt Ministries, Inc., 1979.

Lindsey, Hal. *The Late Great Planet Earth.* Grand Rapids, Michigan: Zondervan Publishing House, 1981.

Mathews, Tom, Rod Nordland, and Carroll Bogert, "The Long Shadow, *Newsweek,"* Vol. CXV, No. 19, May 7, 1990.

McClain, Alva J. *Daniel's Prophecy of the Seventy Weeks.* Grand Rapids, Michigan: Zondervan Publishing House, 1980.

McGee, J. Vernon. *Genesis.* Vol. 1. LaVerne, California: El Camino Press, 1975.

McMillen, D. S. I. *None of These Diseases.* Tappan, New Jersey: Fleming H. Revel Company, 1979.

Meier, John P. *A Marginal Jew.* New York: Doubleday, 1991.

Morris, Henry M. *The Biblical Basis for Modern Science.* Grand Rapids, Michigan: Baker Book House, 1984.

Negev, Abraham, ed. *Archaeological Encyclopedia of the Holy Land.* Englewood, New Jersey: SBS Publishing, Inc., 1980.

Orr, James. *The International Standard Bible Encyclopedia,* Vol. 1–5. Grand Rapids, Michigan: William B. Eerdmans Publishing Company, 1949.

Ostling, Richard N. "Time for a New Temple?" *Time,* New York: The Time Inc. Magazine Company, October 6, 1989.

Otis, Jr., George. *The Last of the Giants.* Tarrytown, New York: Fleming H. Revell Company, 1991.

Payne, J. Barton, *Encyclopedia of Biblical Prophecy.* Grand Rapids, Michigan: Baker Book House Company, 1987.

Petersen, Dennis R. *Unlocking the Mysteries of Creation,* Vol. 1. South Lake Tahoe, California: Christian Equippers International, 1988.

Phillips, Thomas. *The Welsh Revival.* Southampton, England: The Banner of Truth Trust, 1989.

Prince, Derek, *The Last Word on the Middle East.* Lincoln, Virginia: Chosen Books, 1982.

Pritchard, James B., ed. *The Harper Atlas of the Bible.* New York: Harper & Row, Publishers, 1987.

Reiss, Fred. *The Standard Guide to the Jewish and Civil Calendars.* West Orange, New Jersey: Behrman House, Inc., 1986.

Ritchie, John. *Feasts of Jehovah.* Grand Rapids, Michigan: Kregel Publications, 1982.

Rubinstein, Aryeh, ed. *The Return to Zion.* Jerusalem: Keter Publishing House Ltd., 1974.

Schneid, Hayyim, compiler. *Marriage.* Jerusalem: Keter Publishing House Ltd., 1973.

Schultz, Samuel J. *The Old Testament Speaks.* San Francisco: Harper & Row, Publishers, 1980.

Smith, William. *Smith's Bible Dictionary.* Grand Rapids, Michigan: Zondervan Publishing House, 1965.

Smithsonian. Washington, D.C., Smithsonian Associates, May 1987.

Strong, James. *Strong's Exhaustive Concordance of the Bible.* Nashville: Abingdon Press, 1977.

Tenney, Merrill C. *New Testament Survey.* Grand Rapids, Michigan: William B. Eerdmans Publishing Company, 1983.

Unger, Merrill F. *Unger's Bible Dictionary.* Chicago: Moody Press, 1987.

USA Today. Gannett Company, Inc., February 11, 1991.

U.S. News and World Report. Washington D.C.: U.S. News and World Report, Inc., August 28 to September 4, 1989 and April 2, 1990.

Vainstein, Yaacov. *The Cycle of the Jewish year.* Israel: Publishing Department of the Jewish Agency, 1980.

Vine, W.E., Merrill F. Unger, and William White, Jr., editors. *Vine's Expository Dictionary of Biblical Words.* Nashville, Tennessee: Thomas Nelson Publishers, Inc., 1985.

Wilson, Walter Lewis. *Wilson's Dictionary of Bible Types.* Grand Rapids, Michigan: William B. Eerdmans Publishing Company, 1977.

Winter, Naphtali, ed. *Fasting and Fast Days.* Jerusalem: Keter Publishing House Ltd., 1975.

Winter, Naphtali, ed. *The High Holy Days.* Jerusalem: Keter Publishing House, 1973.

Wiesenthal, Simon. *Sails of Hope.* New York: Macmillan Publishing Company, Inc., 1973.

The Wall Chart of 6,000 Years of World History, New York: Barnes and Noble, 1989.

The Washington Post. Washington, D.C.: The Washington Post Company, 1989–1992.

World Atlas, Imperial Edition. New York: Rand McNally & Company, 1971.

The World Book Encyclopedia. Chicago: Field Enterprises Educational Corporation, 1974.

Wurmbrand, Richard. *Marx and Satan.* Westchester, Illinois: Crossway Books, 1987.

Zagoren, Ruby. *Chaim Weizmann.* Champaign, Illinois: Garrard Publishing Company, 1972.

Index

QUESTIONS THIS BOOK ADDRESSES

The following issues offer insight on the crucial importance of this decade, or the next, to each one alive today.

Present Day

1. What is the significance of the sprouting of leaves (coming to independence) of *the fig tree* (Israel) and *all the trees* (nations) (Luke 21:29)? (pp. 13, 313)
2. Why is the generation which was alive when Israel won her independence (1949) of such great importance? (pp. 42, 313)
3. What two events will begin the seven-year transition to Messiah's arrival in Jerusalem to reign on earth? (pp. 2f, 83f)
4. Why may the last three Feasts of Israel fulfill the day of:
   The invasion of Israel? (pp. 237-240; 317)
   The coming of Israel's High Priest/Messiah? (pp. 240, 319)
   The inauguration of Messiah as King in His kingdom? (pp. 247, 319)

5. Why do Israel and all the nations mourn when Messiah arrives upon earth (Zechariah 12:10; Matthew 24:30; Revelation 1:7)? (pp. 193f)

6. Will the Jubilee Year (50th) bring restoration and liberty to God's people and to creation? (pp. 194-197)

7. What factors suggest that the Third Temple will be rededicated on *Hanukkah—Kislev* 25 (p. 198)

General

8. How does the governing principle of seven, six of labor and one of rest, apply to the last 6,000 years of history? (pp. 207-211, 311)

9. How are the three Jewish intervals—4,000 years in the world system, 400 years of captivity in Egypt and 40 years in the wilderness—related? (p. 221)

10. Why were the Israelites told to wait until the fifth year before eating the fruit of the trees they had planted in the Promised Land (Leviticus 19:23ff)? (p. 216)

11. What is the significance of the 430-year intervals that are repeated three times in Jewish history before they were offered: the Land, the Messiah, and nationhood? (pp. 218-220)

12. Why is it noteworthy that Joseph spent 20 years in Egypt among the Gentiles ahead of his brothers? When his brothers entered in the 21st year, they found he was second-in-command. (pp. 90, 223f)

13. Why is the theme of 20 years before fruition or restoration repeated in the Old Testament? (pp. 222f)

14. The ark of the covenant preceded the people by 2,000 cubits when the Israelites entered Israel under Joshua. How does this relate to Messiah and the Jewish Sabbath day's journey? (pp. 224)

15. What is the similarity between the construction of Noah's ark and the rebuilding of Israel and the Church? (pp. 224ff, 296, 303ff)

16. How do the seven religious Feasts of Israel provide the schedule for human gestation (pp. 232-234), pre-Mosaic (pp. 235-237), Jewish and Christian history (pp. 325-327), Israel's agricultural year (p. 160)?

17. What is the parallel between the Church and Israel since 1517? (p. 300f) How has it become more apparent after 1880? (p. 303ff)

18. After the Reformation began in 1517, the authority, inerrancy and knowledge of the Word of God has been under restoration for four centuries in the Church. Since 1901, the Church has been waiting for the utter renewal that the Holy Spirit will bring to the sons of God and to creation. Might this 4:1 ratio apply to the restoration of Israel also? (p. 301f)

19. How does Israel's rejection and later acceptance of both the Law and the Promised Land shed light on their reception of Messiah? (pp. 218-220, 313f)

20. How could one determine long before the event, the seven-year period in which Messiah would be killed? (pp. 228f, 265, 314f)

21. How do Israel's three agricultural harvests and the final "gleanings" provide a perfect picture of God's harvests of the people who will enter His kingdom by the time of Messiah's arrival on earth? (pp. 160-164)

22. Is it possible to reconcile the 240-year difference between the Jewish and the civil calendars? (pp. 4-5)

ORDER INFORMATION

For additional copies of *God Intervenes in the Middle East,* please print your name and address and send a check or money order (no credit cards) to:

God Intervenes, Inc.   God Intervenes, Inc.
P.O. Box 2504   or   P.O. Box 10695
Daphne, Alabama   Burke, Virginia
36526 U.S.A.   22015 U.S.A.

			VA tax
1 copy	+ Shipping/Postage	=$13.00 +	$0.59
2 copies	+ Shipping/Postage	=$24.00 +	1.08
3 copies	+ Shipping/Postage	=$35.00 +	1.58
4 copies	+ Shipping/Postage	=$45.00 +	2.03
5 copies	+ Shipping/Postage	=$54.00 +	2.43
6 copies	+ Shipping/Postage	=$62.00 +	2.79

For seven or more books, please send $10.00 per copy. This includes shipping and postage.

For an order of 20 or more books, please send $6.50 per copy. This includes shipping and postage.

Virginia residents ONLY—Add 4.5% tax.

Available at Christian Bookstores in U.S.

Thank you.